Studies in Historical Linguistics in Honor of George Sherman Lane

UNC | COLLEGE OF ARTS AND SCIENCES
Germanic and Slavic Languages and Literatures

From 1949 to 2004, UNC Press and the UNC Department of Germanic & Slavic Languages and Literatures published the UNC Studies in the Germanic Languages and Literatures series. Monographs, anthologies, and critical editions in the series covered an array of topics including medieval and modern literature, theater, linguistics, philology, onomastics, and the history of ideas. Through the generous support of the National Endowment for the Humanities and the Andrew W. Mellon Foundation, books in the series have been reissued in new paperback and open access digital editions. For a complete list of books visit www.uncpress.org.

Studies in Historical Linguistics in Honor of George Sherman Lane

Festschrift for George S. Lane

EDITED BY WALTER W. ARNDT,

PAUL W. BROSMAN JR.,

FREDERIC E. COENEN AND

WERNER P. FRIEDRICH

UNC Studies in the Germanic Languages and Literatures
Number 58

Suggested citation: Arndt, Walter, Paul W. Brosman, Jr., Frederic E. Coenen, and Werner P. Friedrich, eds. *Studies in Historical Linguistics in Honor of George Sherman Lane: Festschrift for George S. Lane.* Chapel Hill: University of North Carolina Press, 1967. DOI: https://doi.org/10.5149/9781469657035_Arndt

Library of Congress Cataloging-in-Publication Data
Names: Arndt, Walter W., Brosman, Jr., Paul W., Coenen, Frederic E., and Friedrich, Werner P., editors.
Title: Studies in historical linguistics in honor of George Sherman Lane: Festschrift for George S. Lane / edited by Walter W. Arndt, Paul W. Brosman Jr., Frederic E. Coenen, and Werner P. Friedrich.
Other titles: University of North Carolina Studies in the Germanic Languages and Literatures ; no. 58.
Description: Chapel Hill : University of North Carolina Press, [1967] Series: University of North Carolina Studies in the Germanic Languages and Literatures. | Includes bibliographical references.
Identifiers: LCCN 68064591 | ISBN 978-1-4696-5702-8 (pbk: alk. paper) | ISBN 978-1-4696-5703-5 (ebook)
Subjects: Historical linguistics. | Tokharian language.
Classification: LCC PD25 .N6 NO. 58 | DCC 415/ .08

"The Tocharian Verbal Stems in *-tk-*," was originally published in the *Journal of the American Oriental Society,* Vol. 85, No. 1, January-March, 1965, and is reprinted here with permission of the American Oriental Society.

The following essays were originally published in *Language,* and are reprinted here by permission of the Linguistic Society of America: "Problems of Tocharian Phonology," Vol. 14, No. 1; "The Tocharian Palatalization," Vol. 21, No. 1; "Miscellanea, The Tocharian Genitive B *–epi,* A *–(y)ap,*" Vol. 24, No. 3; "Imperfect and Preterit in Tocharian," Vol. 29, No. 3; and "Tocharian Evidence and the Trubetzkoy-Benveniste Hypothesis," Vol. 38, No. 3.

Table of Contents

Dedication IX

Tabula Gratulatoria XIII

Editors' Note. XIX

Part I. Selected Articles on Tocharian Linguistics by George Sherman Lane 1

Problems of Tocharian Phonology 3

The Tocharian Palatalization (I) 27

Miscellanea: The Tocharian Genitive B -epi, A -(y)āp 41

Imperfect and Preterit in Tocharian 44

Tocharian Evidence and the Trubetzkoy-Benveniste Hypothesis. 61

On the Significance of Tocharian for Indo-European Linguistics. . 76

The Tocharian Verbal Stems in *-TK-* 88

On the Interrelationship of the Tocharian Dialects 105

Part II. Studies in honor of George Sherman Lane 135

The Development of Proto-Algonkian **-awe- by Mary R. Haas* . 137

On some Troublesome Indo-European Initials *by Eric P. Hamp* . 146

Hittite *udatis by E. Adelaide Hahn* 154

Ablaut, accent, and umlaut in the Tocharian Subjunctive *by Warren Cowgill* 171

The Correspondences among the Mid Vowels of Tocharian *by Thomas G. Reitz*. 182

Latin *sōns by Calvert Watkins* 186

The Truth, the Whole Truth, and . . . : Problems in old Norse Linguistics *by Ole Widding* 195

The Origin of Irregular *-t* in weak Preterits like *sent* and *felt by Norman E. Eliason* 210

Atertanum Fah *by W. P. Lehmann* 221

European Clothing Names and the Etymology of *girl by Fred C. Robinson* 233

Acknowledgments

The editors wish to thank the following for permission to reproduce these articles by Professor George S. Lane:

'Problems of Tocharian Phonology,' *Language*, Vol. 14, No. 1, January-March, 1938, pp. 20-38.

'The Tocharian Palatalization (I),' *Language*, Vol. 21, No. 1, January-March, 1945, pp. 18-26.

'Miscellanea, The Tocharian Genitive B *-epi*, A *-(y)āp*,' *Language*, Vol. 24, No. 3, July-September, 1948, pp. 293-294.

'Imperfect and Preterit in Tocharian,' *Language*, Vol. 29, No. 3, July-September, 1953, pp. 278-287.

'Tocharian Evidence and the Trubetzkoy-Benveniste Hypothesis,' *Language*, Vol. 38, No. 3, Part 1, July-September, pp. 245-253.

'On the Significance of Tocharian for Indo-European Linguistics,' *Classical Mediaeval and Renaissance Studies*, in Honor of Bertold Louis Ullman, Vol. I, edited by Charles Henderson, Jr., *Storia e Letterature, Raccolta di Studi e Testi*, Vol. 93, Roma, 1964, pp. 283-292.

'The Tocharian Verbal Stems in *-tk-*,' *Journal of the American Oriental Society*, Vol. 85, No. 1, January-March, 1965, pp. 66-73.

'On the Interrelationship of the Tocharian Dialects,' *The Ancient Indo-European Dialects*, University of California Press, Berkeley, California, 1966, pp. 213-233.

Dedication on George Sherman Lane's Sixty-fifth Birthday

It is a difficult and rash thing to do, to write a few pages of deep appreciation of the life's work of a man who dislikes all forms of publicity, whether this aversion comes from shyness or from a form of innate pride. Yet perhaps I can risk the attempt, for we have been friends and colleagues for thirty years, and office-mates for almost twenty years, and we have often grappled with each other about his and my respective fields, Comparative Linguistics versus Comparative Literature (I shall never forget a whole file of 'unaccented vowels' which he kept right behind his desk), and about whether or not graduate students were here exclusively to learn or whether they were also entitled to a share in the disruptive fermentations of all kinds that occasionally shake the very foundations of modern universities. And so, if his colleagues and former students want to honor him who so richly deserves our respect, I am perhaps the logical man to serve as lightning-conductor, even though I can mention my abiding friendship as my one qualification, and certainly not my practically nonexistent knowledge of the field of learning in which he has become such a towering figure.

George Sherman Lane, born in Iowa on September 28, 1902, and superbly trained at the universities of Iowa, Chicago, Reykjavik, Paris and Freiburg by men like Larsen, Buck, and Meillet, was Assistant Professor of Sanskrit and Comparative Philology at the Catholic University in Washington before he came to the University of North Carolina in 1937 and, in 1949, became Kenan Professor of Germanic and Comparative Linguistics. His many professional distinctions need not be enumerated here, from his election as Fellow of the American

Academy of Arts and Sciences and serving as President of the Linguistic Society of America to his teaching and continued studies in Chicago, Göttingen, Oslo, Michigan and Reykjavik; it suffices to state that from the moment of his arrival in Chapel Hill, he served as a mainstay of the Graduate School of our University. I would venture to say that Tocharian and Old Norse are his two favorite fields, even though Comparative Greek and Latin Grammar or Gothic are not far behind.

If we were to single out just two or three of Professor Lane's greatest merits, for which we honor him on this, his 65th birthday, I think that all his former students would urge that his gift as a truly great and devoted teacher should come first. Professor Lane has built for himself a reputation of soundness and solidity in the training of his graduate students which has earned him their gratitude and lasting appreciation and the admiration of his colleagues.

His second great merit probably lies in his role of selfless 'elder' statesman to our University even in his younger days – for whether on the Graduate Board or on selection committees for appointments, George Lane would judge day-to-day academic problems or potential new staff members according to his unalterably high standards. There was no such thing as expediency, for adherence to quality alone was important. To mention but one example of his enriching the good name of our University: it was thanks to his discernment and his single-minded purposefulness that a distinguished scholar from the University of Chicago, a man of the renown of the late Professor B. L. Ullman, was attracted as chairman of our Department of Classics.

And yet, all those who know only this sober, earnest and cautious side of George Lane know only half the man, for his friends are even more aware of his warm smile, his personal loyalty, the amazing scope of his knowledge of all sorts of practical matters extending from the flora and the fauna of a region to manual dexterity in building and growing things, talents in which so many people of our profession are woefully lacking.

This *Festschrift* containing both some of Professor Lane's own contributions and articles by many of his friends and former students is but a small token of our affection and regard for a gentleman of great integrity and a scholar of painstaking thoroughness. Through the following Tabula Gratulatoria, we all join in thanking him and in hoping that his devotion to highest academic standards will serve as an example to those who come after him.

Werner P. Friederich

Tabula Gratulatoria

W. F. Albright
Johns Hopkins University

Raimo Anttila
University of California, L. A.

Walter Werner Arndt
Dartmouth College

Ann Royal Arthur
Tulane University

Samuel D. Atkins
Princeton University

Robert Austerlitz
Columbia University

William M. Austin
Illinois Institute of Technology

Wendy C. Barron
University of North Carolina

Barbara S. Bauer
University of North Carolina

Richard Beck
University of North Dakota

Madison S. Beeler
University of California
Berkeley

Else and Hans Bekker-Nielsen
Copenhagen

Hreinn Benediktsson
University of Iceland

Émile Benveniste
Collège de France, Paris, France

Harry Bergholz
University of North Carolina

George V. Bobrinskoy
University of Chicago

Richard Borth
University of North Carolina

Purabi Bose
University of North Carolina

Wallace R. Brandon
Gallaudet College

Francis J. Brooke, III
Centre College of Kentucky

Paul W. Brosman, Jr.
Tulane University

T. Robert S. Broughton
University of North Carolina

W. Norman Brown
University of Pennsylvania

Rebecca F. Brownlee
University of North Carolina

Nancy Sue Buffaloe
University of North Carolina

James Campbell
University of North Carolina

June N. Campbell
University of North Carolina

Vincent & Baerbel Cantarino
Indiana University

Y. R. Chao
University of California
Berkeley

Allen H. Chappel
The University of Georgia

Frederic E. Coenen
University of North Carolina

N. E. Collinge
University of Durham, England

Emmi Colton
University of North Carolina

J. M. Cowan
Cornell University

Warren Cowgill
Yale University

R. A. Crossland
The University, Sheffield
England

Willard Ticknor Daetsch
Ithaca College

Bruce and Ingeborg Dent
University of North Carolina

Beverly A. Douglas
University of North Carolina

Mark J. Dresden
University of Pennsylvania

Alexander Dunlop
University of North Carolina

Connie C. Eble
University of North Carolina

Norman E. Eliason
University of North Carolina

M. B. Emeneau
University of California
Berkeley

James E. Engel
Vanderbilt University

Erasmus Press
(Dr. L. S. Thompson)
University of Kentucky

Joseph P. Fama
University of North Carolina

Olof von Feilitzen
Kungliga Biblioteket,
Stockholm

Charles A. Ferguson
Center of Applied Linguistics
Washington, D. C.

Joerg Fichte
University of North Carolina

Hugh M. Fincher
University of North Carolina

Werner P. Friederich
University of North Carolina

Harold P. Fry
University of North Carolina

Alice Carol Gaar
University of North Carolina

H. B. Gardner
Pontifical Institute
of Medieval Studies
Toronto

T. Z. Gasinski
University of North Carolina

James R. Gaskin
University of North Carolina

Ignace J. Gelb
The University of Chicago

John A. C. Greppin
University of California
Los Angeles

Finnbogi Guðmundsson
National Library of Iceland
Reykjavík

H. G. Guterbock
University of Chicago

Mary R. Haas
University of California
Berkeley

E. Adelaide Hahn
New York

Halldór Halldorsson
University of Iceland
Reykjavík

Carl Hammer, Jr.
Texas Technological College

Eric P. Hamp
The University of Chicago

James Hardin
University of North Carolina

Jacques Hardré
University of North Carolina

Einar Haugen
Harvard University

Archibald A. Hill
The University of Texas

Carleton T. Hodge
Indiana University

Henry M. Hoenigswald
University of Pennsylvania

Harry Hoijer
University of California
Los Angeles

Lee S. Hultzén
University of California
Berkeley

Catherine Huntington
Philadelphia, Pennsylvania

Henry R. Immerwahr
University of North Carolina

Institut for lingvistik
Statsbiblioteket
Arhus, Denmark

Roman Jakobson
Harvard University

Robert E. Kaske
Cornell University

John E. Keller
University of North Carolina

William W. Kibler
University of North Carolina

Günter Klabes
University of North Carolina

John G. Kunstmann
University of North Carolina

Hans Kurath
University of Michigan
Ann Arbor

Jerzy Kurylowicz
University of Krakow, Poland

Albert L. Lancaster
Virginia Military Institute

Hanne Lauridsen
Copenhagen

Winfred P. Lehmann
The University of Texas

Cornelia S. Lewis
University of North Carolina

Fang Kuei Li
University of Washington

Marcia Rice Lindemann II
Norfolk, Virginia

Albert E. Lindsay
Boston, Massachusetts

Donald Lineback
University of North Carolina

Albert L. Lloyd, Jr.
University of Pennsylvania

Floyd G. Lounsbury
Yale University

R. M. Lumiansky
University of Pennsylvania

Kevin M. McCarthy
University of North Carolina

Pope McClung
University of North Carolina

Raven I. McDavid, Jr.
The University of Chicago

Kemp Malone
Johns Hopkins University

James W. Marchand
Cornell University

Albert H. Marckwardt
Princeton University

Curt Martin
University of North Carolina

Virginia S. Mason
University of North Carolina

Robert T. Meyer
Catholic University of America

Maria Luiza Miazzi
Sao Gaetano do Sul, Brazil

Renate Morris
University of North Carolina

William G. Moulton
Princeton University

Margaret E. Newhard
University of North Carolina

Michael R. Paull
University of North Carolina

Herbert Penzl
University of California
Berkeley

Thomas O. Pinkerton
Davidson College

Edgar Polomé
The University of Texas

Mary Gray Porter
University of Alabama

Jóhan Hendrik Poulsen
Copenhagen

Jaan Puhvel
University of California
Los Angeles

Herbert W. Reichert
University of North Carolina

Thomas G. Reitz
Columbia University

Fred C. Robinson
Cornell University

Kiffin A. Rockwell
Beloit, Wisconsin

Astrid Schneller
University of North Carolina

George C. Schoolfield
University of Pennsylvania

Richard K. Seymour
Duke University

Sam M. Shiver
Emory University

Sidney R. Smith, Jr.
University of North Carolina

Ragnhild Söderbergh
Sollentuna, Sweden

Ronald H. Southerland
Wilmington, North Carolina

Otto Springer
University of Pennsylvania

Ria Stambaugh
University of North Carolina

Carl E. Steinhauser
Georgia Institute of Technology

Einar Ól. Sveinsson
Manuscript Institute of Iceland
Reykjavik

Ransom T. Taylor
University of Nebraska

Gene R. Thursby
University of North Carolina

Hans Vogt
Oslo University, Norway

Richard B. Vowles
University of Wisconsin

Calvert Watkins
Harvard University

Ralph A. West
University of North Carolina

Joseph White
University of North Carolina

Francis J. Whitfield
University of California
Berkeley

Ole Widding
Copenhagen

Werner Winter
University of Texas

Rhea Wood
University of North Carolina

Dean S. Worth
University of California
Los Angeles

John Yelverton
University of North Carolina

Karl E. Zimmer
University of California
Berkeley

A. E. and Lois Miles Zucker
University of Maryland

Editors' Note

The pressure of early deadlines for work commissioned abroad, combined with printing costs for scholarly materials which even in Europe have risen to forbidding levels in recent months, have enforced a reduction of the projected format of this volume by about fifty percent. The most painful omissions of substance imposed by these stringencies comprise a bibliography of George Lane's writings; about half of the articles contributed by pupils and colleagues; any sample of his important contributions to historical-comparative linguistics outside the Tocharian field (including illuminating periodic surveys of the status and needs of the entire discipline); and finally, even in the Tocharian field, his fine edition and translation of the *Punyavantajātaka*, *JAOS* 67.33-53 (1947), and important reviews, particularly of the work of Holger Pedersen and Wolfgang Krause. The latter constituted precious reappraisals and admirably displayed his acute scholarly judgment, salutary caution, and mastery of a difficult field which increasingly absorbed his attention over the years.

The grouping of the articles by contributors is neither alphabetical nor, we trust, entirely arbitrary, but roughly thematic, proceeding from work oriented toward illustrations of general principles of historical linguistics and reconstruction within and beyond Indo-European, as in the Hamp and Haas papers, to those more concerned with specific problems in Hittite, Tocharian, Latin, and Germanic, in that order. Once again, we most sincerely wish that time and space had permitted us to reflect a wider section of the great range of George Lane's interests, and fuller testimony to the devoted friendship of so many in this country and abroad, by including the contributions submitted by N. E. Collinge, Henry Hoenigswald, Harry Hoijer, Raven McDavid, Robert T. Meyer, Richard K. Seymour, Lawrence S. Thompson, and several others that were offered us in addition.

Part I

Selected Articles on Tocharian Linguistics by George Sherman Lane

Problems of Tocharian Phonology

§ 1. The forty odd years which have elapsed since the first publication of a Tocharian text[1] leave much for the comparativist to do. As clear as is the affinity of both dialects A and B[2] to Indo-European, even so inexplicable are still many of the countless special developments that have led to their remarkable appearance alongside the other languages of the family. It is, in fact, the problem of the relationship of Tocharian to the other Indo-European dialects which has most interested scholars from the very beginning, while very little time has been devoted to the comparative study of the two dialects themselves. Indeed, their interrelationship is as yet quite imperfectly understood. As remarked already by M. Sylvain Lévi,[3] in speaking of the vocabulary, the more one observes their fundamental identity, the more one is struck by their divergences. The remark may apply no less appropriately to the phonology.

The phonology of Tocharian has proved disconcerting for the comparativist from the very start. The one order of (voiceless) stops from the three (or four) of PIE renders the etymology extremely ambiguous from the point of view of the consonantism alone, especially when coupled with the fact that the three guttural series likewise fall together. But this is not the worst. The vocalism so far has defied almost every attempt that has been made to bring it to order. In 1924 Feist was forced to conclude his short survey of the Tocharian vocalism with the comment 'Es herrscht völlige Regellosigkeit'.[4] Schwentner in 1935 could do little better: 'Ein anscheinend regelloses Durcheinander'.[5] But in view of the ambiguity of the Tocharian consonant system, it is all the more imperative that the few vowel correspondences of observed regularity be clearly kept in mind. An example of the extreme indifference to vocalism is seen in Poucha's article 'Die tocharische Lautverschiebung',[6] where, for example, A *tseke* 'sculpture' is connected with A, B *tsäk-* 'burn', and A *ko-* 'kill' is compared to B *ken-* (< PIE **gʷhen-*, with reference to Schrader, Reallexikon[2] 2.76, where B *kan-* is given). The same fault is to be found in Grierson's 'Etymologies Tokhariennes',[7] where the comparisons (chiefly with modern Piśāca dialects) are based almost entirely on consonantal resemblances.

The first step, it seems to me, toward clearing up this maze of conjecture is to make a systematic comparison of the vocalisms of the two dialects. In spite of the scattered state of the published B texts and the possible errors in the earlier interpretations, I believe the time is at hand when this is possible. The start already made by Lévi in the vocabulary to his Fragments de Textes Kutchéens[8] is considerable, and many more comparisons are at hand in the Tocharische Grammatik of Sieg, Siegling, and Schulze,[9] especially in the verb list (421-84), where dialect B is cited chiefly in root form.

I have made use of all pertinent comparisons found in these works or elsewhere, with the addition of a few of my own collection. In trying to establish the original vocalism of forms compared, I have sifted the etymologies proposed – and in this regard great care was necessary – and I have added several more which I failed to find mentioned elsewhere, but which seemed probable enough for my purpose.

In this first attempt at a comparative phonological study, I have picked out some of the more striking phonetic variations of the two dialects, namely the presence of monophthongization in A, and the origins of the vowels *e* and *o* in B for which A shows the greatest variety of equivalents. I have expressly avoided, except in a few citations, forms involving the 'reduced' vowel (*ä*) and *ā*. The origins of the former are too varied, and the value of the notation of length still too uncertain for them to be dealt with at present. The correlation A *e* = B *e* (§ 3, 3) involved forms apparently negated by the prefix *en-*; but since this vocalism for the negative prefix is not constant, it was thought better to treat such forms separately in § 5.

Interested scholars will, I think, excuse the omissions and oversights, which of course are numerous, due in part, as they all will know, to the scattered state of the B materials. At any rate I hope that this first attempt at a comparative study of the Tocharian vocalism will add its bit to the eventual clearing up of the most confusing maze that Indo-Europeanists have yet had to face.

§ 2. Monophthongization in Tocharian A.[10] One of the most obvious and commonly recognized vowel changes which places the vocalism of A on a less archaic plane than that of B is monophthongization of original diphthongs. The PIE *i*- and *u*-diphthongs give PToch. *ai* and *au* respectively, which remain in B but become *e* and *o* in A. The situation is remarkably parallel to that of Iranian beside Sanskrit.

1. A *e* = B *ai*. A *e-* 'give', B *ai-* (with sb. A *elune* 'gift', B *ailyñe*, etc.) which, according to Pedersen,[11] probably represent a verbal form of a root hitherto known only in substantives as Grk. αἶσα 'lot, fate', Osc. *aeteis* 'partis', etc. (Walde-Pokorny, Vgl. Wtb. 1.2); that is, a root *ai-* 'give, share', with semantic relationship as in Lat. *pars, portio*: Grk. ἔπορον 'gave, allotted'. Pedersen[12] also connects B *aik-*, *aiś-* 'know' with Goth. *aih* 'owns', Skt. *īçe* 'own, rule, am able' (IE **ēik-*, Walde-Pokorny 1.105). For the meaning compare the Germanic group NHG *können*: *kennen*, etc. To this verb perhaps belongs B *aiśai* (*yāmtsi*) to which corresponds A *eśe* (*yatsi*) '(make) manifest' (Toch. Gramm. 3). A *tre*, B *trai* (masc.) 'three' in all probability represent the nom. PIE **treyes* (Skt. *trayas*, Grk. τρεῖς, etc.).[13] The group for 'write, paint', A *pik-*, *pek-*, B *piṅk-*, *pai(y)k-*, with A *peke* 'picture', vbl. sb. *peklune*, B *paykalñe*, is of

course related to Skt. *piṅçáti* 'adorns', OPruss. *peisāi* 'writes', ChSl. *pĭsati* 'write', Lat. *pingere,* etc. (Walde-Pokorny 2.9).[14] If the preterit participles A *pāpeku,* B *papaikau* are original perfect forms, we are probably dealing with PIE *oi* (rather than *ei*). Another well-defined IE root is represented in A *tsek-,* B *tsaik-* 'form, shape', with sb. A *tseke* 'sculpture': Skt. *dehmi* 'smear, anoint', Lat. *fingere,* etc. (**dheiĝh-,* Walde-Pokorny 1.833).[15] For the original vocalism of the pret. ptc. A *tsātseku,* cf. the remark on *pāpeku* (above). It is useless to conjecture the grade represented in A *tseke* (cf. Grk. τεῖχος neut. or τοῖχος masc.) and *kuntistsek* 'potter'. The conditions for the palatalization of the dental to *ts* are not further elucidated by these examples. The root A *l(y)ip-, lep-* (e.g. pret. pple *lipo, lyipo,* etc., pret. act. 3 pl. *lepar*), B *lyip-* 'be left' is probably cognate with the Germanic group, Goth. *bi-leiban* 'remain', *af-lifnan* 'be left', etc. (Walde-Pokorny 2.403), as Meillet has already suggested.[16] Even these few examples show clearly the normal reflex of the *i*-diphthong, and there are also other rather obvious etymologies bearing out the rule but which I fail to find mentioned. For example A *lit-, let-* 'go away, fall from' (= Skt. *cyu-*), B *lait-* 'transmigrate' must be related to Av. *raēθ-* 'die' (pres. *iriθyeiti,* cf. A pres. mid. *litanträ*), and the Germanic group of Goth. *af-, usleiþan,* OIcel. *līþan* 'go', likewise in Germanic with indication that the original application was to departing from this life, cf. OIcel. *liðinn* 'dead', *leiði* 'tomb', OHG *leita, leiti* 'funeral pomp' (Walde-Pokorny 2.401). Also, though not so identical in formation, A *ritw-* 'be joined, bound', B *ritt-,* with sbs. A *retwe* 'combination, composition', B *raitwe* 'arrangement' (Toch. Gramm. 3.462 f., Fragm. 140), may be compared to the Germanic and Baltic group, Goth. *ga-raiþs* 'fixed, appointed', OE *gerǣde* 'ready', Goth. *garaidjan* 'prepare', etc., Lett. *raids* 'ready', *riedu, rist* 'arrange'. The identity with the Tocharian renders imperative the separation of the Germanic forms from the root **reidh-* 'ride', and the connection with the base *(*a*)*rēi-* 'join, fit' (in Grk. ἀραρίσκω, etc.) all the more probable (cf. Walde-Pokorny 1.75, 2.348). The Tocharian group for 'wash', A *lik-*, *lek-*, B pret. *laik-* (Toch. Gramm. 465) may be cognate with Lat. *liqueō* 'be fluid', *līquor* 'be fluid, melt, flow', OIr. *fliuch*, W *gwlyb* 'damp', etc., from an IE **wleiq^{w}-* (Walde-Pokorny 2.397). For the loss of *w* before *l*, cf. A nom. *wäl* 'king', obl. *lānt*, etc., B nom. *walo*, *wlo* beside nom. *lānte*, etc.: Lat. *valeō* 'be strong', OIr. *flaith* 'ruler, sovereignty', ChSl. *vladą*, *vlasti* 'rule', etc.[17] With A *me-*, *mew-* 'tremble' (e.g. pres. act. 3 sg. *meṣ*, 3 pl. *meyeñc*, verbal noun *mewlune*), B *miw-*, *maiw-* (Toch. Gramm. 456) can be compared OIcel. *mjōr*, *mjǣr*, *mǣr* 'thin, slender' (< **maiwa-*, **maiwi-*),[18] but the treatment of the *w* in A is uncertain. Here also perhaps B *maiwa* = Skt. *dahara-* (Fragm. 46, 127), *maiwaññe* 'childhood' (ibid. 89, 127)? A *met-* 'set out', B *mit-*, *mait-* (Toch. Gramm. 456) may mean more originally 'change (place)', and are in this way to be referred to the group of Lat. *mūto* 'change', Goth. *maidjan* 'alter, falsify', Skt. *mithati*, *methati* 'associates with, disputes' (IE **meit(h)-*, Walde-Pokorny 2.247). The Tocharian verb shows a semantic development parallel to that of Lat. *meō* 'go, wander', Pol. *mijać*, etc. 'pass by, avoid', from the unextended root **mei-* = **mei-* 'change, exchange' (Walde 2.240, 241). A *wek-* 'lie' (pret. ptc. *wāweku*), B sb. *waike* 'lie' (Toch. Gramm. 473), B *waiyke reki* 'parole mensongère' (Fragm. 58, 67, 153), may be connected with OIcel. *vīkva*, *vīkja* 'turn, turn aside, dismiss', OE *wīcan* 'yield, give way, fall down', NHG *weichen*, etc., or Skt. *vējate*, *vijate* 'recoil, flee from', Grk. εἴκω 'give way, retire', etc. (IE **weig-*, **weik-*, Walde-Pokorny 1.233 ff.). For the semantic development 'lie' from 'deviation', cf. Ved. *vīci-* 'deceit, seduction' if it belongs here (so Walde l. c.). Here probably belong also A *wik-* 'disappear' (Toch. Gramm. 471 f.) and B *wik-* 'reject, etc.' (*wikäṣlye* = Skt. supraheya, etc., Fragm. 156). Whether or not A *wek-* 'fall to pieces' (Toch. Gramm. 473 with reference to *wik-*) also goes here is a question, but cf. OE *wīcan* also 'fall down'. A further example of an original diphthong is perhaps A *lek* 'appearance, manner' (Toch. Gramm. 48), without equivalent so far as I know in B. One may compare the Germano-Baltic group Goth. *leik* 'body, corpse', *galeiks* 'like', Lith. *lýgus* 'like', etc. (Walde-Pokorny 2.398). But otherwise no strong-grade form is known. Likewise the new diphthong *oi* in B *soyä* 'son' with *o* < *u* (cf. Grk. υἱός),[19] shows monophthongization in A *se*. There are also numerous examples of the equation A *e* = B *ai* for which I cannot as yet offer plausible connections, e.g. A *ep-* 'cover', B *aip-*; A *ekrä*, B *aikarya* 'empty, desolate'; A *āneñci*, *āneṁśi*, B *anaiśai* = Skt. *su-*; A *keṁ* 'falsely', B *aṅkaiṁ*; A *ne* rel. particle, B *nai* 'in truth';[20] A *treke* 'confusion', B *traike*; A *sem* 'refuge', B *saim* (to A *se-* 'lean upon', Toch. Gramm. 4,479); A *ske-* 'exert oneself', B *skai-*; A *sne* 'without', B *snai*. The relationship of A *pe* 'foot' (du. *pem*, pl. *peyu*, etc.), B *pai* (obl. sg. *paiyne*, du. *paine*) to the PIE **pĕd-*, *pŏd-* remains obscure.[21]

2. A *o* = B *au*. There are several cases where the etymology is clear. A *oks-* 'grow', B *auk-*, *auś-* 'increase' (? cf. Fragm. 113), and A *okṣu*, B *aukṣu* 'old', A *okar* 'plant': Lat. *augeō*, Goth. *aukan* 'increase', with *s*-increment as in Grk. ἀϝέξω, αὔξω, Goth. *wahsjan*, etc.[22] A *ko-* 'kill', B *kau-*: OHG *houwan* 'hew, strike', Lith. *káuti* 'strike, forge', etc. (Walde-Pokorny 1.330).[23] A *ko* 'cow', B *kaurṣu* 'bull': Skt. *gāus*, Grk. βοῦς, etc. (PIE **gʷōu-* Walde-Pokorny 1.696).[24] A *klyos-* 'hear', B *klyau(s)-*: Skt. *çroṣati*, Lith. *klausýti*, etc. (PIE *k̂leu-s-*, Walde-Pokorny 1.494 f.).[25] The palatalization betrays the *e*-grade as opposed to *o*-grade in the words for 'ear', A *klots*, B *klautso*, cf. Ir. *cluas* 'ear', W. *clust* 'hearing'. The palatalization in the weak grade forms A pret. ptc. *kaklyuṣu*, absol. *kaklyuṣuräṣ* (Toch. Gramm. 437), must be analogical. A *lok*, B *lauke* (adv.) 'far': Lith. *laũkas* 'field', loc. *laukè* 'outside', *laukan* 'out'. Here perhaps also the prefix A *lo*, B *lau* 'away, off', shortened in proclitic use.[26] A *śo-*, B *śau-*, *śaw-* 'live' with noun A *śol*, B *śaul* 'life' are best derived

from PIE *$g^wy\breve{\bar{o}}u$- from the *u*-extension of the root *g^wei- 'live' (Walde-Pokorny 1.668 ff.), rather than from the simple *$g^wy\bar{o}$- as usually assumed for Grk. ζώω, Att. ζῶ, etc.[27] The parallel B forms in *ai* (*śai-*, *śay-* 'live', *śailñe* 'way of living') are probably from the simple base *g^wei-, less probably from an (otherwise unknown) extension in *i*, *$g^wy\breve{\bar{e}}i$-. A *śoṣi*, B *śaiṣṣe* 'world' show parallel formations from the two bases. Here probably also A *śom* 'young man', B *śaumo* 'nara-'.[28] The plural B *śāmna* shows simplification of the labials in the group *-wmn-*. There are likewise etymologies proposed for a few isolated words in A or B which appear sufficiently sure to quote. A *yoṁ se* 'grandson', lit. 'young son': Lith. *jáunas*, Lett. *jauns*, ChSl. *junŭ* 'young'.[29] B *ṣñaura* 'sinews, nerves', Grk. νεῦρον 'tendon', Av. *šnāvar-* 'sinew', etc.[30] B *śauk-* 'call, name': Lith. *kaũkti* 'howl' or *šaũkti* 'call, name'.[31] The original *e*-grade of the diphthong is indicated by the palatalization.

But there are other forms found in both dialects for which fairly satisfactory root connections may be proposed. A *koc*, B *kauc* 'high up' may be derived from **qou-d-* parallel to **quo-q-* in Goth. *háuhs*, etc. For dental formation, but with reduplication and weak grade of root, cf. Skt. *kakud-* 'summit, tip'. A *kot-*, B *kaut-* 'split, cut up', are evidently related to Lat. *cūdo* 'strike' (for **caudō*, cf. Walde-Pokorny 1.330, Walde-Hoffman 300 f.). A *koṁ*, B *kauṁ* 'day' (if not loanwords)[32] may be the formal equivalents of Skt. *çoṇa-* 'red', sb. 'redness' (the cerebral appears secondary, cf. Walde-Pokorny 1.368), from a root **keu-* 'shine' seen also in Skt. *çvas* 'tomorrow', Av. *sūrəm* 'early in the morning'. On the semantic side, cf. the usual derivation of Lat. *diēs*, etc. from **dei-* 'shine' (Walde-Pokorny 1.772 ff.). A *koṣt-* 'strike, slay', noun *koṣt* 'blade' (Toch. Gramm. 1 f., 434), B *kauṣ-* 'break, kill' recall forcibly the Indo-Iranian group Skt. *kuṣati*, *kuṣṇāti* 'tears, pinches, kneads', Av. *frakušaiti* 'slays, kills', NPers. *kuštan* 'kill', with different grade of root (cf. Walde-Pokorny 1.331 top). A *cok* 'lamp', B *cauk-* 'light up' may be derivatives of a guttural extension of the root **dheu-* 'shine' in Skt. *dhavala-* 'dazzling white', *dhāvati* 'cleans, rinses', Grk. θοός· . . . λαμπρός, θοῶσαι· . . . λαμπρῦναι Hesych. (Walde-Pokorny 1.835). A *tor*, B *taur* 'dust' are probably from **dhour-* derivative of the extended base **dhewer-* from **dheu-* in words for 'vapor, smoke, dust', frequently transferred to mental states (Walde-Pokorny 1.835 ff.), cf. Russ. *dur'* 'foolishness', *durět'* 'lose one's mind', Ukrain. *dur, dura* 'stupor, giddiness', Grk. θοῦρος 'rushing, furious', etc. (if with genuine diphthong, cf. op. cit. 842 with lit.). I am inclined to derive A *pot-* perhaps 'honor, flatter', B *paut-* (cf. A *potarṣk-*, B *pautarṣke* 'respectful') from the IE root **bheudh-* in Skt. *bodhati* 'be awake, perceive, notice', Grk. πεύθομαι πυνθάνομαι 'find out', etc. (Walde-Pokorny 2.147 f.). The semantic development 'be awake', 'give heed', 'honor' is straightforward enough, and no more remarkable than that of Lith. *baudžiù, baũsti* 'punish' (probably also from an earlier 'notice, heed'). A *lop-*, B *laup-* 'soil, stain', aside from the final labial, recall Grk. λῦμα 'filth, dirt, disgrace', Lat. *lutum* 'mud', Ir. *loth* 'dirt' and with strong grade, as in the Tocharian forms, W. *lludedic* 'muddy' (op. cit. 2.406). A *tsuk-, tsok-* (in imper. *p-tsok*, subj. act. *tsokam*), B *tsauk-* 'drink' (supplementive to present A, B *yok-*) may be cognate with Lat. *dūco*, Goth. *tiuhan* 'draw, lead'. The semantic relation 'draw' > 'drink' is common enough, cf. *pocula Lesbii, nectaris sucos ducere* (Hor.), etc., or μέθυ, οἶνον ἕλκειν, etc., or the relation of NE *draft* to *draw*. The B root form *tsok-*(cited Toch. Gramm. 460) is puzzling, unless it has its vowel by analogy with the present *yok-*. A *nut-* 'disappear', beside B *naut-* 'destroy', shows only a weak grade. The group of Goth. *naus*, ChSl. *navĭ* 'corpse', Lett. *nâwe* 'death', *nâwêt* 'kill' is hard to separate (IE **nāu-*, Walde-Pokorny 2.316). For the remaining examples of A *o* = B *au* I fail to find plausible etymologies, e.g. A *o-, on-* 'begin', B *aun-*;[33] A *oñant* (meaning ? cf. Toch. Gramm. 6), B *auñento*; A *krop-* 'collect', B *kraup-*; A *lotk-* 'turn, become', B *klautk-*, with sbs. A *lotäk* 'manner, way',

B *klautko* (Toch. Gramm. 467); A *muk* ('etwa 'nachlassen'', Toch. Gramm. 456), with adj. *mok* 'old', sbs. *mokone* 'age' (?), *mokats* 'strong', B *mauk-*; A *mrosk-* 'get tired of, renounce', B *mrausk-*; likewise in deriv. suffix, cf. A *prākrone* 'firmness', B *prakrauñe, prakrāwñe* (from A *prākär*, B *prākre* 'firm').

§ 3. B. *e*. The vowel *e*, rare in A except as a result of monophthongization, is extremely frequent in B, and corresponds to at least three different vowels in A, *a*, *o* and *e*. By far the most usual however is the first.

1. A *a* = B *e*. Where the etymology is at all clear we seem to be dealing usually with original *o* which apparently became *a* in PToch., remaining normally in dialect A but becoming *e* in B[34]: A *ak*, B ek 'eye': Grk. ὄσσε, Lat. *oculus*;[35] A *kam*, B *keme* 'tooth': Grk. γόμφος, OIcel. *kambr*, etc.;[36] A *tkaṁ*, B *keṁ* 'earth': Grk. χθον- (χθών, χθονός), Hitt. *tekan*;[37] A *rake*, B *reki* 'word': ChSl. *rokŭ* 'appointed time, goal' (beside *reką* 'say', but also *rěčĭ* 'speech, accusation'); A *lake, leki, leke* 'sleeping place': Grk. λόχος 'ambush, childbirth'. In the middle participle we find A *-amāṁ*, B *-emane* beside Grk. -όμενος.[38] In other forms we may have original *o* but with less certainty, so for example: A *kanweṁ*, B *kenīne* 'knees' (dual): Grk. γόνυ, Arm. *cunr* (but also Skt. *jānu*, Lat. *genu*, Goth. *kniu*, etc.); A *krant-, krañc-* (stem of *kāsu* 'good'), B *krente*, perhaps, with Pedersen[39]: Ir. *carae, carat* 'friend', i.e. a present participle of the type of Grk. φέροντ-, Goth. *baírand-* (not Lat. *ferent-*).[40] Others have no close cognates, but the root connections are clear, and belong clearly to the *e/o* series. The vocalism *o* may be assumed for them as representing the type of Lat. *toga* beside *tegō*, Grk. λόγος beside λέγω, etc.[41] Here I might list A *war*, B *were* 'odor': Goth. *warei* 'cunning', OE *waru*, OHG *wara* 'attention, heed', from the root of Lat. *vereor* 'fear', Grk. ὁράω 'see' (Walde-Pokorny 1.284 f.). The semantic shift between physical and mental, or between the various senses is usual (cf. Lat. *sentīre* > Fr. *sentir*). A *warpi*,

warpiśke, warpäśke, B *werpiśke* 'garden' may be *o*-grade forms belonging with Latin *urbs,* reduced grade of **wer-b(h)-* (Walde-Pokorny 1.275).[42] A *wartsi* 'retinue', B *wertsye, wertsiye* 'company' can be from dental formations to a radical element **wer-* seen in words of similar meaning, cf. Skt. *vṛnda-* 'host, crowd', OIr. *foirenn* 'division, crowd', OE *weorn* 'troop, multitude', and for suffix (but with other root form) Skt. *vrāta-* 'troop', OE *wrǣþ* 'flock' (Walde-Pokorny 1.265 f.). A *kapśañi,* B *kektseñ* 'body' might be compared directly with OIr. *cucht* 'color, outer form, kind', OIcel. *hǭttr* 'mode, appearance' (**qŏktu-,* Walde-Pokorny 1.456). The *p* of the A form is then purely dissimilative. Quite uncertain is the gradation of A *naweṁ* vbl. of *nu-* 'roar', cf. B *newe* 'noise', but perhaps **now-*: Skt. *navate, nāuti* 'roar, shout', Ir. *núall* 'cry, noise' (Walde-Pokorny 2.323), and of A *yśalm* 'sense, sensual pleasure', B *yśelme* 'kāma-' which Pedersen[43] compares with Grk. ἐ-θέλω 'wish', ChSl. *želati* 'desire', but no *o*-grade forms are elsewhere attested (cf. Walde-Pokorny 1.692). Obviously from the root **weq^w-* are A *wak,* B *wek,* 'voice' but whether we are to compare Lat. *vōx,* Skt. *vāc-,* with lengthened *o*-grade, or Grk. ὄσσα (**woq^wyə*), or the *s*-stem Grk. ἔπος, Skt. *vacas-* is dubious. The usual comparison is with Lat. *vōx,* etc., but I doubt if this is correct, in view of A *knān-* 'know': Lat *(g)nōsco,* Grk. γιγνώσκω, etc.; A *āknats,* B *aknāts* 'foolish': Lat. *nōtus,* Grk. γνωτός. Likewise it would appear that A *ṣar,* B *ṣer* 'sister', from PToch. **ṣäṣar* by syncope (cf. Toch. Gramm. 65), would represent PIE **swesor-* rather than the nom. **swesōr.*

A few forms could point to original *a,* with which IE *o* apparently fell together. So the verbal root A *kare-,* B *ker-* 'laugh' (Toch. Gramm. 426, Fragm. 122): Lat. *garriō* 'chatter', Grk. γαρριώμεθα·λοιδορούμεθα (Hesych.),[44] but there are other possibilities. In Iranian loanwords an *ă* is usually treated in the same fashion, e.g. A *pare,* B *peri* 'debt', cf. Av. *pāra-* 'debt', Sogd. *'prtk (apartak)* 'culpable';[45] A *paräṁ,* B *perne* 'position, dignity', cf. Av. *xvarənah-* 'majesty', Sogd. *parn*

(Toch. Gramm. 18); A *ratäk,* B *retke* 'army', cf. MPers. *ratak,* NPers. *rada* 'series, ordo, acies'.[46]

The syllabic liquids seem to have developed the vowel *a* in PToch., if I am right in comparing A *talke,* B *telki* 'offering' with Goth. *dulgs* 'debt', Ir. *dliged* 'duty, law', etc. (Walde-Pokorny 1.868). The original meaning seems to have been 'what is due'. Perhaps we have *r̥* in the verbal root A *ar-,* B *er(s)-* 'arise': Skt. *r̥ṇoti r̥ṇvati,* Lat. *orior,* etc., or (an *o*-grade?) Grk. ὄρνυμι, ὀρούω.[47]

The simplest view of A *nas-,* B *nes-* 'be' (e.g. pres. A *nasam, naṣt, naṣ,* etc., B *nesau, nesäṁ,* etc., cf. Toch. Gramm. 444, Fragm. 132), would be to equate it, as Meillet does,[48] with Grk. νέομαι 'come, go (back, away)', Skt. *násate* 'associates oneself with, joins', as a normal *e*-grade of an unaccented thematic class, but it is possible (and semantically better) to compare rather Grk. ναίω (*νασ-ι̯ω) 'dwell, be situated; cause to dwell', fut. νάσσομαι, aor. pass. ἐνάσθην, etc. If this shows a reduced grade of the root of νέομαι, etc., then Toch. agrees with Greek in its development. Cf. Walde-Pokorny 2.334 f.

The numeral forms, nom. sg. masc. A *sas,* in composition *ṣa-* e.g. *śäk ṣa-pi* '11', *wiki ṣa-pi* '21'), B *ṣeme, ṣe* (*śak-ṣe* '11') deserve special consideration. Meillet[49] assumes an *o*-grade of the root in Grk. εἷς (*ἑνς), μία (*σμια), ἕν, Lat. *sem-per,* etc. (Walde-Pokorny 2.488 ff.). It is possible also that we have representatives of **sm̥-* as in Grk. ἅ-παξ 'once', Lat. *sim-plex* 'simple', though this is commonly only prefixal. Cf. the discussion of *n̥* below § 5.

But there are some cases of A *a,* B *e* which cannot reflect in any fashion a PToch. *a,* whether from *o* or *a* or a reduced vowel of some sort. Here most notably A *mañ* 'moon, month', B *meṁ* 'moon', *meñe* 'month', obviously from **mēn-*: Grk. μήν, Lat. *mēnsis,* Goth. *mēna, mēnōþs,* etc.[50] The vowel of A *want,* B *yente* 'wind' likewise goes back to *ē,* though perhaps shortened prehistorically: Lat. *uentus,* Goth. *winds,* etc., PIE **wē-ntós* to **wē-* 'blow' (Walde-Pokorny 1.220). That of *A* *mank* 'blame, sin', B *menkī* 'less; lack', *menkītse* 'inferiority' was originally short if Meillet's[51] comparison with Lith. *meñkas* 'petty, weak', ChSl. *mękŭkŭ* 'weak' is correct, as may be true also for A *swase*, B *swese* 'rain' if from **suw-eso-* (suffix as in Skt. *rajasas, tamasas*, Lat. *creperum*)[52]: Grk. ὑετός 'hard rain' (**suw-etos*).[53] Provisionally, based on these few examples, one might posit a development of original *mĕ-*, *wĕ-* to *me-*, *we-* in PToch., maintained in B, but become *ma*, *wa* in A (under the influence of the labial?). If this is true we can further define the vocalism of the verbal root A *malyw-*, B *mely-* 'press, trample on', cf. Lat. *molō* (**melō*), Ir. *melim* 'grind', but also Goth. *malan*, Lith. *malù* id., and, more especially for both sense and suffix, Goth. *ga-malwjan* 'crush' (Walde-Pokorny 2.286). This development also renders the forms in A *wa-*, B *we-* (cited above as possible *o*-grades) yet more ambiguous.

There are still other examples of this dialectal correspondence for which I can propose no satisfactory etymology or probable root connection. I cite a few here without intention of making an exhaustive list: A *añcwāṣi* 'of iron', B *eñcuwo* 'iron'; A *aräṁ* 'countenance', B *ere* 'bimba-' (cf. also *arämpāt* 'rūpa-', B *erepate*); A *arkämnāṣi* possess. adj. in *-ṣi*, cf. B *erkenma* 'burial ground' (Toch. Gramm. 26); A *pal* (in *märkampal* 'dharma-'), B *pele* 'pious', neg. *em-pele* 'impious';[54] A *prank* 'moment', cf. B *prenke* perhaps 'circumstance, occasion' (Fragm. 139); A *praṣt*, B *preke* (*preśyaṁ, preściyai*) 'time';[55] A *yats*, B *yetse* 'hide'; A *saku*, B *sekwe* meaning? (cf. Toch. Gramm. 47); A *sark*, B *serke* 'family'; A *spaltäk*, B *spelke*, *speltke* 'effort'.

In A *akälyme* 'zugewendet', B *ekalymi* 'vaçya-, soumis', the variation is evidently in prefix (cf. A *kälyme* 'direction', Toch. Gramm. 248, 285). A *anapär*, *anaprä* beside B *enepre* 'before' and A *ane* 'into', *aneñcāṣ* 'out of' beside B *enenkā* 'interior' are all probably various derivatives of the adverbial stem **en-* (Walde-Pokorny 1.125 ff.).

2. A *o* = B *e*. Forms with this correspondence are much less usual than the preceding (§ 3, 1), and seem to rest for the most part, where there are clear etymologies, on PToch. *a* (IE *o* or *a* or Iran. *a* in loanwords), just as do the majority of the examples of A *a* = B *e*. The special development here probably lies with dialect A, but I fail yet to find a reasonable explanation for it. Here belong A *ñom*, B *ñem* 'name', cf. Grk. ὄνομα, Goth. *namo*, Arm. *anum* (IE *[*o*]*nomen-*). The *e*-grade would be otherwise unknown.[56] Similarly A *ṣom* sg. obl., *ṣome* pl. nom., B *ṣeme*, *ṣe* '1' (but A nom. sg. masc. *sas*, fem. *säṁ*, in composition *ṣa-*, cf. above § 3, 1), probably also *o*-grade forms, cf. Grk. ὁμός 'common, like, same', Goth. *sama* 'same', *etc.*[57] Is it worth noticing that both *ñom* and *ṣom* show palatalization of the initial consonant, indicating that *o* in these cases is of secondary origin? A *porat*, B *peret* 'ax' are probably from an Iran. (Sogd.?) **paraθ* = Skt. *paraçu-*.[58] The other forms showing this correspondence in radical syllable are of uncertain etymology. One, A *omäl*, B *emalle* 'hot' (with derivative substantives A *omlyi*, B emalya), I might connect with Lat. *amārus* 'bitter', Du. *amper* 'sharp, bitter', Skt. *amla-* 'sour' (Walde-Pokorny 1.179). For the semantics cf. Slav. *gorĭkŭ* 'bitter': *gorěti* 'burn'. Another, A *poto*, B *peti* perhaps 'reverence' (Toch. Gramm. 3 with ftn.), is connected by Sieg, Siegling, and Schulze (l.c.) with the verbal root A *pot-*, B *paut-* with orig. diphthong (above § 2, 2), but this is most dubious in view of the B vocalism. Dare I suggest that we have here an *o*-grade derivative of the root seen in the Germanic group, Goth. *bidjan*, *baþ*, etc. (IE **bhedh-*), for which no satisfactory etymology has yet been offered (cf. Walde-Pokorny 2.139 f.)? For A *oṅk*, B *eṅkwe* 'man' (beside *oṅki*? Fragm. 134, cf. § 4, 1) I can offer no suggestion. The variation can be one of suffix in A *cmol*, B *cmel* 'birth' (: A *täm-*, B *tem-*, *täm-* 'beget, be born'), and appears certainly to be one of prefix in A *opyac*, B *epyac*, *epiyac*. The A form reminds us of *opärkā* adv. beside *pärk-* 'rise' and *oklop* beside *klop* 'sorrow'. The meaning of

these forms (and hence the value of the prefix) is uncertain (Toch. Gramm. 249).

3. A *e* = B *e*. Unfortunately most of the forms showing this correspondence remain without plausible etymology. The most likely comparison is perhaps that of A *ents-*, *eṁts-*, B *eṅk-*, *eñc-* 'take, seize' with Grk. ἐν-εγκεῖν (redupl. aorist).[59] The relation of A *eṁts, ents* 'selfishness', B *eṁtse* 'envy' and of A, B *eṅkäl* 'passion' to this verbal stem is uncertain, and semantically difficult (cf. Toch. Gramm. 2, 7). A pret. *weñ-* abbreviated *we-* (pres. *tränk-*), B pret. *weñ-*, pres. *wesk-* 'say' are difficult to separate from A *wak, B wek* 'voice' (cf. above § 3, 1), probably therefore from **weqʷ-ne-* and **weqʷ-sko-*: Skt. *vákti, vívakti* 'speaks, says', Grk. εἶπον 'said', etc., but without exact formal equivalents elsewhere.[60] The gen. sg. of the interrog.-relat. pronoun A *ke,* B *ke-te* (where *-te* is a post-position) can reflect PIE **qʷeso*: Hom. τέο, ChSl. *česo,* OHG *hwes* (Brugmann, Grundr. 2.2.359). A *twe,* B *tweye* 'dust' are perhaps from **dhwes-*: Grk. (Hom.) θέειον, Att. θεῖον 'brimstone' (*θϝεσ-[ε]ιον), from the root of θύω 'rush, storm, rage', etc. (Walde-Pokorny 1.844). The *e* of B is the final increment frequently not found on the corresponding A form, cf. A *war,* B *were*; A *kam,* B *keme*, etc. The *y* is the glide developed in hiatus. For other examples of the correspondence I fail to find outside connections, e.g. A *e-*, *en-*, B *en-* 'command, punish', A *ek,* B *ekañi* 'wealth'; A, B *yepe* 'knife'; A, B *yerpe* 'disc, orb', etc. The list can be considerably lengthened. It is not possible to draw a final conclusion from such doubtful etymologies as I have cited here. However, such as they are, they point to the retention of IE *e* in both dialects. On the other hand we saw IE *ĕ* > A *a* in § 3, 1. As yet I see no solution to the problem.

§ 4. B *o*. The normal in A is *o*, rarely *a*. There is no sure example of *e*.

1. A *o* = B *o*. The only case entirely free of etymological ambiguity is the numeral 'eight', A *okät,* B *okt* from PIE

*$o\hat{k}t\bar{o}[u]$ (cf. Grk. ὀκτώ, Goth. *ahtau*, etc.). Likewise *o* seems original in A *orkäm*, B *orkaṁñe* 'darkness', cf. Grk. ὀρφνός 'dark', Arm. *arǰn* 'dark brown' (Walde-Pokorny 2.367).[61] The original vocalism of A, B *oko* 'fruit' is ambiguous. Lidén[62] is probably correct in connecting it with Lith. *úoga* 'berry', ChSl. *agoda, jagoda* 'fruit', Goth. *akran* 'fruit of the field', etc. (Walde-Pokorny 1.173 f.). Therefore probably *ə*, since it seems probable that *o, a* and *ə* fall together in Tocharian as in Germanic, Baltic, and Slavic. The reason for the retention of IE *o* (or better perhaps the reversion of PToch. *a* to *o*) in both dialects in the first two cases cited is obscure.[63]

In a few cases, some of them of doubtful etymology to be sure, *o* in both dialects seems to be the reflex of a more original *u*. So particularly in A, B *poṣi* 'side, wall' if Fraenkel[64] is right in comparing Lith. *pùse*, Lett. *puse* 'half, side'. For dialect B this development has the indisputable support of *okso* 'ox' (no A equivalent): Skt. *ukṣaṇ-*, Goth. *aúhsa*; *soyä* 'son' (A *se* with monophthongization): Grk. υἱός; *kokale* 'wagon', beside A *kukäl* with more original vocalism (*u* from *e* due to influence of the labiovelar, cf. Grk. κύκλος, PIE *q^we-q^wlos);[65] perhaps also *orocce, orotse* 'large' (no A equivalent): Skt. *urú-*, Grk. εὐρύς 'broad'.[66] For the same development in dialect A can perhaps be counted *por* 'fire', from **puwōr* > **puwr* > **pur*, cf. B *puwār*, or *pwār*, or perhaps original **pur* simply with *r* of nominative but vocalism of oblique cases gen. **punés*, etc. (for inflection cf. Walde-Porkony 2.14, but read A for B).

Slim though our evidence is for the development of *u* to *o* in A, still we may be allowed to apply it to a few other cognates which show *o* in both dialects. So perhaps in A *kos*, B *kos, kosa*, etc. 'yāvat-' if from the interrog.-indef. *u*-stem *q^wu-, but the differentiation from the interrog.-relat. pronoun A *kus, kuc* (Toch. Gramm. 176 ff.), B k_use, k_uce (Lévi-Meillet, MSL 18.418 ff.) is remarkable. Here also may be mentioned the pronominal adj. 'all, each, every', A *poñc-, ponts-*, etc.

(nom. sg. *puk*), B *po*, pl. *ponta* (cf. Toch. Gramm. 161 f., Fragm. 138). In spite of Lévi's (Fragm. 38) reference to Meillet's connection with Grk. πᾶς (παντός, etc.) the resemblance is probably purely fortuitous and Brugmann's[67] derivation of the latter from **k̑wā-nt-*: **keu-* 'swell' (Walde-Pokorny 1.365 ff.) remains preferable. However a similar semantic origin is possible. I would suggest connection therefore with Lith. *puntù, pùsti* 'puff up, swell', Lett. *pūst* 'blow, breathe', cf. especially the nasalized form Lett. *punte* 'bump, belly', all from a dental extension of an onomatopoeic **pū̆-* 'blow, swell'. For meaning, cf. from the guttural extension Skt. *pūga-* 'multitude, quantity', *puñja-* 'heap, mass, quantity' (Walde-Pokorny 2.80). The nom. A *puk* shows the addition of the particle *-k* (Grk. -γε, Goth. *-k*, etc.) common to pronominal forms.[68] The presence of the more original vocalism in A *pu-k* beside B *po* recalls A *kukäl* 'wagon' beside B *kokale* (cf. above).

One is tempted also to connect A *klyom*, B *klyom(n-)* 'noble' with A *klyos-*, B *klyaus-* (above, § 2, 2), as representing a weak grade of the root (**k̑lu-m-*) but this leaves the palatalization of the preceding *l* unexplained.

That Toch. *o* has yet other origins is shown, however, by the comparison of A, B *yok-* 'drink' with Hitt. *ekuzi* 'drinks',[69] and also by that of A, B *kroṅśe* 'bee' with OHG *hornuz*, OE *hyrnet*, Lat. *crābrō*, Lith. *širšė*, Russ.-ChSl. *sŭrŭšenĭ*,[70] which appear to be various derivatives from PIE **k̑ₑrəs-* (*k̑r̥̄s-*), cf. Walde-Pokorny 1.406 f. This development of *r̥̄* is assumed by Fraenkel for A in the isolated *orto* 'up' (: Skt. *ūrdhva-*, Av. *ərəδwa-*, Lat. *arduus*).[71] But the form could as well be derived from **urdh-*, weak grade of the root in Skt. *vardhate* 'increases, grows', Grk. ὀρθός 'up-right, straight' (Walde-Pokorny 1.289).

For the rest of the examples of A, B *o* which I have collected, I have no suggestion, e.g. A *oṅk*, B *oṅki* 'man' (beside B *eṅkwe*, above, § 3, 2); A, B *ottsoyce* (B = asecanaka-, cf. Fragm. 134); A *klyokäśś-*, B *klokaśne* 'pore'; A *kᵤraś*, obl. stem *krośś-*, B *krośce* (*krost-*, *krośc-*, *krośś-*, but also *krauśś-*! cf. Toch. Gramm. 43 f.) 'cold'; A *ṣotre*, B *ṣotri* 'sign'; likewise suffixal in A *śmoññe*, 'place', B *śmoññe*, *ścmoññe* 'base' (: A *ṣtäm-* 'stand'? Toch. Gramm. 433), and A, B *ykorñe* 'negligence' (: *yäk-* 'be careless').

A particularly puzzling case is the relationship of A *poke* (sg. *ā-* case *pokeyā*, du. *pokeṁ*, pl. obl. *pokes*), B *pauke*, but obl. *pokai* 'arm' to PIE **bhāĝhus* (in Dor. πᾶχυς, OE *bōg*, Skt. *bāhu-*, etc.).[72] If there were any other evidence for it, one might be tempted to assume an original gradation **bhā[u]ĝh-*/ **bhəuĝh-*/**bhū̆ĝh-*, B *pokai* then representing the weak grade. The situation would be exactly parallel to that observed in the case of Dor. φᾱγός 'oak', Lat. *fāgus*, OE *bōc* 'beech', beside Icel. *beyki* 'beech(woods)', Russ. dial., Ukr. *boz* 'elder' (PIE **bhā[u]ĝos*/**bhəuĝos*/**bhū̆ĝos*, Walde-Pokorny 2.129).[73]

2. Only a very few cases of A *a* = B *o* have been noticed. In only one of these is the original vocalism quite clear: A *pracar*, B *procer* 'brother' from PIE **bhrāter-* (Lat. *frāter*, etc.), but this does not agree with A *mācar*, B *mācer* 'mother' from PIE **māter-*. The comparison A *waṣt*, B *ost* 'house' with Grk. ἄστυ 'city', Skt. *vastu-*[74] (PIE *a*) is complicated by the loss of the initial in B. B *solme* 'whole', from which I cannot separate A *salu* 'totally', has been compared[75] with Grk. ὅλος, OLat. *sollus*, Skt. *sarva-* (PIE *o*). The comparison of A *praski*, B *prosko*, *proskye* 'fear' with the Gmc. group OHG *forhta*, Goth. *faúrhtei*, Arm. *erkiul* 'fright', etc.[76] (Walde-Pokorny 2.48) tells us little about the original vowel.

3. The only case where A *e* might correspond to B *o* is the difficult group A *es* beside B *oñi* 'shoulder'. But the forms hardly seem cognate, and, if so, their relationship to Skt. *aṁsa-* Grk. ὦμος, Lat. *umerus*, Goth. *ams*, Arm. *us*, is uncertain.[77]

§ 5. IE **n̥-*. There are various correlations in A and B which apparently involve forms negated by the inherited prefix. But there is considerable diversity in its appearance.

For example we have A, B *en-* (by assimilation *em-*) in A *empele* 'powerful', B *empele* 'impious, frightful', to A *-pal* (in *sne-pal* 'unrighteousness', *märkam-pal* 'dharma-', cf. Toch. Gramm. 24, 240, 248), B *pele* 'pious'. The same appearance seems probable in the case of A, B *eñcare* 'aniṣṭa-, apriya-' (Toch. Gramm. 48, 79), possibly for *eñ-ciñcare* by haplology, to A *ciñcär* 'lovely', B *cäñcare, cäñcre* 'priya-'. Isolated B forms are *eneṅka* 'except' which seems to be a neg. cpd. of a verbal adj. to *eṅk-* 'take' e.g. 'non compris' (Lévi, MSS Remains),[78] and *eśuwacca* 'having not eaten' (*śwā-*, *śu-* 'eat'), with loss of nasal before sibilant as in *piś* 'five', *misa* 'meat', but the quality of the vowel is retained, showing that the loss is not of the same antiquity.[79] On the other hand we find *an-* in B *am-plākänte* 'without coming to an agreement',[80] *anākänte* 'anindita-'[81] (for *an-nākänte* ?) and apparently also in *anaiwatse* in Lévi's doubtful translation 'déplaisant' (Fragm. 112), to which A **ānewāts* (dat. pl. *ānewātsnac* and sb. *ānewātsune*) corresponds. Sieg, Siegling, and Schulze (Toch. Gramm. 9, 19, 68 ftn.) make no attempt at interpretation or derivation. It seems probable to me that, as negative forms, they are derivatives of the verbal root A *e-*, B *ai-* 'give' (cf. above, § 2, 1) with a suffix *-wāts* (op. cit. 19). The meaning of the unattested simplex would be near that of Grk. αἴσιος 'boding well, favorable' from the same root. A development parallel to that of Grk. ἀ-, Skt. *a-* is hardly to be assumed on the evidence of A *āknats*, B *aknātse* 'stupid, ignorant' (vb. *knā*(*n*)- 'know').[82] We have rather dissimilatory loss of *-n-* before *kn-*.[83] The relation of B *emprarkre*, which Lévi translates doubtfully 'court' (Fragm. 116), to A *apärkär* (Toch. Gramm. 262 without interpretation) is uncertain. Cf. A *pärkär*, B *pärkre* 'long'? Similarly we find B *empalk* . . . beside A *apälkā* (or *amälkā*? Toch. Gramm. 321). The meanings of both are obscure (Fragm. 116, Toch. Gramm. 1. c.), and so comparison with the verbal root A *pälk-*, B *pälk-*, *palk-* 'appear, shine' is to no purpose.

There are actually then only two probable correspondences for the negative prefix, namely A, B *en-*, and A *ān-*, B *an-*. These are possibly to be explained as variant sandhi forms, originally *en-* from **n̥-* (*ₑn-*) before vowels, *ān-*, *an-* before consonants? This appearance (*ān, an*) for *n̥* is to be assumed (with further reduction, under conditions unknown) for A *känt*, B *känte* '100' from PIE **k̂m̥tóm*, and perhaps also in A *sas, säṁ, ṣa-* 'one' (above, § 3, 1, 2). If this explanation of their origin is true, the two negative prefixes thus arisen have received an entirely new distribution without reference to the following initial, e.g. *em-pele, eñcare*, and **ānewāts, anaiwatse* beside the historically correct B *en-eṅka, am-plākänte*, etc. This confusion is paralleled to some extent in Irish, where correctly we expect *en-* before dental and velar stops and spirants (becoming *in-* before original *d, g*; *ē* before *k, t, s*) but *an-* (*am-*) before vowels, labials and sonants, e.g. *in-derb, ingnāth, ē-coir*, etc., but *an-ecne, aim-brit, amlobar*, etc. However we find also *an-dach* 'worthlessness', *an-glan* 'unclean', *an-cride* 'wrong', etc.[84]

[First published in *Language*, Vol. 14, No. 1, January-March, 1938, pp. 20-38].

1 Hoernle, JASB 62.39 f. (1893).

2 I use here the name 'Tocharian' in the established (American) sense for both dialects A and B, without regard to the appropriateness of the name for both or even one of the dialects. Lévi's 'langue Ārśi' (= A) and 'langue de Koutcha' or 'Koutchéen' (= B) may be preferable on several counts, but the former is yet quite unfamiliar in English. Should we translate perhaps as 'Arshian'? 'Kuchean' is of course familiar in England through the works of Sir M. A. Stein and others. Cf. Lévi, Le 'Tokharien B', langue de Koutcha, Journal Asiatique 1913 (2).311 ff., 1933 (222). 1 ff. (The latter also in Fragments de Textes Koutchéens, Cahiers de la Société Asiatique 1re Série, II, Paris 1933).

3 Fragments de Textes Koutchéens 31 ff.

4 Indogermanen und Germanen 115.

5 Geschichte der indogermanischen Sprachwissenschaft, zweiter Teil, 5, 2 (Tocharisch).35.

6 Archiv Orientální 2.320 ff. (1930).

7 Journal Asiatique 1912 (19).339 ff.

8 Above ftn. 2. Henceforth abbr. Fragm.

9 Göttingen, 1931. Henceforth abbr. Toch. Gramm.

10 Cf. also Feist, Indogermanen und Germanen[3] 115 ftn. 1; Fraenkel, IF 50.7.

11 Le Groupement des Dialectes Indo-européens 19 f. So also now Benveniste, 'Tokharien et Indo-Européen', in Germanen u. Indogermanen, Festschrift für H. Hirt 1.235.

12 Groupement 31.

13 Cf. Meillet, MSL 17.286.

14 Meillet, Indogerm. Jahrbuch 1.18; Schrader, Reallexikon[2] 2.353; Schulze, Kleine Schriften 260, etc.

15 Schulze, Kl. Schr. 240 ftn. 3, 260; Fraenkel, IF 50.97.

16 JAs. 1911 (18).633. Smith's (Videnskabsselskabets Skrifter 2. Hist.-Filos. Kl., 1910, no. 5) early derivation from IE **leiq*^{w}-:Grk. λείπω, etc. is certainly to be discarded (cf. Meillet, l.c.), but is still quoted by Schwentner (Tocharisch 35), Lévi (Fragm. 32) and Reuter, Journal de la Soc. finno-ougrienne 47.4.13.

17 Lidén, Aufsätze Kuhn 142 f.

18 Falk-Torp, Etym. Wtb. 744; Walde-Pokorny 2.242.

19 Meillet, JAs. 1912 (19).116; MSL 17.286; Idg. Jahrb. 1.14; Fraenkel, IF 50.8.

20 Cf. Fraenkel, IF 50.19; Hermann, KZ 50.307.

21 Cf. Schulze, Kl. Schr. 252 ftn. 4; Fraenkel, IF 50.7.
Professor Sapir (Language 12.263) assumes loss of post-vocalic IE *d*

in Tocharian, citing this group and A *kri* 'will', *käryā-* 'bedenken', which he connects with the IE words for 'heart', Grk. καρδία, Lat. *cor, cordis*, etc. To arrive at the proper vocalism in the latter case however he starts from an (otherwise unknown) *kr$_e$d- reduced form of *kred- from dissyllabic *kered-. The comparison of Skt. *çrad-dadhāti* 'believes', Lat. *crēdō*, however, is no support for the base, since the first member of these verbal compounds is probably not a word for 'heart', but rather an Indo-Iranian-Italo-Celtic religious term indicative of the magical properties of an object, cf. MIr. *cretair*, W. *creir, crair* 'relics (of the Saints), holy thing' (Walde-Pokorny 1.423; Walde-Hofmann 287; and especially Vendryes, Rev. celt. 44.90 ff.). Against this loss of post-vocalic *d*, I would cite B *preściye* 'mire, filth': Lith. *brendù, brìsti*, Russ.-ChSl. *bredu, bresti* 'wade', etc. (Lidén, Stud. z. toch. Sprachgesch. 7 f.; but we might have here IE *dh* of course); A *kät-k-* 'überschreiten, vorübergehen' (Toch. Gramm. 427), B *kät-k-* 'tomber, passer, arriver à': Lat. *cadō* 'fall', Skt. *çad-* 'fall off' (so Meillet, in Lévi, MSS Remains 378 f.); A *āti*, B *ǎti* 'grass': Lat. *ador* 'spelt', Goth. *atisk* 'field of grain'.

22 Fraenkel, IF 50.230. But A *oko* 'fruit' = B *oko*, hence more probably (after Lidén, Stud. z. toch. Sprachgesch. 34) to Lith. *úoga* 'berry', Goth. *akran* 'fruit (of the field)', etc. (Walde-Pokorny 1.173), rejected by Fraenkel, 1.c. Cf. below § 4, 1.

23 Fraenkel, IF 50.222 ftn. 2. For Schrader's A *ko-*, B *kan-*, Poucha's A *ko-*, B *ken-*, cf. above.

24 Schrader, Reallex.[2] 2.255.

25 Meillet, JAs. 1912 (19).113; MSL 15.327 ff.; Schrader, Reallex. 1.635; etc.

26 Fraenkel, IF 50.16 f.

27 Meillet, Idg. Jahrb. 1.16; Fragm. 37 (quoted by Lévi). Connection with A, B *śwā-, śu-* 'eat' (as e.g. Fraenkel, IF 50.7) seems highly improbable.

28 So Fraenkel IF 50.8 (but eventually with different IE root connection, cf. ftn. 27). The older comparison with Lat. *homō*, Goth. *guma*, old Lith. *žmuõ*, etc. 'man' is certainly to be discarded.

29 So Schrader, Reallex. 1.246 and cited also by Poucha, Arch. Or. 2.323. Toch. Gramm. gives only *yoṁ* 'Spur'.

30 Schulze, Kl. Schr. 261.

31 Fraenkel, IF 50.227 ftn.

32 Meillet, Idg. Jahrb. 1.19 suggests Turkish origin without closer identification, but apparently with reference to the group of Osmanli *gün*.

33 Connection with any one of several roots in *au-*, or *eu-* is of course

possible, cf. e.g. **au-* 'weave' (Walde-Pokorny 1.16), possibly orig. 'begin weaving', cf. Lat. *ordīrī* in the wider sense 'begin'; or perhaps **eu-* 'put on', of clothing, etc. (op. cit. 1.109f.), had a more general sense originally. But such connections cannot of course be demonstrated.

[34] I fail to find evidence to support Meillet's statement (Introduction[7] 99) that Tocharian keeps IE *o* and *a* distinct. For the cases of retained *o* in both dialects cf. § 4, 1.

[35] Meillet, JAs. 1912 (19).113.

[36] Reuter, Jour. de la Soc. Finno-ougr. 47.4.9.

[37] Meillet, JAs. 1911 (18).147, Idg. Jahrb. 1.19; Kretschmer, Glotta 20.66 f.; Benveniste, Hirt-Festschrift 2.235. But no one seems to have envisaged the difficulty that Toch. *ṁ* does not equal final *m* but *n*. Greek and Hittite show simply the extension of *n* from *m*, phonetically correct in final position, to the oblique cases (Hitt. gen. *taknas*), cf. Sturtevant, Hitt. Gramm. 136. The root has *m*, cf. Grk. **χαμαί**, Lat. *humus*, etc. (Walde-Pokorny 1.662 ff.).

[38] Cf. also Meillet, MSL 17.284.

[39] Groupement 28.

[40] Contrary to Meillet's assumption (MSL 18.18) based on the palatalized *ṣṣ* from *sk*.

[41] Cf. Meillet, MSL 17.284.

[42] Reuter (Jour. Soc. Finno-ougr. 47.4.13) revives again the ghost of labial development from labiovelars by deriving the group from **wer-gʷ-* an otherwise unattested formation (cf. Walde-Pokorny 1.272).

[43] Groupement 20 f.

[44] Poucha, Archiv Orientální 2.324.

[45] Meillet, MSL 19.159.

[46] Schulze, Kl. Schr. 257.

[47] Meillet, MSL 19.159.

[48] JAs. 1911 (17).456.

[49] MSL 17.284 f.

[50] Schrader, Reallex.[2] 2.70, etc.

[51] JAs. 1912 (19).112; Walde-Pokorny 2.267.

[52] Cf. Brugmann, Grundr.[2] 2.543.

[53] Meillet, JAs. 1912 (19).115 f.; Boisacq, Dict. étym. 999.

[54] Pedersen's comparison (Groupement 32) with MHG *un-bil* 'ungemäss' is surely erroneous because of the A vocalism.

[55] Holthausen's comparison (IF 39.66) with NHG *Frist*, etc. wrecks on the guttural of the B forms, and also on A *tāpärk* 'now', which is probably related. For the Gmc. group cf. Walde-Pokorny 2.34.

[56] Meillet, JAs. 1911 (17).451; MSL 17.284.

[57] Ibid.

[58] Lidén, Studien zur toch. Sprachgesch. 1.17 ff., but without B *peret*.

[59] Meillet, MSL 18.28; Fraenkel, IF 50.227 ftn. 1.

[60] Meillet, JAs. 1911 (18).148; Toch. Gramm. 2.

[61] Benveniste, Hirt-Festschrift 2.236.

[62] Stud. z. toch. Sprachgesch. 34, but probably not from *ā* as he assumes.

[63] Sapir (LANGUAGE 12.179 ftn. 15) invokes Brugmann's *å*, that is *o* not of the *e/o*-series (and for which he substitutes *ǫ*), to explain the retention of A *okät*, and in *opäśśi*, *opśi* 'dexterous, skilful', which he connects with Lat. *opus*, etc., as opposed to IE *o* in gradation with *e* which gives A *a*. This explanation comes to grief on at least two points. First *å* (*ǫ*) also gives A *a* in PIE **oqʷ-* (Walde-Pokorny 1.169 ff., Brugmann, Grundr.[2] 1.153 ff.), cf. A *ak* (B *ek*, cf. above 3, 1) 'eye', and in PIE **potis* (Walde-Pokorny 2. 77 f., Brugmann, l.c.), cf. A *pats* 'husband' (no B equivalent). Secondly IE *o* (alternating with *e*) gives also A *o*; cf. *ṣom* sg. obl., *ṣome* pl. nom. of *sas*, fem. *säṁ* 'one' (above § 3, 2 with reference), and also Grk. ὀρφνός, A *orkäm*, B *orkaṁñe* probably stand in ablaut relationship to Grk. ἔρεβος, Goth, *riqis*, etc. cf. Walde-Pokorny 2.367; Benveniste, Hirt-Festschrift 2.236.

[64] IF 50.229.

[65] Schulze, Kl. Schr. 239; Benveniste, Hirt-Festschrift 229.

[66] Pedersen, Groupement 39.

[67] Begriff der Totalität 23, 35, 53, 60.

[68] Toch. Gramm. 306 f.; Meillet, MSL 18.416. Holthausen (IF 39.65) takes the *k* as radical and connects with Grk. πυκνός 'close, thick', but does not envisage the forms in *-nt-*.

[69] Sturtevant, Hitt. Gr. 91; Benveniste, Hirt-Festschrift 2.235.

[70] Schrader, Reallex.[2] 2.645; Walde-Hofmann 283; Benveniste, op. cit. 234.

[71] IF 50.6. But on the interrelationship of the forms cited, cf. Walde-Pokorny 1.148, 289; Walde-Hofmann 64 f.

[72] Cf., for example, Meillet, Idg. Jahrb. 1.18; Schulze, Kl. Schr. 255 ftn. 1; Fraenkel, IF 50.7.

[73] In his criticism of my paper on Tocharian vocalism (LSA meeting Chicago, December, 1936), and later by personal letter, Professor Sapir suggests the presence of a sort of *u*-epenthesis in Tocharian. That is, PIE **bhāǵhu-s* > Pre-Toch. **pāku-* > PToch. **pāᵘku-* > **pauk-* whence A *pok-e*, B *pauk-e*. This view is exceedingly fascinating for these particular words, in as much as it affords an ex-

planation also for B obl. *pokai*, which may then represent the vocalism inherited from another IE case, e.g. dat. **bhāĝhewai*, loc. **bhāĝhēu*, **bhāĝhewi*, etc. – provided, of course, that IE *ā* may give Toch. *o*.

74 Schrader, Reallex.[2] 1.443.

75 Meillet, MSL 18.386.

76 Cf. Holthausen, IF 39.65 without the B forms.

77 Meillet, JAs. 1911 (18).150; Schulze, Kl. Schr. 255 ftn. 4; Fraenkel, IF 50.7.

78 Manuscript Remains of Buddhist Literature Found in Eastern Turkestan, ed. by A. F. R. Hoernle, Oxford 1916.

79 Cf. Pedersen, Groupement 32 ftn., but for B *ekalymi* 'subject' (to which corresponds prob. A *akälyme* 'zugewendet') cf. above, § 3, 1 end.

80 Meillet, Idg. Jahrb. 1.14; MSL 18.20.

81 Meillet, JAs. 1911 (17). 456, MSL 18.20.

82 But so apparently Petersen, LANG. 11.197 with ftn. where he derives A from **n̥-gnətos*.

83 So Meillet in Lévi, MSS Remains 377.

84 Cf. Pedersen, Vgl. Gramm. d. kelt. Sprachen 1.46 ff., 2.7 f.; Thurneysen, Hdb. d. Altir. 493 f.

The Tocharian Palatalization (I)

[This is intended as the first of a series of detailed discussions of the so-called Tocharian palatalization. All that is attempted here is an examination of the actual appearance of the sound change, to determine what are the original and what are the secondary consonants.]

Few detailed studies of the so-called Tocharian palatalization have appeared, though off-hand mention of it has been current. Perhaps the first serious treatment was that by W. Schulze in an article dealing with the reduplicated preterit in Tocharian and Germanic (BSB 166-74 [1924], phil-.hist. Kl. = Kl. Schr. 239-48),[1] but there the discussion was only incidental to the main topic. Recently two more discussions have appeared, one by A. J. van Windekens in his monograph De indo-europeesche Bestanddeelen in de tocharische Declinatie 56 ff., esp. 66 (Louvain, 1940), the other by H. Pedersen in his recent volume Tocharisch vom Gesichtspunkt der indoeuropäischen Sprachvergleichung 235 ff. (Copenhagen, 1941).

That the subject is a confused and difficult one is generally recognized – but so are most of the problems of Tocharian phonology. And perhaps in this case, as already in others, we have been too prone to jump at conclusions by drawing analogies from our experience in other languages. Indeed the very term 'palatalization' shows our preconception of the nature of these consonant changes before we have established their conditions. In fact, even the consonant changes themselves are established only in the most general outlines.

There is general agreement however that the affricates *c* [tʃ′] and *ts*, the sibilants *ś* and *ṣ*, the nasal *ñ*, and the lateral *ly* have, in most instances at least, arisen secondarily. And there is also general agreement that both *c* and *ts* arise from dentals which are normally reflected by Tocharian *t*; that *ṣ* arises from *s*, and *ś* from velars, labio-velars and palatals which appear usually as *k*; and that *ñ* and *ly* reflect normal *n* and *l*. There is less agreement that *my* and *py* bear a similar relationship to *m* and *p*, or that *y* may be actually the 'palatalized' form of *w*.[2]

In view of this nebulous situation, it seems to me that it might perhaps be profitable to review the whole phenomenon without prejudice, in the first place to establish once and for all, if possible, what its appearance actually is; and then, but only later, when we are sure of this, we should examine the phonetic conditions which have led to the changes under consideration. For any one who has been over the ground already, the prospect of a review in the latter regard is anything but encouraging.

Now in dealing with such a phenomenon as palatalization in Tocharian, or in any language for that matter, it is patent that we should be extremely careful to base our conclusions on its appearance in isolated forms, where sound laws have perhaps had the best chance to take their course unmolested by the analogy of grammatical categories. Hence we should avoid in Tocharian particularly the use of forms from preterit, subjunctive, and imperfect stems where palatalization seems to have acquired a functional significance (cf. SSS 349 f.).

In taking up the first of our assigned tasks, a clarification of the actual appearance of the sound change, we shall consider the altered consonants in the order mentioned above: *c*, *ts*, *ś*, *ṣ*, *ñ*, *ly*, *my*, *py*, *y*.

1. That *c* is normally a reflex of Tocharian *t* is generally agreed, and seems particularly clear from such internal relations as *cämp-* 'be able' beside *tampe* 'might'; A *cmol*, B *cmel* 'birth' beside A *täm-*, B *täm-*, *tem-* 'be born'; or the second singular pronoun obl. A *cŭ*, beside nom. *tu*; and the masculine singular demonstrative obl. A *cam* beside the corresponding feminine *tām* or neuter *täm*, etc.

As regards the original (Indo-European) order of the dental involved, we are, in most cases, dealing with the voiceless unaspirated stop, and so in the last two instances cited above and clearly also in the case of the primary endings of the second and third persons plural in A, e.g. *-c* and *-ñc*, from IE *-te* and *-nti*. But we cannot assume, with van Windekens (Toch. Decl. 62), that this is always the case, nor can we assume that *ts* (below) is reserved for the Indo-European aspirates, though entirely unimpeachable etymologies are to be desired. However, A *ckācar* 'daughter' certainly shows *dh* reflected by *c* in that dialect, though B *tkācer* shows the initial dental unaltered. Likewise A *cmol*, B *cmel* 'birth', already cited above beside the verb, are quite plausibly to be derived from the root seen in Skt. *dhāman-* 'dwelling place', Av. *dāmi-* 'creation', Lat. *familia* etc. The evidence of the subjunctive middle verb forms A *cmatär*, B *cmetär* from this root, like that of the preterit A *casäs, casär* from *tas-* (*tā-, täs-*) 'put, lay' (IE *dhē-*), would of course by itself be inconclusive for the reason mentioned above. According to V. Pisani (KZ 62.43), we could add here A *märc* 'head' as from IE **mr̥dh-*: Skt. *mūrdhan-* etc., but the connection of the latter with OE *molda* may seem preferable to many.[3] On the other hand, van Windekens' connection of *mrāc* with Gk. βρεχμός, βρέχμα[4] is surely to be rejected on the ground that Toch. *c* cannot reflect the Indo-European gutturals (see below). Another possible example of IE *dh* reflected by *c* would be perhaps A *cok* 'lamp', B *cauk-* 'light up', if from the base **dheu-* seen in Skt. *dhavala-* 'dazzling white', Gk. θοός· λαμπρός (Hesych.), etc., as I have already suggested elsewhere.[5]

Furthermore *c* seems to reflect the voiced unaspirated dental in A *koc*, B *kauc* 'high', IE **qou-d-*, cf. Skt. *kakud-* 'summit' (beside **qou-q-* in Goth. *hauhs*, etc),[6] and possibly also in A *plāc* 'word': Gk. φλεδών 'chatter', according to van Windekens.[7] The same scholar's connection of *pāci* 'right' (? 'right' or 'left', SSS) with the root of OHG *fazzōn* 'seize' (IE

**ped-*)[8] seems too doubtful however to cite for further support.

It was often assumed earlier, but more recently also by van Windekens (cf. above), that *c* may also reflect an Indo-European guttural. I am able to verify this only after nasals, e.g. A *añcäl* 'bow': Gk. ἀγκύλος 'bent', OHG *angul* 'hook' etc.; B *eñcīmar, eñciträ*, opt. 1 and 3 sg., beside *eṅkasträ*, 'takes': Gk ἐνεγκεῖν.[9] (On A *eṃts-*, cf. below). Pedersen[10] has indicated that this is purely a secondary development, by way of *ñ* + *śi* > *ñci*, analogous to that seen in possessive adjectives like A *atroñci* (from *atär* 'hero') or *kᵘleñci* (from *kᵘle* 'woman'), which contain a double suffix -(*e*)*ṃ* + *ṣi*. Thus the guttural has here its normal palatalization to *ś* first (see below).

2. That *ts* is also of dental origin seems clear. Clean-cut etymologies like A *tsek-*, B *tsaik-* 'form, mould': Skt. *dih-* 'anoint', Lat. *fingō* 'form', or A, B *tsäk-* 'burn': Skt. *dah-* 'burn', Gk. θέπτανος (Hesych.) 'kindled', τέφρα 'ashes', Lith. *dègti* 'burn', prove conclusively that it may reflect IE **dh-*. But that this is the only origin, as van Windekens (Toch. Decl. 46) would maintain, seems to me unlikely, for I would hesitate to discard the connection of A, B *tsär-* 'divide' with Gk. δέρω 'flay', Goth. *dis-taíran* 'tear apart' etc. (IE **der-*),[11] or that of A *tsuk-*, B *tsauk-* 'drink' (pret. and subj. stem of *yok-*) with Lat. *dūcō*, etc.[12] Even clearer is the evidence that *ts* may reflect IE t, e.g. A *pats* 'husband': Skt. *pati* 'lord'; A *lānts*, B *lāntsa* 'queen' (**wlantyā*); A *klots*, B *klautso* 'ear': Av. *sraota-* 'hearing', Goth. *hliuþ* 'hearing, attention'; A *tsru* 'little': Gk. τέρυς 'weak'[13] etc. The frequent assumption, however, that *ts* may represent an original guttural has, for the most part, poor etymological support. The best is possibly van Windekens' suggested connection (Toch. Decl. 58 f.) of A *tsärw-*, B *tsärw-* perh. 'take courage' (= Skt. *ā-śvas-*, *pra-grah-*[14]) with Skt. *háryati* 'desires', Gk. χαίρω' rejoice' etc. The lack of a formation in -(*e*)*u-* from this base is however against the etymology. Even less likely on grounds of formation seems to me the same scholar's connection of A *tsru* 'little'

(cf. above) with Skt. *hrasva-* 'short'. Schwentner's connection (IF 57.251) of A *tsär* 'rough, sharp', with Skt. *khara-* 'hard, rough' is not objectionable in itself, but should perhaps be discarded in favor of Pedersen's suggestion (Toch. 242 f.) of relationship between *tsär* and *tsrasi* 'strong', B *tsirauñe* 'force'. The one remaining apparent example of guttural origin for *ts* is then the oft cited A *tsar* 'hand': Gk. χείρ. However, the corresponding B *ṣar* was always embarrassing. As Pedersen notes (Toch. 236), however, the Hittite *kessar* (*ki-eš-šar*) indicates that this was not a direct development of the guttural, but rather by way of syncope from PToch. **śesar* to **śsar* > **śṣar*, whence simplification of the initial cluster to *ts* in A but *ṣ* in B. And furthermore, Pedersen[15] disposes, in similar fashion, of the bothersome A *eṃts-* 'seize' beside B *eṅk-*, *eñc-* (above under *c*). Presumably the *ts* arose in the infinitive suffix *-ti*, i.e. original *ṅk-ts* > *ṅts* > *nts* (*ṃts*), and thence *ts* spread throughout the paradigm in place of *ṅk* (or *ñc*, its palatalized form) in dialect A but not in B. Support for this view is afforded by the related A *eṃts* 'selfishness', which shows the same change also in B *entse* 'greed'. The suffix here was probably *-tyo-*.

With regard to the further change of *ts* to *ś*, see below.

3. As a product of palatalization, *ś* has several origins. The most immediate seems to be any of the various Indo-European gutturals, though, apparently by chance, clear-cut examples of a few of these are lacking.

Of the palatals, IE *k̑* may be reflected in B *aiśträ* 'vijānāte' beside *aikemar* 'janāmi': Goth. *aih* 'owns', Skt. *iśe* 'rule, am able';[16] and IE *ĝ* is evident in A pres. mid. sg. 3 *āśträ*, pres. pple. *āśant* beside pres. act. pl. 3 *ākeñc*, from *āk-* 'lead': Gk. ἄγω, Skt. *ajāmi* etc., and is probably likewise to be recognized in A and B *śwā-*, *śu-* 'eat' as from **ĝyeu*, cf. OE *cēowan*, OHG *kiuuan*, Russ. *žujú*, *ževát'* '*chew*', etc.[17] IE *ĝh-* seems probable for A *śew-* 'gape, yawn': OHG *anagiwēn*, Lat. *hiāre*, OCS *zeją* 'gape', Skt. *vi-jihīte* 'gape apart'.[18]

For the plain velars there is little definite evidence. IE *k* may be reflected in A *śiśri* perhaps 'points (of the ears)',[19] which might thus be a reduplicated form from the same root as Lat. *crīnis, crista,*[20] and in A *śur-* 'be sad, care', possibly: Gk. κοέω 'notice', Skt. *kavi-* 'wise; poet' etc.;[21] but neither etymology is particularly convincing. As for B *śauk-* 'call' one can compare equally well either Lith. *šaũkti* or *kaũkti,* and A *śanweṃ* (dual) 'cheeks' is of course to be connected with GK. γένυς, Goth. *kinnus,* Skt. *hanu-,* a group with particularly ambiguous initial.[22] Likewise in the case of A and B *śpāl* 'head' beside Gk. κεφαλή, OHG *gebal,* the initial is ambiguous in the absence of a satem-form.[23]

On the other hand, the labiovelars are well attested. IE *kʷ* is clear for A *śtwar,* B *śtwer* 'four'; for A *aśaṃ,* B *eśane* dual beside sing. A *ak,* B *ek* 'eye'; and for B *piś* 'five' (with loss of nasal as opposed to A *päñ*).[24] IE gʷ is surely represented in A *śäṃ,* B *śno* 'wife' (Gk. γυνή, Boeot. βανᾱ́, etc.), and probably also in A *śo-,* B *śau-, śaw-* and *śai-, śay-* 'live' (: Gk. ζώω, Lat. *vīvō,* Skt. *jīvate* etc.).[25] Likewise IE *gʷh-* is quite probable for A *śärme* if the meaning, which is not sure, allows connection with Skt. *gharma-,* Gk. θερμός, etc.[26]

The form of the initial of the word for 'ten', A *śäk,* B *śak,* has caused some confusion. The explanation is obviously assimilation, e.g. PIE **deḱṃ* > PToch. **tek-,* then by assimilation of first to second consonant, **kek-,* whence by palatalization **śek-.*[27] Thus the chief support of the view that IE dentals may give Toch. *ś* directly is done away with.

In a number of forms, however, A *ś* is actually of dental origin, but only as a 'secondary' development of more original *ts* or perhaps of *c.* Most important here, as a category, are the verbal forms which show parallel stems in *ts* and *ś,* e.g. A *tsär-,* B *tsär-, tsar-* 'divide' (Gk. δέρω etc., cf. above), beside caus. pret. act. sg. 2 A *śaśrāst,* derivative substantive *śral* 'separation'; A *tsuk-,* B *tsauk-* 'drink', pret. act. sg. 3 A *śuk;* A *tsälp-,* B *tsälp-, tsalp-* 'go across, be saved', pres. mid. sg. 3 A *śalpatär*, inf. *śalpatsi* etc.; A *tsäm-*, B *tsäm-*, *tsam-* 'grow', pres. mid. pl. 3 A *śamantär*; A *tsip-*, B *tsip-*, *tsep-* 'dance', imperf. act. pl. 3 A *śepär*; A *tsārt-* 'weep', pres. mid. sg. 3 A *śercär*, pres. mid. pple. *śertmāṃ*; A *tspäṅk-* (meaning?), caus. pret. pple *śaśpäṅku*. This is obviously a secondary change which must have arisen properly in certain forms and was then extended to whole categories. The resulting alternation *ts/ś* is partially parallel to *k/ś* in verbal roots having an original guttural, but here the change extends to B also (e.g. A *käm-*, *kum-*, B *käm-*, *kam-* 'come', subj. stem A *śm-*, B *śem-*; A, B *kärs-* 'know', pret. stem A *śärs-*, B *śārs-* *etc.*), and is not found in present stems as is the case with *ts-/ś-* (cf. above A *śalpatär* etc. from *tsälp-*, or *śercär* from *tsārt-*).

Outside of these verb forms, the change of *ts* to *ś* is observed also in *aśśi* (emphatic particle), no doubt an extended form of *ats* (= Skt. *eva*), and in *pākraśi* 'apparently' beside B *apākärtse* (to A *pākär*, B *pākri* 'indeed').[28] Likewise, if the gen. ending *-nts* in B lies behind the obl. pl. *-s* in A, then the extended genitive *-śśi* in A may be considered to show more original *ts* palatalized secondarily to *ś*.[29]

In the inflection of one noun and two adjectives with stems in *-t-*, we find after a nasal an alternation of *ś* with *c* instead of the normals *ts*, e.g. A, B obl. *lānt* 'king' (nom. A *wäl*, B *walo*, *wlo*), nom. pl A *lāñś* but B *lāñc*, obl. p. A *lāñcäs* etc., beside nom. sg. fem. *lānts* 'queen' (etc. with *ts*). In the inflection of the two adjective stems *pont-* 'all, each' (nom. sg. masc. and fem. *puk*) and *krant-* (nom. sg. masc. *kāsu*) 'good', we have the parallel forms nom. pl. masc. *poñś*, *kraṃś*, beside obl. pl. masc. *poñcäs*, *krañcäs* (nom. and obl. pl. fem. *pont*, *krant*) etc.

Yet a third origin of *ś* lies in original *st-* (normally B *st-*, but A *ṣt-*). This is clear from examples like A *śreñ* (nom. pl.), B *śiriṃ*, *ściriṃ* (obl. pl.) 'stars' (: Gk. ἀ-στήρ, Goth. *stairnō* etc.). That this is likewise of secondary origin is clear from the alternate B form with *śc*, e.g. *st* > *sc* > *śc*, whence always simplification to *ś* in A but only partially in B.[30] Another example is A *śmoññe,* B *śmoñña, ścmoñña* 'place', obviously related to A *ṣtäm-,* B *stam-* 'stand, stay' (IE **st*(*h*)*ā*), of which the preterit stem likewise has *ś* in A (e.g. 3 sg. *śäm*), with the alternation *ṣt*/*ś* just like *ts*/*ś* and *k*/*ś* (above). Further we have A *kaśśi* 'hungry' beside *kaṣt* 'hunger' (: Hitt. acc. *kastan*), A *krośśune,* B *krośśaññe, krostaññe* 'cold' (subst.) beside A *kᵘraś, krośś-,* B *krośce* 'cold' (adj.).[31]

4. Examples of the change of original *s* to *ṣ* are plentiful. Certain etymologies are beyond question – thus the etymology of A *ṣäk,* B *ṣkas* 'six' (: Lat. *sex* etc.), or of A *ṣpät* (in cpds. *ṣäpta*), B *ṣukt* 'seven' (: Lat. *septem*), or even of A *ṣom* obl. to *sas* 'one', B *ṣeme* 'id.' (: Gk. εἷς, ἕν etc.), and of A *ṣälyp* 'fat, oil': Skt. *sarpis-,* Gk. ἔλπος (Hesych.), etc. The change occurs likewise before *w* in A *ṣpäṃ,* inflected stem *ṣäpn-,* B *ṣpäne, ṣpane* 'sleep' (: Skt. *svapnas,* OE *swefn,* etc.), and possibly in A *ṣar,* B *ṣer* 'sister' (: Skt. *svasar-,* Goth. *swistar*) if from PToch. **ṣäsar* with syncope. Likewise an intervening *p* does not seem to affect the change, according to the evidence of A *ṣpin-ac* (dat.) 'peg, hook': Lat. *spīna,*[32] and Fraenkel[33] has already compared the bird name A *ṣpār-āñ* with Goth. *sparwa* etc. 'sparrow', Gk. σπαράσιον (Hesych.).

Of an alternation *s-*/*ṣ-* in the verb, comparable to the alternations *k*/*ś, t*/*c* etc. (cf. above), I find only one example: A *spärk-* 'disappear', causative 'destroy', pret. pple. *ṣaṣpärku,* vbl. sb. *ṣpärkaslune* (but preterite mid. 3 pl. *saspärkānt* with *s*, cf. SSS 371, 481).[34]

Quite different from these changes of *s* to *ṣ* is that of *st* to *ṣt* in A as opposed to B, e.g. A *ṣtäm-, ṣtam-,* B *stam-* 'stand, stay' (IE **st*(*h*)*ā-*); A *ṣtām,* B *stām* 'tree' (cf. OHG *stam* 'stem' etc.); A *waṣt,* B *ost* 'house' (Gk. ἄστυ, Skt. *vastu-*) etc. On the mutation of *st* to *ś*, cf. above.

5. A few examples of *ñ* with clear-cut etymology will suffice. A *ñom,* B *ñem* 'name'; A, B *ñu* 'nine'; A *mañ* 'moon, month', B *meñe* 'month' (*meṃ* 'moon'). A *päñ* 'five' < **pañś* (IE **peŋkʷe*) has retained the palatal after the simplification

of the final consonant group. In B *piś* we see the loss of the nasal as in *mīsa* 'flesh' (IE **mēmso-*, Goth. *mimz*, Skt. *māṃsa-* etc.); see below. Whether by analogical extension or by correct development, the alternation *n*/*ñ* is likewise found in the verb, e.g. A *näk-* 'disappear', (caus.) pret. stem *ñak-* (SSS 445), *nu* 'roar', pret. *ñañwār* (SSS 446) etc. Here also a following *w* does not seem to prevent the change of *n* to *ñ*, cf. A (pres.) *päñwäs* 'pulls', but strangely enough the pret. stem appears with *n* in *panwar* (3 pl.), *pänwo* (pple.) etc. (SSS 448). B shows assimilation of *w* and loss of palatalization, *pänn-* or *pann-* (see below).

6. The etymological interpretation of words showing initial *ly-* is for the most part difficult. Some possible connections with Indo-European groups are, however, to be mentioned: A *lyäk*, pl. *lyśi*, B *lyak*, pl. *lyśi* 'thief' (Boh. *lakáti* 'ambush', OHG *luog* 'lair'?[35]); A *lyäm* 'sea' (Lett. *láma* 'puddle, low spot in a field', Lat. *lāma* 'bog, swamp'?[36]); A *lyāk* 'visible' (with derivative abstract *lyāktsune*) is probably related to the verbal root *läk-* 'see' (: OE *lōcian* 'look' etc.?[37]); A *lykäly*, *lyäkly*, B *lykaśke* 'fine', possibly, with diminutive suffix from the base **legʷh-* (Gk. ἐλαχύς etc.); A *lymeṃ* (dual) 'lips', possibly from the same base as Skt. *lambate* 'hangs down' etc.[38] (for the loss of stop after *m*, cf. A *kam*, B *keme* 'tooth': Skt. *jambha-*); A *lyutār*, *lyᵘtār*, *lytār* 'exceedingly' (: OCS *ljutŭ* 'fearful', Gk. λύσσα 'rage'?, cf. English *awfully*). And there are still other examples of *ly-* for which even less probable etymologies might be proposed.

The expected alternation of *l*/*ly* occurs also in the verb, e.g. A *läk-* (pres. act. sg. *lkām*, *lkāt*, *lkāṣ* etc.) 'see', imperf. act. sg. 3 *lyāk*, pl. 3 *lyākar*; A *länk-* 'hang' (pres. act. pl. 3 *läṅkiñc*), caus. pret. pple. *lyalyäṅku*; A *lip-* 'be left', caus. pret. act. sg. 3 *lyepäs*; cf. also A *lyipär*, B *lyipar* 'remainder'; A *lu-*, *law-* 'send', pret. A *lywā*, B *lyuwa* (SSS 366).

It is worth noting also that palatalization of *l* is not prevented by intervening *w* or labials, e.g. A *malywät* 'you crush'

(2 sg.), cf. Goth. *gamalwjan* 'id.' but B *melyeṃ* 'they crush' (Lévi, Frag. 129) with loss of *w* (see below), A *kälyme*, B *kälymye* (*-iye*) 'direction', and A *ṣälyp*, B *ṣalype* 'oil, fat' (: Skt. *sarpis-* etc.).[39]

7. More difficult is the question of mutation in the case of the labials. But it seems probable that these too were subject at one time to similar changes of articulation, though the evidence is left only in isolated relics, particularly in dialect B[40]; e.g. of *my*, B *kälymiye*, *kälymye* 'direction' (beside A *kälyme*); of *py*, A *pyāpi*, pl. *pyāplāñ*, adj. *pyāpyāṣi*, B *pyāpyo* 'flower', which could conceivably be related to Lett. *pāpa*, *pāpis*, *pāpulis* 'pimple', Lith. *pãpas* 'dug', *pupuolo* 'bud' etc., but the vocalism of the group[41] is too fickle to be helpful in the matter of palatalization. Likewise little can be concluded from a comparison of A *pyākäṣ* (dat. *pyākṣac* etc.) 'sacrificial post' with Gk. πήγνυμι, πήσσω 'make fast', Lat. *pangō* etc., though the etymology seems probable enough. Further evidence for the regular mutation of the labials is found also in B *piś* 'five', *mīsa* 'flesh', *mit* 'honey', from IE **peŋkʷe*, **mēmso-*, **medhu-*. The following *ĕ̄* palatalized the preceding *p* or *m*, under the influence of which, in turn, the *ĕ̄* became *i*; and in *piś* and *mīsa* the nasal was lost before the sibilant.

As regards the palatalization of initial labials, expected in certain verbal forms, Schulze has already pointed out how such a causative preterit form as B *spyārta* shows palatalization in contrast to the reduplicated A *saspärtu* (root B *spärt-*, A *spartw-* 'turn' intrans.) just as roots in *t*, *k* or *l* show the palatalized initial *c*, *ś* and *ly*, e.g. B *cāla*, *śārsa*, (mid.) *lyāmate* beside the likewise palatalized (and reduplicated) A *cacäl*, *śaśärs*, *lyalyäm*.[42] A parallel form is B *pyautka* beside A *papyutäk* from A *pyut-k-* 'zu Stande kommen',[43] for here the palatalization of the root has no 'functional' value (i.e. it occurs in all forms of the verb, e.g. pres. ind. act. *pyutkäṣ*, subj. mid. *pyutkāsmār* etc.), nor has it any such value in A *pyāṣtäṣ* (= Skt. *chadayati*), caus. pres. act. sg. 3 to pres. mid. *pyaṣtatär*. Also *m* shows parallel palatalization to *my* in B *myāska* 'changed' (no A equivalent?). Of course, the originality of such palatalization depends upon the cause and original scope of the phenomenon in the verb system.

Palatalization of stem-final *m* or *p* is also to be observed in some preterit forms in dialect B, e.g. *śānmyāre* 'they proclaimed',[44] *cämpyāre* 'they were able'[45] etc.

8. The question of the palatalization of *w* is even more complex. It has long been recognized that Toch. A *w* (= IE *w*) might correspond to *y* in dialect B in many instances, especially in initial position. Examples where the etymology is clear are A *want*, B *yente* 'wind' (Lat. *ventus* etc.), A *wäs-*, B *yäs-* 'dress' (Goth. *wasjan* etc.), and (with later loss of *y* before *i* in B) A *wiki*, B *ikäṃ* 'twenty'. Equally clear-cut examples of the correspondence, but where the etymology is doubtful or obscure, are A *wṣe* 'night', *wṣeññe* 'couch', B *yaṣi* 'night' (Skt. *vásati* 'dwells'?); A *wärkänt* 'wheel', B *yerkwantai* (obl.) 'wheel' (: Skt. *vṛṇákti* 'turns' etc., IE **werg-*?[46]); A *wäs* 'gold', *wsaṣi*, B *ysaṣṣe* 'of gold' (possibly: Lat. *aurum* etc.[47]); A *wkäṃ* (inflected stem *wäkn-*), B *yäkne*, *ykne* 'manner, way'; A *wälts*, B *yältse* '1000' (perhaps, in spite of the absence of dental suffixes,: Slav. *velь-* prefix 'very', *velikŭ* etc. 'great'[48]).

That this change might be considered a sort of 'palatalization' comparable to the other phenomena which we have been discussing seems to have been recognized first by Schulze in his article on the reduplicated preterit, which has already been mentioned.[49] Schulze's conclusion arose from his recognition of such preterit forms as B *yaika* beside A *wawik* 'destroyed', and B *yātka* beside A *wotäk* (**wa-wtäk*) 'command', as parallel to B *spyārta*: A *saspärtu*; B *pyautka*: A *papyutäk*; B *cāla*: A *cacäl*; B *śārsa*: A *śaśärs* etc. (cf. above), where palatalization has become as sign of function whatever its origin or original scope may have been. Still other examples of this palatalization of *w* to *y* in B may be cited, e.g. *yairu* pret. pple to *war-* 'exercise'; *yaitkormeṃ* 'according to the order', probably with *yātka* (above) to *wätk-* 'command'. Likewise *yärpo* 'punya' is probably to be connected with *wärp-* (3 sg. pres. mid. *wärpnātr*) 'enjoy, experience'.[50]

As has been already noted by Schulze,[51] the later loss of *y* before *i* explains the contrast between A *wiki* and B *ikäṃ* 'twenty'. Likewise the loss of *w* after *ṣ* in A *ṣpäṃ* (in cpds. *ṣäpna-*), B *ṣpäne* 'sleep' (OE *swefn*, Skt. *svapnas*) and in A *ṣar*, B *ṣer* 'sister' (Goth. *swistar*, Skt. *svasar-*) seems more easily explained by way of *ṣy-*. There is evidence that *sw-* was maintained when not palatalized, cf. A *swase*, B *swese* 'rain' (Gk. ὕει 'rains' etc.[52]), and furthermore the initial cluster *ṣw* does not to my knowledge occur. On the other hand we find *ṣyak* 'together' and *ṣya-wkäm* 'in the same way', with *ṣy-* retained, but the forms are etymologically obscure.

In the light of what has been concluded, I believe another explanation may now be offered for such a form as B *mely-* 'crush' beside A *malyw-*, e.g. IE **molwy- e/o-* > PToch. [mel'w'-], whence B [mel'-], but A, with loss of *w*-palatalization later, [mal'w-]. We are not dealing simply with a loss of *w* in B but with the loss of *w'*. The relation between A *pänw-* or *pañw-* 'pull' and B *pänn-*, *pann-* is apparently of a different sort.

[First published in *Language*, Vol. 21, No. 1, January-March, 1945, pp. 18-26.]

[1] The less obvious abbreviations used in this article are: BSB = Sitzungsberichte der Preussischen Akademie der Wissenschaften zu Berlin; Kl. Schr. = W. Schulze, Kleine Schriften, Göttingen, 1933; SSS = E. Sieg, W. Siegling, und W. Schulze, Tocharische Grammatik, Göttingen, 1931; WP = Walde-Pokorny, Vergleichendes Wörterbuch der indogermanischen Sprachen, Berlin, 1930-32; WH = Walde-Hoffmann, Lateinisches etymologisches Wörterbuch, 3d ed., vol. I, Heidelberg, 1938; BSOS = Bulletin of the School of Oriental Studies of the University of London; KZ = (Kuhn's) Zeitschrift für vergleichende Sprachforschung, etc.; IF = Indogermanische Forschungen; Phil. Stud. = Philologische Studien (Université Catholique, Louvain); JAs. = Journal Asiatique; MSL (BSL) = Mémoires (Bulletin) de la Société de Linguistique de Paris; AOr. = Arkív Orientálni (Prague); Frag. = S. Lévi, Fragments de Textes Koutchéens, Paris, 1933. The oft-cited monographs of van Windekens and Pedersen (above) are abbreviated respectively as Toch. Decl. and Toch.

[2] That some of these consonants may also arise in totally different fashion is likewise recognized. For example, *ts* may come from *t* + *s* as in *läntseñc* 'they go out', *letseñc* 'they depart (?)', where the verbal root ends in *t* and the present suffix is -*(ä)s* (cf. Pedersen, Toch. 263, SSS 358 ff.). Likewise, inherited *s* always appears as *ṣ* before *t* in A as contrasted to B, e.g. A *ṣtām*, B *stām* 'tree' (see below).

[3] Cf. WP 2.295.

[4] BSOS 10.939.

[5] Lang. 14.27.

[6] Ibid. 26; Pedersen, Toch. 266.

[7] Toch. Decl. 56; so already Holthausen, IF 39.66.

[8] Phil. Stud. 183-5.

[9] Meillet, JAs. 17.451 (1911), MSL 17.248.

[10] Toch. 96, 251.

[11] Poucha, AOr. 2.325.

[12] Lang. 14.27; cf. also now Pedersen, Toch. 190, anm. 2.

[13] Pedersen, Toch. 243 f.

[14] Cf. SSS 481, Lévi, Frag. 152.

[15] L.c. ftn. 1.

[16] Pedersen, Groupement des dialectes indo-européens 31.

[17] But there is of course evidence for a parallel root in *g*-, cf. WP 1.642. The connection with Skt. *śavas* 'strength', *śūra*- 'strong; hero', etc. (WP 1.365) made by Fraenkel (IF 50.7) is much less preferable.

[18] WP 1.548 f.

[19] Cf. Sieg, Aufsätze Kuhn 151, lines 5-6.

20 WP 2.572, WH 1.292.

21 Van Windekens, BSOS 10.397 f.

22 Cf. WP 1.587; Sturtevant, Indo-Hittite Laryngeals 86.

23 WP 1.571.

24 Cf. Pedersen, Toch. 91.

25 For the phonology, cf. LANG. 14.26.

26 Cf. Schwentner, KZ 64.266; SSS 4.

27 Pedersen, Toch. 252.

28 Ibid. 237 f.

29 Ibid. 79 ff., 237.

30 Ibid. 242.

31 Possibly, in spite of unexplained vocalism (A *o* usually equals B ***au*** representing an IE *u*-diphthong), from ****krus-t-***: Gk. κρύος 'frost', κρυσταίνω 'freeze', Lat. *crusta* 'rind, crust' etc. (WP 1.479 f.).

32 Schwentner, IF 55.297.

33 IF 50.229.

34 I am not clear on the corresponding B forms. SSS 480 says merely 'Ebenso B' without citation, Lévi, Frag. 147, gives only the causative stem *ṣparkṣ-* 'détruire' without citing any forms.

35 WP 2.377–8.

36 Ibid. 2.385.

37 Ibid. 2.381.

38 Ibid. 2.432–3.

39 Cf. Pedersen, Toch. 241.

40 Ibid. 241 f.

41 WP 2.107.

42 Kl. Schr. 243 ff.; SSS 371, ftn. 1; Pedersen 187.

43 SSS 452: 'Ebenso B', but without citing root or forms.

44 Pedersen, Toch. 180 f., 242; MSL 18.2.

45 Lévi, Frag. 114.

46 WP 1.271 f.

47 WH 1.96.

48 WP 1.295 f.

49 Kl. Schr. 245.

50 Lévi, Frag. 154.

51 L.c.

52 Meillet, JAs. 1.115 f. (1912); WP 2.468.

Miscellanea

THE TOCHARIAN GENITIVE B *-epi*, A *-(y)āp*

Already a considerable amount of print has been devoted to the explanation of this most peculiar-looking of the Tocharian genitive singular endings: B *-epi*, A *-(y)āp*. It belongs originally, as everyone agrees, to the singular of the masculine adjective: B *kreñcepi* from *krent* 'good' (Frag. p. 57, S 2a2; p. 65, S 8b2; p. 86, K 2b3: *kreñcepi wat yolopi no wat yāmorntse* 'of either good or evil deed'; cf. Sieg, KZ 65.9 line 18), *alyekepi* from *alyek* 'another' (Frag. p. 59, S 3b1; p. 95, K 10a5), etc. In A the ending has been extended from the masculine adjectives to masculine nouns indicating reasoning male beings, e.g. *kuntistsek* 'potter', *lokit* 'guest', *amokäts* 'artisan', *pekant* 'painter', *käṣṣi* 'teacher', etc., gen. *kuntistsekāp, lokitāp, amoktsāp, pekäntāp, käṣṣyāp*. See SSS 82, 88 f.

The ending is usually compared with the Greek adverbial particle -φι, and so eventually with the IE instrumental ending *-bhis*. The comparison, however, is only a desperate way out.[1] Semantically better, it seems to me, is the suggestion that we may be dealing with a postposition related to Gk. ἀπό (Hermann, KZ 50.310) or even to Gk. ἐπί (Couvreur, Hoofdzaken 40). I believe, however, that Pedersen is right when he concludes (loc.cit.) that we are dealing here not with a postposition but with a suffix, and that the vowel (B *-e-*, A *-ā-*) is a stem vowel, not part of the suffix itself.

I should therefore be inclined to suggest that we have here originally a possessive adjective. This hypothesis is in line with the well-known excessive development of the use of possessive adjectives in Tocharian, as compared with the preference of most IE languages for the use of genitive case forms to express possession (cf. SSS 21 ff.). The principle of 'group inflection' – i.e. inflection of only the final member of a series of nouns or of a noun preceded by modifiers – would readily give rise to an inflectionless (oblique) form of the possessive adjective in genitive function (op. cit. 206 ff.). The development would then be similar to that of Latin pronominal genitives like *cuius*.

It seems probable to me, then, that we have here the suffix *-bho* seen in adjectives like Gk. ἄργυ-φος 'silver-white, (: ἄργυ-ρος 'silver', ἀργός 'white'), Lith. *ankstý-bas* 'of an early sort' (: *anksti* adv. 'early'), *vėlý-bas* 'of a late sort' (: *vėlùs* 'late'), Goth. *bairhta-ba* adv. 'brightly' (: *bairhts* 'bright'), and so on. More important, of course, is the use of the suffix in substantivized adjectives; Gk. φλήναφος 'chatter; chatterer', κόλαφος 'slap', OCS *zŭlo-ba* 'evil' (*zŭlŭ* 'bad'), etc., and especially animal names like Skt. *vr̥ṣabha-*, *r̥ṣabha-* 'bull', Gk. ἔλαφος 'deer'.[2] The notion 'pertaining to, related to' carried by this suffix in some of the secondary derivatives is quite clear. Further development to the value of a possessive adjective would be natural.

If this is indeed the origin of the suffix, as I believe it is, then the additional *-i* in B *-(e)pi* needs an explanation. One might, in desperation, compare the whole with the variant form of our suffix seen in Greek diminutives like θηράφιον 'little animal', ξυράφιον 'little razor'.[3] But the fact that this seems to be a peculiarly Greek innovation, as well as the dubious hypothesis that a final *-yo-* would give *-i* in Tocharian B,[4] renders this view doubtful. Moreover, I do not like to separate the B and A forms in this fashion. I believe that the correct way to connect them is to assume the addition of another genitive ending *-i*, which seems to have its origins in the pronouns: B *cwi*, *cwī* (*cpi*, *cpī*), genitive of demonstrative *su*, *sū*; A *ñi* masc., *nāñi* fem. 'my', *tñi* 'thy', etc. This ending has already been extended to nouns: B *seyi* to *soy* 'son', A *pācri* to *pācar* 'father', *mācri* to *mācar* 'mother', etc.[5] It would seem logical to suppose that if a pronominal ending is extended, the extension will proceed by way of the adjectival inflection, not directly from pronoun to noun.

[First published in *Language*, Vol. 24, No. 3, July-September, 1948, pp. 293-294.]

[1] Cf. Pedersen, Tocharisch 52: 'Lautlich möglich ist zur Not die Identifikation mit gr. -φι (mit Dehnung des -*i* in B, nicht aber in A?).' A. J. Van Windekens would apparently separate B -*epi* from A -*āp*, comparing only the latter with Gk. -φι; B -(*e*)*pi*, instead, he compares with the Germanic preposition (and preverb) OHG *bi*, *bī*, Goth. *bi*, etc. Cf. Bestanddeelen 92 ff., Morphologie 152 ff.

[2] For further illustration of use, cf. Brugmann, Grdr. 2.1.399 f.

Imperfect and Preterit in Tocharian

[The Proto-Tocharian imperfect, based on IE optative formations, is preserved in Kuchean (Toch. B) but lost in Turfanian (Toch. A) except for two relics, the imperfects of the verbs 'be' and 'go'. The remaining Turfanian imperfects are in origin identical with preterit formations found in Turfanian or in Kuchean or in both, which are all derived from IE perfects and aorists.]

As I have stated several times on other occasions, the more one attempts to compare the two Tocharian 'dialects' with a view to concluding something about the nature of Proto-Tocharian and its position among the Indo-European languages, the more one becomes impressed with the remarkable divergence of development which took place from the period of Proto-Tocharian unity to the time between 500 and 800 A.D. when the dialects appear. About all that really connects the language of Turfan in the east to that of Kucha in the west is a close similarity of grammatical system and a fairly high coincidence of vocabulary. Everywhere we find either the same grammatical function served by morphemes of entirely different phonetic shapes and of different formal origins, or else formal elements the same in origin but serving different grammatical functions. Nowhere is this situation more apparent than in the verbal system.

Both Turfanian (Toch. A) and Kuchean (Toch. B) possess four modes – indicative, subjunctive-future, optative, and imperative – and, in the indicative, a present, an imperfect, and a preterit tense. But there the coincidence all but ceases. There are of course some close parallelisms in stem formations in most verbal categories, but there are also marked discrepancies; and of all the verbal categories, it is the formation of the imperfect in Turfanian and its relation to the present system on the one hand and to the preterit system on the other that is most confounding. It is also in the formation of the imperfect that the two languages go farthest asunder. The present paper treats the identification of so-called imperfects and preterits and their ultimate origins. Some of the facts are obvious and already pretty well agreed upon, others are in dispute, and some of the problems have received no attention at all. In our treatment we shall in general proceed from what is most certain to what is more obscure.

The formation of the imperfect in Kuchean seems clear enough. It is formed by the addition of a characteristic sign *-i-* (*-ī-*, *-y-*) or *-ai-* (*-ey-*) to the present stem. Before this sign, an immediately preceding consonant or consonant group is subject to palatalization: *k* > *ś*, *ṅk* > *ñc*, *tk* > *cc*, *sk* > *ṣṣ*, *t* > *c*, *tt* > *cc*, *nt* > *ñc*, *n* > *ñ*, *l* > *ly*, *s* > *ṣ*.[1] Exceptions to this rule are the imperfects of Present Classes III and IV (cf. below),[2] and the present stems in original *ā*, which form the imperfect in *-oy-*. A brief survey will elucidate the formation: Cl. I *käln-* 'resound', pres. pl. 3 *kalneṃ*, impf. act. sg. 3 *kalñi*; *kläṅk-* 'doubt', pres. mid. sg. 3 *klyenträ*, impf. act. sg. 3 *klyeñci*; *pälk-* 'shine', pres. act. sg. 3 *palkäṃ*, impf. act. sg. 3 *palyśi*; Cl. II *aik-* 'know', pres. mid. sg. 1 *aikemar*, impf. act. sg. 3 *palyśi*; Cl. II *aik-* 'know', pres. mid. sg. 1 *aikemar*, impf. *aiśimar*; *klyaus-* 'hear', pres. act. sg. 3 *klyauṣäṃ*, impf. sg. 1 *klyauṣim*; Cl. III *sruk-* 'die', pres. mid. sg. 3 *sruketrä*, impf. mid. pl. 3 *sruky* (*enträ*); *mäsk-* 'be', pres. mid. sg. 3 *mäsketär*, impf. mid. sg. 3 *mäskītär*; Cl. IV *kārp-* 'descend', pres. mid. sg. 3 *korpotär*, impf. mid. pl. 3 *korpyentär*; *yāt-* 'be capable', pres. mid. sg.. 3 *yototär*, impf. mid. sg. 3 *yotiträ*; Cl. V *kwā-* 'call', pres. mid. sg. 3 *kwātär*, impf. mid. sg. 3 *kwoytär*; *śwā-* 'eat', pres. act. sg. 3 *śuwaṃ*, impf. act. sg. 3 *śuwoy*; Cl. VI *kärs-* 'know', pres. act. sg. 3 *kärsanaṃ*, impf. act. pl. 3 *kärsanoyeṃ*; *tärk-* 'release', pres. act. sg. 3 *tärkanaṃ*, impf. act. sg. 3 *tärkänoy*; Cl. VII *pärs-* 'sprinkle', pres. act. sg. 3 *prantsäṃ*, impf. mid. sg. 3 *präntsitär*; Cl. VIII *er-* 'produce', pres. act. sg. 3 *erṣäṃ*, impf. mid. pl. 3 *erṣyenträ*; *lik-* 'wash', pres. mid. sg. 3 *lyikṣtär*, impf. mid. sg. 3 *līkṣītär* (caus.?); Cl. IX (primary) *ai-* 'give', pres. act. sg. 1 *aiskau*, 3 *aiṣṣäṃ*, impf. act. sg. 3 *aiṣṣi*; *yām-* 'do', pres. act sg. 1 *yamaskau*, 3 *yamaṣṣäṃ*, impf. act. sg. 3 *yamaṣṣi*; *kälp-* 'get', pres. act. sg. 1 *kälpāsk(au)*, sg. 3 *kälpāṣṣäṃ*, impf. act. sg. 2 *kälpāṣṣit*, 3 *kälpāṣṣi*; (causative) *kärs-* 'know', pres. act. sg. 3 *śaräṣṣäṃ*, pl. 3 *śäräskeṃ*, impf. act. sg. 3 *śaräṣṣi*; *wätk-* 'decide', caus. 'command', pres. act. sg. 1 *watkäskau*, 3 *watkäṣṣäṃ*, impf. act. sg. 3 *watkäṣṣi*; Cl. X *lät-*, *länt-* 'go out', pres. act. sg. 1 *lnaskau*, 3 *lnaṣṣäṃ*, impf. act. sg. 3 *lnaṣṣi*; *mäl-* 'oppress' pres. mid. sg. 3 *mällăsträ* (*ll* < *ln*), impf. mid. sg. 3 *mälläṣṣitär*; Cl. XI *āks-* 'announce', pres. act. sg. 1 *aksaskau*, 3 *aksaṣṣäṃ*, impf. act. sg. 3 *aksaṣṣi*; Cl. XII *mänt-* 'injure', pres. act. sg. 3 *mäntaṃ*, pl. 3 *mäntaññeṃ*, impf. mid. sg. 3 *mäntaññīträ*.

To these 'regular' imperfects are to be added those of the verbs 'be' and 'go':[3]

	'be'		'go'	
	Sg.	Pl.	Sg.	Pl.
1	*ṣaim, ṣeym*	*ṣeyem*	*yaim*	
2	*ṣait*	*ṣaicer, ṣeycer*	*yait*	
3	*ṣai, ṣey*	*ṣeyem, ṣeṃ*	*yai, yey*	*yeyeṃ*

The corresponding imperfects are found also in Turfanian, where these two verbs are the only examples of the '*i*-imperfect':[4]

1	*ṣem*	*ṣemäs*	*ye(m)*	
2	*ṣet*		*yet*	
3	*ṣeṣ*	*ṣeñc*	*yeṣ*	*yeñc*

It is generally assumed that the origin of this imperfect is to be sought in an optative, showing either an extension of the Indo-European 'weak' athematic optative sign *ī* or possibly the thematic *oi*, reduced to *ĭ* in atonic position, or a combination of both.[5] There is no reason to doubt this on either formal or semantic grounds. Pedersen has pointed out the similarity with the iterative use of the optative in Greek in temporal and relative clauses, and Couvreur has indicated certain Indo-Iranian parallels.[6] Krause has recently noted also the coincidence of the Tocharian development with that which may be assumed for certain of the British Celtic imperfects.[7] In order to add greater plausibility to this view (if it is still doubted on semantic grounds), I would call attention to the use of the English conditional with *would* as a sort of habitual past, as in *When I was on vacation I would take a walk before breakfast every day, When we were in New York last month we would see a show every night.*

It is to be assumed, then, that this imperfect is a reflex of the Indo-European optative (thematic or athematic or both, cf. above). Its endings, however, except the 1st and 3rd sg. in Kuchean, are identical with those of the present indicative, e.g. from *camp-* 'be able' (act.), *aik-* 'know' (mid.):[8]

	Active		Middle	
	PRESENT	IMPERFECT	PRESENT	IMPERFECT
Sg. 1	*campau*	*cämpim*	*aikemar*	*aiśimar*
2	*campät*	*campit*	*aiśtar*	*aiśitar*
3	*campäṃ*	*campi*	*aiśtär*	*aiśitär*
Pl. 1	*campem*	*campim*	*aikemt(t)är*	*aiśyemt(t)är*
2	*campcer*	*campicer*	*aiśtär*	*aiśitär*
3	*campeṃ*	*cämpyeṃ*	*aikentär*	*aiśyentär*

It is noteworthy that *campim* and *campi*, the two forms of the imperfect which contrast with the indicative, also show what may be readily interpreted as the (originally athematic) primary ending *-mi* and the secondary (thematic and athematic) ending *-t*. The latter is of course proper to the optative; the former shows, as in Greek (Attic and elsewhere), the transfer from the μι inflection (e.g. φέροιμι as opposed to the historically correct Arcad. ἐξελαύνοια[9]).

It is debatable whether this imperfect use of the optative was a feature of Proto-Tocharian lost in Turfanian except for the roots *s*- and *i*-, or whether it was a special development in Kuchean after the separation of the dialects, originating in these two roots. I should think, however, and I believe the arguments of this paper will show, that the former is the more reasonable view. This would seem a logical conclusion, since in many other respects Kuchean is the more archaic of the two languages.

This being my assumption, I am compelled to look for the origin of the so-called imperfect in Turfanian, which must then be secondary. Perhaps a review of these formations will be helpful; the following outline retains the order and numbering of SSS:[10]

I includes the imperfect of *s*- 'be' and *i*- 'go', cf. above.

IIa lengthens the radical vowel and palatalizes the initial consonant if possible, and adds the stem vowel *a* before the endings (no ending in act. sg. 3): act. sg. 3 *lyāk*, pl. 3 *lyākar* to *läk*- 'see' (present act. sg. 3 *lkāṣ* etc.); act. pl. 3 *cārkar*, mid. sg. 3 *cārkat* to *tärk*- 'let, let go' (present act. sg. 3 *tärnāṣ* etc.); act. pl. 3 *śārsar* to *kärs*- 'know' (present act. sg. 3 *kärsnāṣ* etc.); mid. sg. 3 *pārat*, pl. 3 *pārant* to *pär*- 'carry' (pres. mid. sg. 3 *pärtär* etc.); mid. sg. 3 *śālpat* to *kälp*- 'find, get' (pres. mid. sg. 3 *kälpnātär* etc.); mid. pl. 3 *śākant* to *tsäk*- 'pull out' (present mid sg. 3 *tsäknātär* etc.).

IIb shows the strong form of the root (*a*, *e*), to which the stem vowel *ä* is added before the endings (act. sg. 3 in -*s*), and likewise palatalizes the initial: act. sg. 2 *crañkäṣt*, 3 *crañkäs*, pl. 3 *crañkär* to *träñk*- 'say' (present act. sg. 3 *träñkäṣ* etc.); act. pl. 3 *śepär* to *tsip*- 'dance' (present act. pl. 3 *tsipiñc*).

III is formed from the present stem, of which the final consonant is palatalized if possible, and adds the stem vowel *ā* (which is retained without ending in the act. sg. 3). This is the most common formation. Some seventy-five or more forms are listed by SSS; only a few examples will be cited: act. sg.

3 *eṣā*, pl. 3 *eṣār* to *e*-'give' (pres. act. sg. 1 *esam*, 3 *eṣ*); act. sg. 3 *kātäñśā* to *kātk*- 'stand up, arise' (pres. act. sg. 3 *kātäṅkāṣ*), *keñā* to *ken*- 'call' (pres. act. sg. 3 *kenäṣ*); mid. sg. 3 *kropñāt*, pl. 3 *kropñānt* to *krop*- 'collect' (pres. mid. pple. *kropnmāṃ*).

IV may be based upon the subjunctive stems in *-ās-* and in *-ñ-*: cf. mid. pl. 3 *(tä)kwāṣānt* and a fragmentary *täkwāṣā*.., apparently beside vbl. sb. *täkwāṣlune*, which is then from the subjunctive stem of the causative verb to the root *täkw-* (inf. *täkwātsi* etc., cf. SSS 439 with no meaning given for the verb). As possible examples of imperfects from the subjunctive in *-ñ-* are cited (SSS 387) the following: mid. pl. 3 *tpukñānt*, act. sg. 3 *wātñā* and *tsākñā*. For only the last of these is either the meaning clear or the present formation attested, viz. pres. mid. sg. 3 *tsākäṣtär* 'glows'. The other attested forms are pret. mid. pl. *tsāksānt* and opt. mid. pl. 3 *tsāśinträ* (cf. SSS 481). The fact that the preterit middle is in *s* (Cl. III) makes it possible that the subjunctive is in *ñ*, e.g. act. sg. 3 **tsākñäṣ* etc.; but no such form is attested, and actually the optative *tsāśinträ* makes it more probable that the subjunctive is of a 'thematic' type, e.g. act. sg. 3 **tsākäṣ*, since for the *ñ*-subjunctive we would expect rather opt. **tsākñinträ*. These imperfects then can very well have been formed (as already suggested by SSS 337) from unattested presents in *nă̈*, and belong rather to Cl. III. Indeed, there is no conclusive evidence for an imperfect based on the subjunctive stem in *ñ*, or in fact on one in *ās*, owing to the fragmentary nature of the quotable forms. We have then primarily three formations to examine: IIa, IIb, and III.

A fundamental assumption of this paper will be that like formations had in origin like grammatical meanings, and that differences of meaning between identical formations in the same language or in closely related languages are secondary. If we accept this assumption, I believe we can identify some at least of the Turfanian imperfects.

For type IIa, the key lies in the identification of Turf. impf.

lyāk, lyākar (above) with Kuch. pret. *lyāka, lyakāre,* etc. This identity, which has been assumed over and over again, would seem indisputable;[11] Pedersen[12] adds to it that of Turf. impf. pl. 3 *śārsar* and Kuch. caus. pret. sg. 3 *śārsa* (pl. 3 *śarsāre*) from *kärs-* 'know' (Turf. pres. sg. 3 *kärsnāṣ*, Kuch. *kärsanaṃ*). He continues, however, to follow Wilhelm Schulze[13] in the view that the Kuch. caus. *śārsa* results from contraction and is to be equated therefore also with Turf. (uncontracted) caus. pret *śaśärs*. As a result, he is faced with two problems: (1) the origin of the distinction in meaning, i.e. between non-causative imperfect and causative preterit; and (2) the reason for the presence of both contracted and uncontracted forms in Turfanian. As regards the first, Pedersen decides that the contrast between the contracted and uncontracted forms had in origin nothing to do with their grammatical (non-causative or causative) meaning, nor with dialectal differentiation; and as regards the second, he concludes that contraction took place properly only in longer forms. The resultant distribution in Turfanian and the elimination of uncontracted forms in Kuchean are due to analogy.[14] With the view that the difference in grammatical meaning was not originally bound to the contrast in form, I heartily agree. But I have never been able to accept Schulze's view that Kuch. *śārsa* results from contraction and is to be equated to Turf. *śaśärs* – a view which is all the less acceptable if (with Pedersen) we equate to it also the Turf. imperfect *śārsar*.

Schulze's theory of the identity of these forms was supported by the assumed parallelism with the development of the seventh class of strong preterits in Germanic: for example Goth. *haihait*, OE *heht* on the one hand, vs. OHG *hiaz*, OE *hēt* on the other. One cannot of course prove one improbable phonetic development by recourse to another just as improbable. Many students of Germanic, I among them, have long given up the contract origin of unreduplicated seventh-class preterits in North and West Germanic.[15] As in the case of the

Germanic forms so also in that of the Tocharian, I am convinced that the long-vowel preterits and imperfects in question have in origin nothing to do with the reduplicated forms. The coincidence in grammatical meaning between causative preterits like Kuch. *śārsa*: Turf. *śaśärs*, or Kuch. *cāla*: Turf. *cacäl* (to *täl-* 'lift') is purely accidental, as is so often the attachment of any particular meaning to a formal category. As to what these forms are from the Proto-Indo-European point of view, I can only reiterate my earlier opinion[16] that the possibility of a connection with the 'long-vowel' perfects of Latin and Germanic should not be as categorically denied as it seems to be by Pedersen and others. The equation Turf. (imperf.) *pārat* (to *pär-* 'carry') with Goth. *bērum* etc., and even of Turf. *lyāk* (imperf.), Kuch. *lyāka* (pret.) with Lat. *lēgī*, is hard for me to reject. The comparison of these long-vowel perfects with the Hittite *ḫi*-conjugation makes it almost certain that these were originally Indo-European 'perfects' (and Indo-Hittite presents) denoting a present state or the result of an action performed in the past.[17] I believe that the shift from the notion of aspect to that of relative time, which took place in Tocharian as it did eventually in most of the other Indo-European languages as well, could quite easily transfer such formations to a developing category of imperfects (e.g. in Turfanian), or make them simple preterits to an originally iterative-durative or simply imperfective present system. This seems to be the original value of the *sk* formation in Indo-Hittite,[18] and is still a common characteristic of some *sk* (*ṣṣ*) presents in Tocharian,[19] though of course their predominant value in both dialects is causative. Kuchean preterits of Cl. II (caus.) like *śārsa* (= Turf. impf. *śārsar*, cf. above), *ñyārsa* (*närs-* 'crowd'), *pyālka* (*pälk-* 'shine'), *myārsā-ne* (*märs-* 'forget'), *ṣārkate* (*ṣärk-* 'excel'), *ṣpyārta* (*spärtt-* 'turn'), *ṣpyarkatai* (*spärk-* 'pass away'), *tsyālpāte* (*tsälp-* 'redeem'), probably have their long vowel by analogy with stems ending in a single consonant, like *cāla* and *lyāma*. It is most unlikely that the length of the vowel here reflects the original quantity. A parallel is shown in the West Germanic seventh-class strong verbs of the type of OHG *hialt, giang, fiang,* (after *hiaz, liaz,* etc.), where Gmc.$\bar{e}^2$ (< PIE *ēi*) cannot possibly be original. Kuchean Cl. II preterits in the diphthongs *ai* and *au* can reflect normal PIE perfects (without reduplication) with initial palatalization on the analogy of the 'long-vowel' type. Examples are *klyautka, klyautkate* (*klutk-* 'turn about', caus. 'make into'), *traika-ne, traikate* (*trik-* 'go astray'), *pyautka, pyautkare* (*pyutk-* 'come into being'), *raittate, raittǎnte* (*ritt-* 'be bound', caus. 'become bound'), etc. These Kuchean 'causative' preterits of Class II are then identical, so far as the vocalism of the root is concerned, with 'non-causative' preterits of the type of Kuch. *kāka, kakāte* = Turf. *kāk* (from pres. Kuch. *kwā-*, Turf. *ken-* 'call'), Kuch. *kamāte* = Turf. *kāmat* (*kām-* pret. stem to Kuch. and Turf. *pär-* 'carry'), Kuch. *kārpa* = Turf. *kārp* (Kuch. and Turf. *kārp-* 'descend'), Kuch. *paiykāte* = Turf. *pekat* (Kuch. and Turf. *pik-* 'write'), Kuch. *kraupāte* = Turf. *kropat* (Kuch. *kraup-*, Turf. *krop-* 'gather'), etc.[20] The only difference is the lack of initial palatalization in both dialects. No palatalization is to be expected, of course, if these forms are reflexes of the PIE normal perfect singular of the *e/o* series (Gk. λέλοιπα, οἶδα, etc.). It would appear then that the forces of analogy worked in two different directions: on the one hand, the causative preterits and noncausative imperfects all assumed the palatalization after the model of the 'long-vowel' type (*lyāka, lyāk,* etc); on the other, the non-causative preterits rejected it where one might expect it to have occurred originally, as in *kāka, kāk, tāka, tāk.* It hardly seems possible to assume that these latter are all reflexes of 'long-vowel' perfects of other series (like Goth. *stōþ, stōþum,* Lat. *fōdī, scābī*). The principle of 'vowel balance' or vowel weakening in connection with the primitive accent position and number of syllables[21] seems to work more uniformly in the Kuchean pret. Cl. Ib than in Cl. II; but this can hardly be significant, especially in view of the great irregularity of its application in all categories of forms. A few examples will make this principle clear: Kuch. Cl. Ib act. sg. 3 *kāka* but mid. *kakāte,* mid. sg. 1 *kāmmai,* but sg. 3 *kamāte,* act. sg. 3 *kārpa* but sg. 1 *karpāwa,* etc., as opposed to Cl. II act. sg. 3 *cāla* and sg. 1 *cālawa,* act. sg. 3 *kyāna,* sg. 1 *kyānawa,* act. sg. 3 *lyāma,* mid. 3 *lyāmate,* and the like. The alternation of *ā* in dissyllabic forms with *a* in trisyllabic ones is thus the rule in Kuchean Class Ib but not in Class II. That the stem vowel (between root and ending) was originally long in the latter class also is clearly shown by forms like *myārsā-ne* with suffixed pronoun (*märs-* 'forget'), *raittānte* beside *raittante* (*ritt-* 'be joined'), *tsyālpāte* (*tsälp-* 'be redeemed').

Let us turn now to Turfanian imperfect IIb. This, as we have already seen, is represented by only four forms, all active: sg. 2 *craṅkäṣt,* 3 *craṅkäs,* pl. 3 *craṅkär* from *träṅk-* 'speak', and pl. 3 *śepär* from *tsip-* 'dance'. These are identical in formation with preterits of Class III, e.g. act. sg. 3 *ñakäs* (*näk-* 'disappear'), *lyepäs* (*lip,* 'remain, be left'), *lyokäs* (*luk-* 'light up'), pl. 3 *caṅkär* (*täṅk-* 'hinder, obstruct'), *crakär* (*tärk-* 'let, release'), *śarkr-äm* (*kärk-* 'bind'). It follows, if my fundamental assumption is correct, that they are in origin the same formation. This is also the Class III 's-preterit' of Kuchean, cf. sg. 3 *neksa* (: Turf. *ñakäs*), *lyauksa* (: Turf. *lyokäs*) etc. The coincidence of forms in the two dialects is extremely close.[22] Both dialects show both causative and non-causative values, and both show both palatalized and non-palatalized initials. In Turfanian the palatalization is largely confined to the active, and therefore agrees with that of the imperfect IIb (SSS) which I identify with it, although only active forms of the latter are attested.

As regards the history of the *s*-preterit (and hence of the Turfanian *s*-imperfect IIb), I am inclined to agree with Krause[23] that it is probably of mixed origin. The Indo-European *s*-aorist furnished the endings with *-s,* e.g. act. sg. 3 Kuch. *neksa,* *lyauksa, lyautsa,* Turf. *ñakäs, lyokäs,* and the entire Kuchean middle (*neksate, lauksāte, lyutsāmai, lyutstsante*), but in Turfanian only the middle of the second type (e.g. *rise, risāte, risāt, risānt,* cf. SSS 376).[24] The Indo-European perfect, on the other hand, probably lies back of the radical in Kuch. act. 1 *nek-wa,* 2 *nek-asta,* 3 *nek-sa,* which must represent PIE *o*-grade forms, (cf. Lat. *nocuī, nocuistī, nocuit*). Since the *e* < IE *o* in these forms is probably to be equated with the Turf. *a* in *ñakäs* (cf. Kuch. *keme* = Turf. *kam* 'tooth': Gk. γόμφος, OIcel. *kambr,* etc.),[25] the Turfanian palatalization in such forms is clearly not original. It could arise, however, in forms of the *s*-aorist, which regularly had the *e*-grade (cf. Gk. ἔδειξα, ἔπεισα, etc.). Hence such forms as Turf. preterit *lyepäs, lyokäs* (with PIE *ei, eu*) and imperfect *śepär* are probably correct, and so are the Kuchean *s*-preterit forms with initial *ly* cited above.[26] It is very doubtful that the initial palatalization in the Turf. imperfect *crañkaṣt, crañkäs, crañkär* (to *träñk-* 'speak') is original; it is of course parallel to that observed in the pret. pple. *caccrīku* (beside *tatriku*) to *trik-* 'be confused, err', which may likewise be 'functional' rather than original. The palatalization of consonants across an intervening 'unpalatalizable' consonant is of course not unknown in Turfanian; thus – across *w*: Turf. *ṣpäṃ,* Kuch. *ṣpane* 'sleep' (: Skt. *svapnas,* OE *swefn*); Turf. *ṣar,* Kuch. *ṣer* 'sister' (: Skt. *svasar-,* Goth. *swistar*); – across *p*: Turf. *ṣpin-ac* (dat.) 'peg' (:Lat. *spīna*); Turf. *śaśpäñku* caus. pret. pple. from *tspäñk-* (SSS 484).[27] But there is no good reason to assume that this was not also analogical palatalization and that the form is therefore an original perfect.

It remains to discuss the most widely represented class of imperfects in Turfanian, Class III – those derived from the present stem by addition of the stem vowel *ā* (< PIE *ē*) with preceding palatalization. That some of these are identical with aorists has been already noted by Pedersen:[28] 'Einige *ē*-Imperfekte haben die Geltung als Präterita erworben. Das hängt mit der Wortbedeutung zusammen.' He cites the three Turfanian roots *klyos-* 'hear', *wles-* 'perform, practice', and *pās-* 'keep, observe'. According to SSS 386, the forms act. sg. 1 *klyoṣā*, pl. 1 *klyoṣāmäs*, 3 *klyoṣār*, mid. sg. 1 *wle*[*ṣe*], 2 (*pā*)*ṣāte*, 3 *wleṣāt*, *pāṣāt* are imperfects, but the same forms are cited also (381-2) as preterits of Class IVc. To these must be added (*wi*)*nāṣār* to *winās-* 'honor' (likewise cited in both places by SSS), and possibly *wināṣā-ṃ* (cited as imperf. SSS 472). Again the identity of the forms – here within one dialect – is the key to their identification in the total system of imperfects and preterits in both dialects. In Kuchean the corresponding forms are of course preterits only: sg. 1 *klyauṣāwa*, 3 *klyauṣa*, pl. 3 *klyauṣāre*, etc., mid. sg. 2 *paṣṣatai*, 3 *laṃṣṣāte*, pl. 3 *laṃṣṣānte*, *lāṃṣānte*, all classed by Krause as Class Ib (= SSS Ia); and act. sg. 3 *wịnāṣṣa-me*, pl. 3 *wināṣṣā*(*re*), *wināṣṣar-ne*, classed by Krause as IV, since the latter is clearly derived from the present stem in *-sk-*. Actually the formation of the pret. *wịnāṣṣa*, beside the present *winās k-*, is identical with that of *klauṣa*, *paṣṣatai*, *laṃṣṣāte*, and all the other preterits which Krause classed as Ib and which show as their characteristic the palatalization of the final radical consonant or consonant group, e.g. *aklyamai*, *aklyyatai* from *ākl-* 'learn'; *akṣāwa-me*, *akṣāsta* from *āks-* 'announce' (pres. *aksaskau*); *kaccāre* from *kātk-* 'rejoice' (pres. *kātkau*, *kāccäṃ*).[29] This formation has no parallel among the corresponding Turfanian preterits (SSS Cl. Ia), except in the preterit-imperfect forms (SSS IVc) cited above. On the other hand it has been retained and enlarged as the regular imperfect when formed from the present stem: *eṣā* to *e-* 'give' (pres. *esam*, etc.), *karyā* to *kar-* 'laugh' (pres. *karyeñc*), *kātäñśā* to *kātk-* 'arise' (pres. *kātäṅkāṣ*), etc.; cf. the survey given above.

As to the ultimate Indo-European provenience of this formation, Pedersen[30] has already connected it with the *ē*-verbs of the other Indo-European languages, which, as is generally conceded, expressed states or conditions rather than actions;

cf. Lat. *pendeō, jaceō, taceō* (= OHG *dagēn*). In general, the verbal stem in *ē* gives non-present forms in other IE languages (specifically in Greek, Baltic, and Slavic) which are frequently parallel to present formations in *yo/ye;* cf. the Gk. second aorist ἐχάρην, ἐμάνην, ἐφάνην, beside the presents χαίρω 'rejoice', μαίνομαι 'rage', φαίνω 'show'; Lith. preterits *smirdėjau, sėdėjau,* beside presents *smirdžu, sėdžu* 'sit'; OCS aorists *smrĭděchŭ, mĭněchŭ, viděchŭ* beside presents *smĭrždą* 'stink', *mĭnją* 'think', *viždą* 'see'.[31] In Latin and Germanic, however, the stem in *yo* may form an originally transitive verb. parallel to the originally intransitive present in *ē*; cf. Lat. *jaciō* 'throw' beside *jaceō* 'lie (thrown)'. In Germanic the original difference is usually obscured: Goth *hafjan,* OHG *heffen* 'lift' = Lat. *capiō* beside Goth. *haban* (*habaiþ*), OHG *habēn* (*habēt*) 'have' (i.e. originally the state of lifting); Goth. *hatjan* 'hate': *hatan,* OHG *hazzēn* 'id.'.

It seems clear to me that these imperfects (and/or preterits) of Turfanian and the preterits of like formation in Kuchean are to be equated (disregarding differences of ending) with the second aorists of the type of Gk. ἐχάρην. This view is considerably strengthened by the fact that in Tocharian also we find them coexisting with present stems in *yo/ye.* A conspicuous example is Turf. *kar-* 'laugh', act. pres. pl. 3 *karyeñc,* impf. sg. 3 *karyā.* In Kuchean, unfortunately, only present forms (act. pl. 3 *keriyeṃ,* mid. pple. *keriyemane*) and the pret. pple. *kek(e)ru* are attested. I believe, however, that this verb can be confidently equated, sound for sound and form for form, with Gk. χαίρω, ἐχάρην.[32] Other examples of *yo/ye*-presents beside *ē*-preterits are seen in Turf. *käl-* 'stand, be', pres. mid. sg. 1 *kälymār,* 3 *kälytär,* pl. *klyanträ,* imperf. mid. sg. 3 *klyāt,* pl. 3 *klyānt*; and *malyw-* 'crush', pres. act. sg. 2 *malywät,* impf. act. sg. 3 *malywā.* Both verbs are also *yo*-presents in Kuchean (pres. mid. pl. 3 *klyentär,* etc., sg. 3 *melyan-me,* pl. 3 *melyeṃ*). Again no preterit is attested in Kuchean to either of these stems (the preterit of *käly-* is from the suppletive *stäm-*), but the preterit active to the Kuchean *yo-* present *pänn-* 'stretch', pres. mid. sg. 3 *peññaträ*, is clearly of the expected formation: sg. 3 *piñña* (mid. sig. 3 *pännāte*, however, without palatalization).[33] To the corresponding Turf. *panw-* (also *yo*-present, act. sg. 3 *pañwäṣ*), no imperfect of any sort is attested. Another possible *yo*-present, act. sg. 3 *pañwäṣ*), no imperfect of any sort is attested. Another possible *yo*-present is Turf. *me-*, *mew-* 'tremble', pres. act. sg. 3 *meṣ*, pl. 3 *meyeñc*, with *ē*-imperfect *meyā*. The Kuchean correspondent is *miw-*, pres. sg. 3 *miwäṃ*, pret, act. sg. 3 *maiwa*, mid. sg. 3 *maiwāte*. But in the absence of a clearly palatalizable consonant and a convincing etymology, there is no real evidence.

Two other Kuchean preterits seem to me to belong definitely to this formation: *karṣṣa* (*karṣṣ-* 'shoot') and *kälpyawa* (*kälyp-* 'steal'), inasmuch as they may show the expected reduced-grade vocalism (cf. ἐχάρην above). Here, however, no present forms are attested. Kuch. pret. *camyāwa*, *campya* (to present *campäṃ* 'can') and pret. pl. 2 *memyas* (present not attested) probably show analogical 'secondary palatalization'.[34]

This formation *ā* has of course been extended in Turfanian as an imperfect to all sorts of presents, including those in *-nā* (*klisñā*, pres. *klisnāṣ* 'sleeps'), those in *-näs* (*kumṣā*, pres. *kumnāṣ* 'comes'), and particularly those in *-s-*, primary and causative (e.g. *eṣā* to *e-* 'gives', *kātkṣāt* to *kātkäṣtär* caus. to *kātk-* 'rejoice'), as well as to denominatives in *iñña-* (e.g. *tuṅkiññā*, inf. *tuṅkiñtsi*, pple. *(t)uṅkiññant-*). As a preterit formation we find the identical suffix also in Class IV b (SSS 380 f.): *ākṣiññā*, *okṣiññā* (from *āks-* 'teach' and *oks-* 'grow', presents *āksiṣ* and *oksiṣ*). The same formation is found (only as a preterit, of course) in Kuchean, e.g. *kwipeññate* (to *kwip-* 'be ashamed', pres. *kwipeññentär*). Pedersen has already identified the formation as a *yo*-suffix added to an *n*-stem, and has compared Skt. *iṣaṇyati* 'incites'.[35] Another parallel is OHG *giwahanen* 'mention', PIE **wokʷn-yō*. The latter etymology is important here, since it shows the present formation to be expected beside the Tocharian preterit of the verb 'say': Turf. act. sg. 1 *weñā*, 2 *weñāṣt*, 3 *weñā-* = Kuch. *weñāwa, weñāsta, weña*. The present of this verb, however, is furnished in Kuchean by an *sk*-formation (act. sg. 1 *weskau*, 3 *weṣṣäṃ*) and in Turfanian by a suppletive verb (act. sg. 1 *träṅkäm*).

The remaining Turfanian imperfects, those presumed to be derived from subjunctive stems (Class IV, SSS 386), are too inadequately attested for detailed discussion. Purely on the basis of form, however, they too are identical with known preterits: *(tä)kwāṣānt* (mid. pl. 3) and fragmentary *täkwāṣā*.. are to be identified with Turf. pret.-impf. *wināṣā-ṃ*, *(wi) nāṣār*, Kuch. pret. *wināṣṣa*; Turf. *tpukñānt*, *wātñā*, and *tsākñā* are identical with *weñā*, etc., above.[36]

In conclusion, I believe that the evidence brought forth here supports the view expressed at the outset: that the Kuchean imperfect of optative origin is to be attributed to Proto-Tocharian, and that in Turfanian it was replaced by forms originally identical with those which came to be used as preterits. This identity is for the most part demonstrable within Turfanian itself, but is even more obvious in the light of comparisons with Kuchean. These 'preterits' of Proto-Tocharian are probably derived from Proto-Indo-European perfects and aorists. The eventual developments of some of them into Turfanian imperfects must be explained by the meaning of the verbs themselves; but their origins must be identified exclusively on the basis of form.

[First published in *Language*, Vol. 29, No. 3, July-September, 1953, pp. 278-87.]

[1] For further details of the palatalization, cf. *Lg*. 21.81 ff.

[2] For the convenience of the reader who may want additional information not pertinent to this paper, the numbering of classes (whether present, preterit, subjunctive, or optative) follows the system advanced by W. Krause, *Westtocharische Grammatik*, Band 1. *Das Verbum* (Heidelberg, 1952; abbr. Krause).

[3] Krause 255 and 222 respectively.

[4] Cf. Sieg, Siegling, and Schulze, *Tocharische Grammatik* (abbr. SSS) 384 ff.

[5] Cf. Krause 103–4, 113–4.

[6] Pedersen, *Tocharisch* 204 f.; W. Couvreur, *BSL* 39.247 f.

[7] Krause, *Journal of Celtic Studies* 1.24 ff. Cf. also Pedersen, *VKG* 2.348.

[8] Several of these forms are of course assumed for the particular verbs for the sake of uniformity of comparison.

[9] Cf. Buck, *Introduction to the study of the Greek dialects*[2] 112.

[10] Op. cit. 384 ff.

[11] Cf. SSS 385 fn. 1; Couvreur, *Hoofdzaken van de tochaarse klank- en vormleer* 66; Pedersen, *Tocharisch* 178.

[12] Loc. cit.

[13] *Kleine Schriften* 239 ff. = *Sitzungsberichte der preuss. Akad. der Wissenschaften* 1924 166 ff.

[14] Op.cit. 176.

[15] Cf. Prokosch, *A Comparative Germanic grammar* 176 ff., with literature.

[16] Cf. *Lg*. 24.307–8.

[17] On the identity of the Indo-European perfect with the Hittite *ḫi*-conjugation, cf. Sturtevant, *Comp. Gramm. of the Hittite language*[2] 131 ff.

[18] Cf. Sturtevant, op. cit. 129-30; Couvreur, *Revue des études indo-européennes* 1.89 ff.

[19] Cf. Krause 83.

[20] These are Krause's Class Ib, but SSS Ia.

[21] Krause 10 ff.

[22] Cf. Krause's list 181 ff.

[23] Op. cit. 180.

[24] The question of the identity of the 2nd sg. ending Kuch. *-sta*, Turf. *(ä)ṣt* with Lat. *istī* need not concern us here; cf. Krause, loc. cit.

[25] *Lg*. 14.28-9; Pedersen, *Tocharisch* 219.

[26] Krause's remark (180) that palatalization is unknown in the Kuchean preterit of Class III is in general true, but initial *ly* occurs.

[27] *Lg*. 21.22, 23.

[28] Op. cit. 180.

[29] Krause 167-8.

[30] Op. cit. 179-80.

[31] Cf. Brugmann, *Grdr.*[2] 2.3.158 ff.; Buck, *Comp. Gramm. of Gk. and Lat.* 269.

[32] In such a case then PIE *ər* (or *r̥r* or *r̥* before vowel, however we write it) fell together in its development with PIE *o* and *a*. The etymology that I proposed in *Lg.* 14.29 (connection with Lat. *garriō* 'chatter'), is therefore to be abandoned, as is also that of Van Windekens, *Lex. étym.* 37.

[33] Cf. Krause 166 Anm. 1.

[34] Krause 165 (§ 164) compares these last-mentioned preterits, *karṣṣa, kälypawa, comyāwa, memyas,* with Baltic preterits like Lith. *tempiaũ* (to *tempiù, tem̃pti* 'stretch'), *tapiaũ* (to *tampù, tàpti* 'become'), as formations in *-yā*. I prefer the standard view (as in Brugmann, *Grdr.*[2] 2.3.176-7), that these Baltic forms are also *ē*-stems, not *yā*-stems; cf. sg. 2 *tempeĩ*, 3 *tem̃pė*, pl. 1 *tem̃pėme*, 2 *tem̃pėte*. They are then indeed comparable to our Tocharian formation, but only in the way that I have indicated.

[35] *Tocharisch* 170.

[36] Couvreur (*Hoofdzaken* 66) may be right in suspecting that we are actually dealing here, at least in part, with preterits and not with imperfects. In fact, while throughout this paper I have accepted the classification as imperfect or as preterit as I found it in SSS or Krause, I am not at all sure that when all texts are eventually analyzed such a classification will hold for Turfanian.

Tocharian Evidence and the Trubetzkoy-Benveniste Hypothesis

In the *Festschrift für Paul Kretschmer* 267-74 (1926), in an article entitled Gedanken über den lateinischen *ā*-Konjunktiv, N. S. Trubetzkoy proposed very convincingly the theory that the *ā*-subjunctive of Italic and Celtic was, in reality, originally an optative not a subjunctive. His thesis was that beside the athematic optative in *jē/ī* (Lat. *siem, siēs, siet / sīmus,* etc., Gk. *eíēn/eîmen,* Skt. *syām,* etc.), there were two distinct optatives for thematic indicatives, one in *oi* (Gk. *phéroi,* Skt. *bharet,* Goth. *bairai,* etc.), which is the one generally recognized, and another in *ā* found in Italic and Celtic to the exclusion of the *oi* optative.

Trubetzkoy emphasized (273) that both formations, *oi* and *ā*, were equally 'old', i.e. both of PIE origin, and that the individual dialect development of the *ā*-subjunctive in Italic and Celtic was to be ruled out. He was inclined to the view that those dialects which had the *oi*-formation did not have the one in *ā* and vice versa, but did not rule out completely the possibility that the latter was found also (beside the *oi*-optative) in Slavic and Germanic.

In *BSL* 47.11-20 (1951), in an article Prétérit et optatif en indo-européen, Benveniste, basing his thesis on his acceptance of the Trubetzkoy theory that the *ā*-subjunctive is really of optative origin, argued also for the optative origin of the *ā*-preterit (imperfect) in Italic. That is, the (originally) auxiliary verb forms Lat. *-bam, -bās, -bat, -bāmus,* etc. (< PIE **bhwām, *bhwās,* etc.) were in origin optatives. The equation of Lith. *bùvo* '(he) was' with Lat. *-bat* is purely fortuitous, since *bùvo* is probably an analogical form (*bùvo*: inf. *búti*:: *žùvo*: *žúti,* etc.) for dialectal *bìt,* OLith. *biti* (cf. Lett. *bija*).[1]

The other Latin '*ā*-preterit', *eram*, would be a new creation on the model *-bō*: *-bam*:: *erō*: *eram*. Likewise in Irish we find both *ā*-subjunctive *ba* and an imperfect *ba*. The former has been explained as a modal use of the latter. Benveniste suggests the reverse.

In support of the view that the optative can lend itself to preterit (imperfect) use, Benveniste cites copiously from other IE languages, including Tocharian, where, as is well known, the imperfects of 'be' and 'go' in both dialects are originally optatives, and where in dialect B the entire imperfect is of that origin.

Benveniste had, however, to revise Trubetzkoy's theory to the extent that the '*ā*-optative' was not limited exclusively to the thematic indicatives, but was also established (perhaps secondarily) for certain athematic forms, notably root aorists (cf. 19).

Such, in brief, is the Benveniste-Trubetzkoy hypothesis.

Neither of the two scholars, however, considers the wider problem of the '*ā*-preterit' in the other IE languages, that is, in Baltic and Slavic and especially in Tocharian, to see whether these languages have any evidence to offer for or against the hypothesis. To be sure, Benveniste does reject, following Stang, the comparison Lith *bùvo*: Lat. *-bat* (< **bhwāt*), and suggests also that the Armenian aorist in *-eaç*, which has been derived from *-is-ā-ske-*, shows the same evolution of an '*ā*-optative', derived from an aorist in *-is-*, cf. Lat. plperf. indic. *lēgeram* < **lēg-is-ā-m*.[2]

Let us examine the situation briefly in Tocharian, for it is here that the closest relationship between an *ā*-subjunctive and an *ā*-preterit is to be observed. In dialect A, a great number of subjunctive and preterit stems are identical; where there is no vocalic alternation in the root, they are distinguished only by choice of ending, e.g. act. 3 pl. subj. *tākeñc*: pret. *tākar* (*tāk-* 'be'); mid. 3 sg. subj. *pekatär*: pret. *pekat* (*pik-* 'write'); subj. *kälpātär*: pret. *kälpāt*, mid. sg. 1 subj. *kälpāmār*: pret. *kälpe* (*kälp-* 'find'). To be sure, subjunctives of the 'ablauting' class are further distinguished in the active forms by gradation, where the subjunctive has 'strong grade' in the singular but 'weak' in the plural, as opposed to the preterit, which shows the weak grade in the singular but the strong in the plural, e.g. subj. act. sg. 1 *kalkam*, 3 *kalkaṣ*, pl. 1 *kälkāmäs*, 3 *kälkeñc*, but pret. act. sg. 2 *kälkāṣt*, 3 *kälk*, pl. 3 *kalkar*. The stem suffix alternates correspondingly between *a* after strong root and *ā* after weak.[3] The correlation of subjunctive and preterit stems is so regular that the authors of *SSS* have seen it descriptively feasible to treat the preterit and subjunctive classes together, even where they are not formed from the same stem.[4]

In dialect B, the systematization of the relationships between preterit and subjunctive stems is not nearly so thorough. However, the vast majority of preterits in *ā* (Cl. I) show beside them *ā*-subjunctives (*WtG.* and *TElb.* subj. Cl. V), e.g. act. pl. 3 subj. *tākaṃ*: pret. *takāre*; mid. sg. 3 subj. *paiykatär*: pret. *paiykate*; but beside pret. *kälpāwa* etc. we have subj. *kallau* etc., *nā*- subjunctive (subj. Cl. VI), though most of the B preterits Cl. Ia (*WtG* 160 f.) show also *ā*-subjunctives, e.g. to *käl*- 'bring', mid. sg. 3 subj. *kalatär*: pret. *klāte* (= A *klāträ*: *klāt*); to *tärk*- 'release', act. sg. 3 subj. *tārkaṃ*: pret. *carka* (A act. sg. 1 subj. *tarkam*: pret. sg. 3 *cärk*, pl. 3 *tarkar*, beside '*s*-pret.' *crakär*).

Deviations from this pattern are rare in dialect A. One instance has just been noted above where an '*s*-preterit' (pret. Cl. III, *SSS* 375, *WtG* 179 ff.) *crakär* is found beside *ā*-preterit and *ā*-subjunctive. Similar is the case of *spārksā-m* (pret. III), beside *spärkā-ṃ*, vbl. subst. *s[pä]rkālune* (*ā*-pret. and subj.). In the case of *as*- 'dry up', only pret. III *asäs* is attested beside *ā*-subj. *āsaṣ*, vbl. subst. *āslune*.

For *pkät*, ppl. *pko* (*päk*- 'intend') and pple. *yko* (to *yäk*- 'neglect'), all pointing clearly to *ā*-pret., no subjunctive forms are attested, but the optatives are completely anomalous: *päknāśi(t)rä* and *(yäk)nāśśiträ* (*SSS* 370).

Somewhat less regular is the situation in dialect B. Here, though the vast majority of *ā*-preterits show *ā*-subjunctives, there is quite a scattering of other subjunctives (*WtG* 159 ff.). Of the verbs with preterits Cl. Ia (Krause, *WtG* = *SSS* Ib, i.e. preterits with short root-vowel), about fifty-six have attested subjunctives, of which about nine are of other formation. For preterits of Cl. Ib (*WtG* = *SSS* Ia, i.e. preterits with long root-vowel) about fifty-two have attested subjunctives, of which about a dozen, perhaps fourteen, seem not to be *ā*-formations. But it is a significant fact that those forms which might be called the 'regular' preterits of both types (i.e. Ia with pple. in unreduplicated *-au, -oṣ*, Ib in reduplicated participle in *-au, -aṣ*) rarely show anything but *ā*-subjunctives.

On the other hand, so far as I am able to judge, all *ā*-subjunctives in both dialects have beside them *ā*-preterits within the limits of our evidence. This situation, as opposed to the fact that approximately twenty-five percent of the *ā*-preterits in dialect B show other subjunctive formations, is possibly significant for our purpose. I shall attempt to interpret it later.

Before one can begin to evaluate the facts regarding the relationship between *ā*-subjunctive and *ā*-preterit in Tocharian with regard to its effect on the validity of the Benveniste-Trubetzkoy hypothesis, two very fundamental questions must be answered: (1) Is the Tocharian *ā*-subjunctive identical in origin with the *ā*-subjunctive of Italic and Celtic? (2) Is the Tocharian *ā*-preterit to be equated to the *ā*-imperfect seen in Lat. *-bam* etc., Osc. *fufans* 'erant', and possibly OIr. *ba*? To answer these questions, the origins of Tocharian *ā* should be examined, and the conditions for the fluctuation between *ā* and *a* in Tocharian itself should be determined.

Tocharian *ā* = (1) IE *ā* in B *sā*, *sā-u*, *sā-ṃ*, A *sā-s*, *sā-m*, *sā-ṃ*: Gk. *hā* (Att. *hē*), Goth. *sō*, etc.; A *mācar*, B *mācer*: Gk. *mḗtēr*, Lat. *māter*; etc.; (2) IE *a* in A *ākeñc*, B *āśäṃ*: Lat. *agō*, Gk. *ágō*, etc.; A *ārki*, B *ārkwi* 'white': Gk. *árguros* etc.;

(3) IE *ə* in A *pācar*, B *pācer*: Skt. *pitár-*, Gk. *patḗr*; A *ckācar*, B *tkācer*: Skt. *duhitar-*, Gk. *thugátēr*, etc.

Toch. *ā* can also reflect IE *o*: A *āle, ālyi, āli* (obl.) 'palm of the hand': Arm. *ołn* 'spine', Goth. *aleina* 'cubit'; B *āsta* (pl.) 'bones': Gk. *ostéon* etc.; and IE *ē* in AB *mā* 'not': Gk. *mē*.

On the other hand IE *ā* is clearly reflected by A *a*, B *o* in A *pracar*, B *procer* 'brother', and IE *a is* probably represented in the same way in A *waṣt*, B *ost* 'house' (: Gk. *ástu*).

As regards the alternation between *ā* and *a* in dialect B, it can be assumed that we are dealing with a single phoneme, with length a matter of stressed position, cf. 3 sg. *tāka*, pl. *takāre* (pret. of verb 'to be') probably with IE *ā*; sg. 3 *āśäṃ*, but with suffixed pronoun *aśan-ne* (pres. of *ak-* 'lead' with certain IE *a*); pl. nom. *pacera*, perl. *pacerasa*, gen. *paceraṃts* to *pācer* with certain IE *ə*. But there are frequent instances of *a* where we expect *ā*, e.g. *aśäṃ*, or even *ā* where we expect *a*, e.g. *pācera*.[5]

In dialect A, *ā* and *a* appear to be distinct phonemes, though one can establish rules for the appearance of one or the other vowel in certain categories of forms in accordance with what has been termed a type of 'vowel balance'. This phenomenon is of particular importance in the very forms we are dealing with here, e.g. in the alternation of 'strong' and 'weak' root with *a*/*ā* of the stem vowel in pret. Ia (*SSS Ib*): pret. act. sg. 2 *kälkāṣt*: pl. 3 *kalkar*, mid. sg. 2 *kälpāte*, pl. 3 *kälpānt*; subj. act. sg. 3 *kalkaṣ* pl. 2 *kälkāc*; or in the retention of a 'strong' root throughout and *a* (or zero) as stem vowel in Ib (*SSS* Ia): pret. act. 2 sg. *tākaṣt*, pl. 3 *tākar*, mid. sg. 2 *kropte*, 3 *kropat*, pl. 3 *kropant*; subj. act. sg. 3 *lotkaṣ*, pl. 2 *lotkac*. What these regular alternations have to do with the actual accent it is impossible to say, nor is it easy to deduce a reasonable accent system for Proto-Tocharian which might be responsible for it. I believe, however, that both Toch. A *a* and *ā* as stem suffixes go back to PToch. /*ā*/, or to whatever phoneme gave Toch. B /*a*/ = [ā] and [a]. Compare the forms quoted from

B above. This then will be our assumption, and when necessary I shall write the phoneme in question merely *ā*.

But even if this is correct, we cannot say conclusively that we are here dealing with PIE *ā*. We have seen above that Toch. *ā* can have several origins, and that PIE *ā* is reflected by different vowels in Tocharian. In fact, it has been suggested that the only sure example of the development of PIE *ā* is A *a*, B *o* in the word for 'brother'. This opinion seems also to be reflected in W. Winter's discussion of some aspects of the *ā*-subjunctive in his report for Tocharian in *Evidence for laryngeals* 173-86, especially 181f. (Austin, Texas, 1960).

Winter's discussion has some bearing on our problem here. If I understand him rightly, he would derive the stem vowel of presents Cl. IV (B *o*, A *a*) from PIE *a*, and that of the corresponding subjunctive (B *a*, A *a*/*ä*) from PIE *ə*. He considers the formation to be denominative, but cites only B pres. *klautkoträ* 'becomes', subj. *klautkaträ* beside noun *klautke* 'turn'.[6] The present of this verbal root in A is found only with a nasal infix: sg. 3 *lotäṅkaṣ*, parallel to B pl. 3 mid. *kluttaṅkentär* 'turn around (intrans.), become'. The corresponding noun in A is *lotäk*. It is difficult for me to see how these verbs (i.e. Cl. IV) can be denominative, especially if the present stem has original *ā* (alternating with *ə*). A *lotäk*, B *klautke*, both masculine, have all the earmarks of *o*-stems. I am not inclined, however, to follow Winter in his derivation of the present-stem vowel B *o* = A *a*, or of the subjunctive stem *a*, from *ā* or *ə*.[7]

As for the *o* in B *procer* = A *pracar* I am inclined to leave it unexplained in the face of the other evidence that the 'regular' development of PIE *ā* is Toch *ā*.[8] I fail to see any reason to assume *ə* in the subjunctive in particular, nor do I understand why we should expect an ablaut alternation in the stem vowel between indicative and subjunctive. In similar fashion Winter apparently assumes that the present-stem vowel of class III, B *e*, beside the *ā* of the subjunctive,[9] represents PIE *ō* alternating with *ə*. I know of no good evidence for the development of PIE *ō* > Toch. *e*. Instead, as far as there is any evidence, it suggests that *ō* fell together with *ā̆* and *ə* (e.g. A *āknats*, B *aknātsa*: Lat. *ignōtus*).[10]

I believe, then, that we may assume with some degree of confidence that the *ā* of the subjunctive in question does actually reflect PIE *ā*. The next question that arises is whether it is to be derived from the same source as the *ā*-subjunctive of Italic and Celtic (as has up to now been generally assumed) and, if so, how this affects the theory of its optative origin. Speaking for this identity is the retention by Tocharian of other archaisms of the 'periphery' found likewise in Italic and Celtic, in particular the mediopassive in *r*, the long-vowel perfect, and the *ui*-perfect. The first two of these are found also in Hittite, the second also in Germanic,[11] and the last possibly also in Indic (Skt. *ja-jñāu* etc.).[12]

In an article on the Tocharian subjunctive published in 1959, I followed current opinion in taking the identity of the Tocharian and the Italic-Celtic subjunctive for granted. In that article I argued for the original identity of the *ā*-subjunctive and the *ā*-present; that is, I held that not only is Latin *secās* formally indistinguishable from *tegās*, but that they are originally the same formation, which I suggested was merely another present (indicative) type, possibly with a developing sense of futurity already in at least these three IE dialects.[13]

This hypothesis seemed appropriate in view of the actual Tocharian B relationship between present (indicative) and subjunctive. In Tocharian the majority of the formations are identical, and – even more to the point – many verbal stems do not distinguish formally between indicative and subjunctive. In the particular instance of the *ā*-formation, of the twelve verbs that have *ā*-presents, seven have attested subjunctives and five of these are identical in form with the present. Two others show *ā*-preterits, hence certainly *ā*-subjunctives, which would probably be identical with the presents if they were attested. Two more show *ā*-subjunctives from a different stem, and one shows an *ā*-subjunctive from a grade of root different from that of the present.[14]

Furthermore, the *ā*-subjunctive in Tocharian B is in no way to be connected with the thematic present system. Of the sixteen (or seventeen) verbs of the latter class (pres. II) for which the subjunctive is attested, only one clear instance of an *ā*-subjunctive is found (*klātsät*, to *kälṣtär* 'threatens').[15] The majority of thematic presents (nine out of ten) show also thematic subjunctives which are identical in form with the indicative. The *ā*-subjunctive is, on the other hand, formed especially alongside presents in *e* (Cl. III), *o* (Cl. IV), *ā* (Cl. V), (*a*)*na* (Cl. VI), and the nasal infix (Cl. VII).[16]

There is of course no valid evidence with regard to the connection of the *ā*-subjunctive with the thematic aorist, since we have only two presumable relics of the latter: pl. 1 *kmem*, 3 *kameṃ* to *käm-* 'come' and sg. 3 *lac*, pl. 3 *lateṃ* to *lä*(*n*)*t-* 'go out'. The former has a thematic subjunctive. The latter is uncertain, but is clearly not an *ā*-subjunctive.[17]

Thus Tocharian in no way supports Trubetzkoy's theory, modified by Benveniste, that the *ā*-subjunctive was originally an optative, characteristic of thematic presents or aorists. Indeed, the evidence, though of a negative sort, points in the opposite direction. And, so far as Tocharian is concerned, the existence of the subjunctive as a category originally independent of the indicative is a very dubious assumption. This was my conclusion in the article mentioned above,[18] and the considerations presented here do not cause me to change my mind. But before reaching a definite conclusion let us examine the Tocharian preterit in the light of Benveniste's theory.

It is, in fact, Benveniste's hypothesis that the *ā*-imperfect of the root **bhew-* in Italic and Celtic is of optative origin, which adds greatly to the credibility of Trubetzkoy's theory that the *ā*-subjunctive is an optative. As Benveniste has demonstrated (cf. above), the transfer of the optative to preterit (imperfect) use is widespread and not to be denied, whatever the semantic shift involved. However, we have *ā*-preterits in languages where there is not and probably never has been an *ā*-subjunctive, in particular Baltic and Slavic.

Stang, in his extremely important monograph on the Slavic and Baltic verb system,[19] would distinguish between the Baltic *ā*-preterit with intransitive meaning (e.g. *bùdo*: pres. *buñda*, inf. *bùsti* 'wake up'; *liñko*: pres *liñgsta*, inf. *liñkti* 'bow down') and what he terms 'das rein-präteritale *ā*' in *pir̃ko*: pres. *pe̒rka*, inf. *pir̃kti* 'buy'; *riñko*: pres. *reñka*, inf. *riñkti* 'collect'; *sùko*: pres. *sùka*, inf. *sùkti* 'turn', etc. This 'rein-präteritales *ā*' is found also in the Slavic aorist: OCS *bĭra*: pres. *berą*, inf. *bĭrati* 'gather'; *gŭna*: pres. *ženą*, inf. *gŭnati* 'drive'; *kova*: pres. *kovą*, inf. *kovati* 'forge'. Stang would also draw into comparison with the 'rein-präteritales *ā*', the Armenian aorist in- *ç*, e.g. act. sg. 3 *gorceaç* '(he) made', with a suffix *-is-ā-sk-* which he equates[20] to the Latin *-isā* > *-erā-* in the pluperfect (*legeram* etc.). These Armenian and Latin formations, as we have seen, have also been discussed by Benveniste in connection with the hypothesis of the optative origin of the *ā*.

As Stang has pointed out,[21] this purely preterital *ā* is generally accompanied by a weak-grade root. And, as he notes, this *ā* – no matter what its origin, whether radical or not – has long since reached the status of an independent suffixal element. The question, so far as this paper is concerned, is whether the purely preterital *ā* is identical with that of the *ā*-preterit of Tocharian, and eventually also with the *ā*-formation in question (*ā*-subjunctive) in Italic and Celtic.

In the article on the Tocharian subjunctive referred to above,[22] I examined the evidence not only in Tocharian but also in Germanic, Italic, and Celtic, to determine whether the gradation of the root supported the view that both the *ā*-subjunctive (and present) and the *ā*-preterit were to be derived from aorist and preterit bases of the type seen in Gk. *édrān*, *étlēn* (Dor. *étlān*), Skt. *átrāt, áyāt.* I concluded that for these languages no decision could be reached on this point.

J. Vendryes[23] has examined the Italic and Celtic (primary) present formations in *ā* of two types: (1) Latin *occupāre* 'get hold of, occupy' (beside *capiō* 'seize'), *comparāre* 'get' (beside *pariō* 'give birth to'), with fundamentally mediopassive value – whereas the verbs in *yo/i* indicate the action pure and simple; (2) the intensive-duratives *ducāre* (beside *dūcō, -ere*), *dicāre* (beside *dīcō, -ere*). He concluded that both types are derivative of an aorist stem in *ā*. The difference in function, mediopassive vs. intensive-durative, is due to their opposition to presents in *yo/i* on the one hand and *o/e* on the other. In this latter conclusion I believe that Vendryes was surely correct. Leaving aside for the moment the Italic and Celtic (and Tocharian) *ā*-subjunctive, I feel that all the indicative *ā*-formations – presents, preterits, and aorists, mediopassive-intransitives and active-transitives – must go back ultimately to the same original *ā* element. This is of course implied in the treatment accorded them by Brugmann.[24] The starting point of the *ā* is obscured, however, by extensions and analogical formations in all the IE languages, and especially in Italic, Celtic, Germanic, Baltic, and Slavic – exactly those languages with which Tocharian, in my opinion, shows the closest affinities.

As we know, and as has been implicit in the discussion above, the preterit in *ā* is one of the significant common dialect features of Baltic and Slavic. It would seem most injudicious of me to attempt to separate from it the *ā*-preterit of Tocharian, where it has been extended most widely.

But to return to the *ā*-subjunctive in Italic and Celtic. The older view of its origin is that sponsored by Brugmann,[25] according to which the formation was originally an 'injunctive', i.e. an unaugmented preterit (aorist or imperfect) used in modal value (imperative, subjunctive). That is, the preterit formation is the more archaic. Later, in modal use, it was assimilated in Italic and Celtic to the present system.

Holger Pedersen is even more specific:[26] 'Die italisch-keltischen Konjunktivformen sind mit den slavisch-baltischen indikativischen Aoristformen ganz identisch; derartige mit einem Indikativ identischen Konjunktivformen nennt man in der idg. Grammatik gewöhnlich Injunktive.' And as regards the Tocharian *ā*-subjunctive he remarks:[27] 'Er ist natürlich mit dem italisch-keltischen *ā*-Konjunktiv zu vergleichen.'

In his Note liminaire to *L'apophonie en indo-européen*, J. Kurylowicz makes the following statement with regard to the relationship between the definite past (aorist = Eng. perfect, Fr. perfect = passé défini) and the optative: 'Conformément à notre schéma d'en haut, l'optatif est en règle une forme de B_1 'déclassée'. Cela n'est pas évident pour l'optatif en *-i̯ē/ī-*, formation sans doute trop archaïque, sans rapport intime avec les formes attestées de l'aoriste. Un tel rapport s'impose, par contre, pour le subjonctif (= ancien optatif) italoceltique en *-ā-* (déradical dans le type lat. *attigat*, *venat*, v. irl. *cria-* de *crenaid*, etc.), apparenté à l'aoriste balto-slave en *ā* (type lit. *lìko*, v. slave *bĭra*).'

If I interpret Kurylowicz's meaning rightly (and I am not sure I do), this would indicate that while he believes the *ā*-subjunctive is in origin an optative, he considers the change in meaning to be from aorist to optative, rather than the other way around as Benveniste would have it and as the numerous parallels from other IE languages indicate. I would agree that the evidence which I have presented supports the shift aspect > mood. But I would not agree that the *ā*-formation was an optative, except so far as there is no opposition between subjunctive and optative in Italic and Celtic; in Latin the old optative in *yē/ī*, where it occurs, serves as both. On the other hand, Tocharian has both subjunctive and optative, the latter reflecting the IE formation (cf. above).

In my article on the formation of the Tocharian subjunctive, I expressed the view that the subjunctive in *ā* was in form ultimately identical with the (present) indicative, and that it stood in formal relationship to the *ā*-preterit as the thematic present indicative stands to the imperfect or thematic aorist. I see no reason to alter that view in any fundamental way. I would only add the following explanation of the gradual elimination of the primary present indicative in *ā*. As the injunctive in *ā* (formally a preterit) was assimilated to the present system in a modal sense and assumed primary endings, it competed with the indicative, with which it was formally identical. By analogy, then, the larger share of such indicatives assumed subjunctive value, leaving only scattered relics in their original use. This, I hope, will satisfy Puhvel's objection[28] that 'It is difficult to believe that Italic and Celtic . . . changed their -*ā*-presents to subjunctives and kept them too.' Actually this is no real objection anyway: the difference between indicative and subjunctive is merely one of contrast elsewhere, where other types of subjunctives are identical with indicatives, e.g. the 'short-vowel' subjunctive of Greek and Indic, as pres. Gk. *édomai* (> future), *íomen*, aor. *kheúomen*, Skt. *hanati*, *hanat*, *gamanti*, *gamat*.[29] Per se, there is nothing to distinguish these from the corresponding forms of thematic indicative formations.

The Tocharian situation is remarkable to this extent, that in a few *ā*-subjunctives, as well as in most of the other subjunctive formations, one and the same formation for the same verbal root serves both as subjunctive and indicative. This indicates to me that the development of a contrast between the two stems had not progressed here as far as in some other Indo-European languages.

Furthermore, as we have seen, practically all *ā*-subjunctives are accompanied by *ā*-preterits in both Tocharian dialects; but in dialect B, the more archaic of the two, a considerable number of the *ā*-preterits (about one-fourth) show other subjunctive formations. So far as Tocharian is concerned, then, it appears that the subjunctive is clearly the derivative of the preterit, not the reverse. This agrees conclusively with the Baltic and Slavic situation, where preterits did not develop into subjunctives at all. In Italic and Celtic, on the other hand, the development from preterit to subjunctive was almost complete. In Latin only the form **bhwām* etc. remained as a preterit, and then only in composition as *-bam* etc. to form the new imperfect. It was this formation (originally periphrastic) which eliminated the simple *ā*-preterit, while it remained Baltic, Slavic, and Tocharian.

[First published in *Language*, Vol. 38, No. 3, Part 1, July-September, 1962, pp. 245-253.]

[1] Cf. Chr. S. Stang, *Das slavische und baltische Verbum* 197 (Oslo, 1942).

[2] Op. cit. 20.

[3] Cf. Sieg, Siegling, und Schulze, *Tocharische Grammatik* 341 ff., 363 ff. Abbreviated hereafter as *SSS*.

[4] In *SSS* the type of *tāk-*, *pek-*, etc. (nonablauting *ā*-preterit) is called Ia, whereas the type of *kalp-/kälp-*, *kalk-/kälk-* (ablauting *ā*-preterit) is called Ib. W. Krause, *Westtocharische Grammatik* I (abbreviated *WtG*) reverses the subdivisions a and b. The latter order is followed also by W. Krause and W. Thomas, *Tocharisches Elementarbuch* I (abbreviated *TElb.*).

[5] Cf. the detailed exposition *WtG* 10 ff., *TElb.* 43 ff.

[6] So Krause in *GGA* 1943.25, but apparently no longer, cf. *TElb.* 53.

[7] Actually the particular subjunctive form cited is not registered by Krause in *WtG* 241. While the basic meaning of the verb is 'turn', that of the noun appears to be secondary only: 'Art, Funktion' (*WtG* 50), 'Art und Weise, Verhalten, Abwandlung, Modifikation' (*Toch. Sprachreste*, Spr. B. 1, p. 118).

[8] Cf. Pedersen, *Zur toch. Sprachgeschichte* 43 f. (Copenhagen, 1944). The other instance of Toch. *o* < PIE *ā* in A *poke*, B *pokai* (obl.) 'arm', is in my opinion due to *u*-umlaut (: Gk. *pêkhus* etc.).

[9] The author cites no example but I suppose he has in mind the type of pres. *triwetär* subj. *triwātär* (from *triw-* 'mix' intr.).

[10] Cf. Pedersen, *Tocharisch vom Gesichtspunkt der indoeur. Sprachvergleichung* (Copenhagen, 1941) 226.

[11] I am not ready to accept many of J. Kurylowicz' brilliant but from the comparative point of view frequently unfounded hypotheses on the origin of lengthened-grade vowels as arising in the individual IE languages. Cf. *Apophonie en indoeuropéen* 308 ff., *Proceedings of the Eighth International Congress of Linguists* 228.

[12] On the *ui*-perfect, cf. Krause, *Corolla linguistica: Festschrift F. Sommer* 137-44.

[13] *Lg.* 35.157-79, esp. 171 f., 179 (1959).

[14] For the forms cf. *WtG* 70.

[15] The abstr. II *maṃtsalyñe*, which points to an *ā*-subjunctive, hardly counts, since we also have a nasal present *mantsana(tär)* beside the thematic *meṃṣtär*. The adherence of opt. *makoymar* and inf. *makatsi* 'run' to thematic present *maś(c)e(r)* is most uncertain. Cf. *WtG* 65.

[16] Cf. the statistics op. cit. 130, and *Lg.* 35.169 ff.

[17] *WtG* 140.

[18] Fn. 13.

[19] Op. cit. (fn. 1) 75 ff., 188 ff.

[20] After Maries, *Rev. des études arm.* 10.167 ff.

[21] Op. cit. 189, bottom.
[22] Fn. 13.
[23] *MSL* 16.300 ff. (1910-11).
[24] *Grundriss*[2] 2.3.116 ff.
[25] Op. cit. 539 ff.
[26] *Vergl. Gramm. d. kelt. Sprachen* 2.354 f.
[27] *Tocharisch* 199. E. Adelaide Hahn, in her significant monograph *Subjunctive and optative: Their origin as futures* (New York, 1953), is in essential agreement with this view of the origin of the *ā*-subjunctive. She differs, however, in claiming that the so-called 'injunctive' as a mood is actually a fiction: 'The injunctive is a creation of Delbrück's, christened by Brugmann' (38). Miss Hahn goes on to demonstrate that the modal value lay not in the verb form, which was of course identical with the indicative (she would perhaps say 'was indicative'), but rather in the negative particle accompanying it, i.e. originally in the particle **mē* > Gk. *mḗ*, Skt. *mā* (41). The preference for the aorist aspect is of course to be expected in a prohibition.
I am in complete agreement with Miss Hahn in denying the existence of an injunctive as a separate mood. I can see no harm, however, in continuing the word for this specific use of an originally preterit indicative form. As for the explanation of the modal value as arising from the accompanying negative particle, I find it most enticing. In addition to the support which she has adduced (40 ff., 52 ff.), I would call attention to the use of Toch. B *mā*, A *mar* (= B *mā ra* 'nor', after negative) in prohibitions. For details, cf. W. Thomas, Zum Gebrauch des prohibitiven *mā* bzw. *mar* im Tocharischen, *Cent. As. jour.* 3.289 ff. (1958).
On the other hand, as I have often stated elsewhere, I do not consider the subjunctive an IE mood, at least not on a par with the optative, as Miss Hahn apparently does. In this I am in close agreement with Holger Pedersen.
It seems a pity that many of our colleagues, especially in Europe, have largely ignored Miss Hahn's monograph. Even if one does not agree with some of her conclusions, the book is invaluable as a history and a digest of research on the Indo-European subjunctive and optative, both formal and syntactic.
[28] Jaan Puhvel, *Laryngeals and the Indo-European verb* 59 (1960).
[29] Cf. Schwyzer, *Griech. Gramm.* 1.790; Brugmann, op. cit. 524 ff.

On the significance of Tocharian for Indo-European linguistics

The above title would, at first glance, seem to be rather barren in its promise of significant results. As all who have any particular acquaintance with Tocharian know, we have here two medieval languages, chronologically on a par with the earliest records of West Germanic. And even these two languages, which, following long-established custom, we shall call here dialect A and dialect B, show in many points such great dissimilarity that it is impossible by the comparative method to establish a satisfactory notion of Proto-Tocharian – a prerequisite to their competent comparison with other IE languages.

However we have perhaps, all too long now, based our notions of the parent speech on the skeleton which the dissection of Greek and Sanskrit exposed to our view. To be sure Hittite has given us a few shocks in recent years and caused considerable modifications with which the author of a new edition of Brugmann's *Grundriss* will have to cope. Moreover, the word 'significance' in my title can always be interpreted in a negative as well as a positive sense, and disagreements with our long-established conceptions are themselves significant.

Least propitious of all for my purpose would seem to be an examination of Tocharian phonology where we have a system of only three voiceless stops, *p*, *t*, *k*, in the face of voiceless and voiced stops, both aspirated and unaspirated of each series in Indo-European, and not only that, but where the voiceless *k* may represent any member of the three guttural series, palatal, plain velar or labiovelar – or at least so is our normal statement in relating the Tocharian consonants to the Indo-

European system as usually conceived. However in Hittite there is no evidence for a distinction between aspirated and unaspirated stops. And likewise there is no evidence, I believe, for assuming that the IE labiovelars were in origin unit phonemes rather than two separate phonemes consisting of guttural plus labial semivowel. Certainly there is no evidence for a phonemic distinction between palatals and velars. Now how does this affect our Tocharian problem? If we assume the separation of Tocharian from the parent speech at a very early stage, we need only assume a loss of the phonemic distinction of voice, not aspiration. I wonder also if I would be going too far if I call attention to the fact that those languages of the Indo-European family with which, in my opinion, Tocharian had its last IE contacts, namely Baltic and Slavic, show likewise no distinction between aspirated and unaspirated stops, nor for that matter do those with which it had, again in my opinion, its closest contacts in the original Indo-European community, namely the Celtic languages.

This does not mean that I hold to any theory of a special Hittite-Tocharian, Balto-Slavo-Tocharian or Celto-Tocharian linguistic unity any more than I do to any imaginable combination indicating a special relationship between Hittite, Balto-Slavic and Celtic. Much to the contrary, I would rather point out merely that other branches of the Indo-European family likewise fail to show evidence for certain phonological distinctions in the parent speech which we have generally since the 1890's considered fundamental and not to be questioned.

As regards traces of laryngeals in Tocharian (beyond the evidence of the presence of long-vowel series), I am entirely unconvinced that any can be produced, just as I am by laryngealist explanations of various and disparate phenomena in other IE languages known only from a comparatively late date.[1]

With regard to the development of the labiovelars in Tocharian, it has often been said that it is a 'centum' language. But this refers only to the coincidence of palatals and plain velars. But it is also possible that some distinction between original labiovelar and palatal (or plain velar) plus labial sonant can be shown.[2] This is a characteristic of the 'satəm' languages.

A phonological feature which Tocharian seems to share with Celtic and Germanic is extensive vowel assimilation in adjacent syllables. To be sure the details of this Tocharian 'Umlaut' have not been worked out, but many of the irregularities of vowel development are, no doubt, to be explained in this fashion. In particular back umlaut seems especially important, e.g. A *okät*, B *okt* 'eight' < **oktō*. Otherwise IE *o* should appear as A *a* (*ä*), B *e*, cf. A *kam*, B *keme* 'tooth': Grk. γόμφος. The influence of *u* is probably to be noted in A *waṣt*, B *ost* 'house': Grk. ἄστυ; and in B *mit* 'honey': Grk. μέθυ. Compare especially OIr. *mid*, gen. *medo*, OHG *mito* (beside usual *metu*, *meto*).

In view of the fact that the Tocharian declension is built up by the addition of (original) postpositions (alike for singular and plural) to the oblique (or accusative) case forms, there would seem to be little historical or comparative significance in an examination of nominal inflection. However it is possibly worthy of notice that the oblique singular in *-ṃ* (= final *n*), which is a property of nouns indicating 'rational' beings, is probably merely the *n*-stem suffix which remained after the case endings themselves were lost, e.g. A B *käṣṣi* 'teacher', sg. obl. *käṣṣiṃ*; A *śom* 'young man,' sg. obl. *śomäṃ*, B *śaumo* 'man', sg. obl. *śaumoṃ*, etc. This seems to be a development of the use of the *n-stem* suffix to form terms indicating characteristics of the persons to which applied and is a use of the suffix shared also by Latin (*Catō*: *catus*), and Greek (Στράβων: στραβός), and with extreme consequences in Germanic where it not only forms epithets (especially tribal names *Saxones*,

Frankones), but in particular furnished the weak adjective inflection.[3]

The importance of the *n*-stem inflection in Tọcharian is seen further in the plural nom., A B *-ñ*, which is certainly to be derived from PIE nom. **-n-es*.

An astonishing, but apparently correct, comparison is that which has been made between the Tocharian plural ending A *-nt* (*-änt*, *-unt*) and B-nta (*-enta*, *-inta*, *änta*, etc.), and the (originally) collective *-nt*-suffix in Hittite (e.g. *utneyant* 'population, country' beside *utne-* 'land', *parnant-* 'Häuser-komplex (?)' [Friederich, *Wtb.* 162), beside *parn-*, *pir-* 'house'), and the Luvian pl. in nom. *-nzi*, acc. *-nza*.[4] This *-nt-* suffix is no doubt to be identified with similar formations elsewhere in IE, but the particular development to collective > plural would appear common to Tocharian and Anatolian.

One of the more striking features of Toch. B inflection over against that of dialect A is the oblique sing. ending *-ai* (*-yai*). It occurs for a variety of nom. sg. forms: *arṣaklai*, nom. *arṣaklo* 'serpent', *wertsyai*, nom. *wertsya* 'retinue', *kaumai*, nom. *kaumiye* 'sea', etc. The stem in *-ai* is found also even in the plural: obl. pl. *proskaiṃ*, sg. obl. *proskai*, nom. *proskiye* and *prosko*, 'fear'. Only one possible instance of this ending appears to be found in A, namely *k*$_{\hat{u}}$*le*, nom. *k*$_{\hat{u}}$*li* 'woman' which can be identified with B *klai*, nom. *kliye*, *klyiye*. But A *-e* can be of several other origins. One can hardly refrain from comparing this ending *-ai* with the stem shown in the very archaic type of *i*-stem seen in Hittite *ḫurtaiš* 'curse', acc. *ḫurtain*, gen. *ḫurtiyaš*, dat. *ḫurtiya*, *ḫurtai*, abl. *ḫurtiyats*, etc., and possibly also in the type of Grk. ἠχώ, πειθώ, and the isolated Skt. *sakhā*, acc. *sakhāyam*.[5]

In the derivation of the personal pronouns, one of the puzzles is the 1st person sing. nom. -obl. A masc. *näṣ*, fem. *ñuk*, B (both genders) *ñäś* (*ñiś*), gen. A masc. *ñi*, fem. *nāñi*, B (both genders) *ñi*. Of the various suggestions that have been offered possibly the most probable would seem that of

Professor Krause[6] as from **ne-kwe* for **me-kwe* by dissimilation (cf. Goth. *mik*. Venet. *mexo*). But another possibility might be to resort to the connective particle *nu*, i.e. $nu + m^{e}/_{o}$- > $n(u)m^{e}/_{o} > n(m)^{e}/_{o} >$ *ñ*- before orig. *e*, but *n*- before *o*. Such an assimilation would have to be very old and would remind us forcibly of the use of *nu*- in Hittite *nu-mu* 'and me', *nu-tta* 'and thee', etc.[7] It would be strange, however, that traces of the coalescence of *nu* with other pronominal stems do not appear.

When one turns to the verb, it is of course the medio-passive in -*r* which strikes one at first because of its obvious, even if superficial, similarity to that of Italic and Celtic. Compare, for example the endings of the present: sg. 1 A *mār*, B *mar*, 2 A *tār*, B *tar*, 3 A B *tär*; pl. 1 A *mtär*, B *mt* (*t*)*är*, 2 A *cär*, B *tär*, 3 A B *ntär*; with the Irish deponent (absolute): sg. 1 *ur*, 2 *ther*, 3 *thir*; pl. 1 *mir*, *mar*, (2 *d*, *th*), 3 *tar* (*tir*); and Latin: sg. 1 *or*, 2 *ris*, *re*, 3 *tur*; pl. *mur*, (2 *mini*), 3 *ntur*. This similarity, along with the misinterpretation of Toch. *p* as a reflex of a labiovelar, led to an early suggestion that Tocharian was indeed a Celtic language.[8] However a close examination of the formation of the Tocharian endings in comparison with either the Irish or the Latin shows little or nothing that may be considered as innovations common to the three. Rather, the *r*, which is really the only common feature not found in other IE medio-passives, is merely a relic from the parent speech which they all have preserved and independently extended. Moreover a deponent or mediopassive in *r*- is found also in Phrygian and in the Anatolian languages (Hittite, Luvian). To be sure our evidence from the former is too meager to arrive at hard and fast conclusions about its closer relationships within IE, but the oft cited αδδακετορ ('joins' (= formally *adficitur*?) seems proof that Phrygian too must be brought into any discussion of the *r*- ending. Better evidence of the antiquity and of the original wide distribution of the '*r*-element' is to be found in Hittite where the medio-passive present may be characterized by an optional *ri*, e.g. (for the *mi*-conjug.): sg. 1 *hari* (*hahari*) beside *ha*, 3 *tari* beside *ta*; pl. 2 *dumari* beside *duma*, 3 *antari* beside *anta*.[9] It is obvious I believe from the Hittite evidence that the '*r*-element' was in origin an independent particle of optional use in the parent speech. Its incorporation into the endings of the present medio-passive in Tocharian, Italic and Celtic cannot in itself be indicative of a common development unless there are other more fundamental agreements in the verbal system that can only be explained in that fashion.

As regards tenses, Tocharian is one of those IE languages which show no distinction between an imperfect, i.e. a form with secondary endings derived from the present stem, and an aorist from a contrasting stem. In fact the PIE distinction between an imperfect and aorist is based on the situation in Greek and Indo-Iranian, but here, as we all know the formal distinction is one of contrast for the particular verbal stem, since like formations are found for both present and aorist stems, e.g. ἔγραφον impf. is identical with ἔλιπον aor. and similarly Skt. *átudam* impf. with *ásicam* aor.

In Slavic in particular the distinctions between aorist and imperfect formations usually attributed to the parent speech are completely gone and both are found instead in the 'aorist', e.g. ChSl. 2, 3 sg. *reče* (< IE imperf. **rekes*, **reket*) beside 1 sg. rěxŭ, pl. rěchomŭ, *rěste*, *rěše* (< IE s-aorists), to pres. 1 sg. *rekạ*, *receši*. Original thematic (or at least thematized) aorists are represented by *dvigŭ*, *dviže*, *legŭ*, *leže*, etc.[10]

Likewise in Armenian the 'radical' aorist corresponds formally to thematic forms with secondary endings of Greek and Sanskrit, e.g. *eber* 'he carried' = Grk. ἔφερε, Skt. *abharat* imperf.; *elik* 'he left' = Grk ἔλιπε aor., etc.[11]

The Slavic and Armenian situations are usually considered later confusions of an old distinction observed in Greek and Indo-Iranian. But these are the only two IE dialects that make the distinction. All other IE languages that develop an 'imperfect' do it quite independently of each other. Could it not rather be possible that it is Greek and Indo-Iranian that have developed an imperfect out of one original category, namely the aorist (or better perhaps 'preterit') of the parent IE speech? Moreover these two dialects may show contradictions in 'tense', whether aorist or imperfect, in identical formations, e.g. Grk. ἐγένετο aorist = Skt. *ájanata* imperfect, etc.

So far as I am able to judge at the present, there are no Tocharian preterits or imperfects which may be identified in form with Greek or Indo-Iranian 'imperfects'.[12] However we do at least have here one more branch of IE that shows no trace of any original distinction between imperfect and aorist.

From the variety of formations (aorist and perfect) that were combined to create the Tocharian preterit, one of the more interesting for the purposes of this paper is the long vowel preterit (= A imperfect) of the type act. sg. 3 A *lyāk* impf. = B *lyāka* pret. (*läk-* 'see'); 3 pl. A *śārsar* impf. = B *śārsare,* 3 sg. *śārsa* pret. (*kärs-* 'know'); 3 pl. mid. A *śakant* impf.: 3 sg. act. B *tsā*(*ka*) pret. (A *tsäk-* mid. 'pulls out' = B *tsăk-* act 'bite, sting'); 3 pl. mid. A *pārant* impf. (*pär-* 'carry'); etc. My view (op. cit. below, ftn.[1]) that these are to be identified with 'long vowel perfects' elsewhere (Lat. *sēdī,* Goth. *sētum,* etc.) has in general not been accepted. However the equation Toch. A *pārant*: Goth. *bērum,* and the possible identification of A *lyāk,* B *lyāka-*: Lat. *lēgī* should not, I think, be ignored, especially when these three branches of IE show other common features inherited from the parent speech.[13]

One of the most striking agreements between Tocharian and Italic and Celtic is the subjunctive in *ā.* That is, if we assume that the *ā* (weakened to *a* in both dialects in certain positions) is really PIE *ā.*[14]

I do not intend to repeat or even resume much of that which I have already said about the Tocharian subjunctive in general or the assumed *ā-* subjunctive in particular.[15] Suffice it to say here that Tocharian gives no support to the view that the parent speech had a subjunctive formation in conformity with the picture formed by Greek-Sanskrit comparisons, i.e. a thematic subjunctive to athematic indicatives, a long vowel subjunctive to thematic indicatives. Rather, almost every present indicative formation may also be used to form subjunctive stems, and almost every subjunctive stem will also be found in the indicative. The only clear agreement outside Tocharian is in the instance of the *ā*- subjunctive.

In my discussion of the development of the Tocharian subjunctive, referred to above, I attempted to show that the *ā*- subjunctive was identical in origin with the (primary) *ā*-present of IE (type Lat. *secāre, domāre*, etc.), and that it was related to the *ā*-preterit (type Lat. *-bam, -bās*, etc., Lith. *bùvo*) in much the same way that thematic presents are related to thematic imperfects and aorists. I ignored there an article by Émile Benveniste in *BSL* 47 (1951), pp. 11-20, entitled 'Prétérit et optatif en indo-européen'. Benveniste there uses as a point of departure an article of N. Trubetzkoy 'Gedanken über den lateinischen *Ā*-Konjunktiv', published in the *Festschrift P. Kretschmer* (1926), pp. 267-74. Trubetzkoy's thesis there was that the *ā*-subjunctive of Italic and Celtic was actually an optative in origin and was a characteristic optative formation for thematic presents alongside the thematic optative in *oi* (Greek φέροι, Goth. *bairai*, Skt. *bharet*, etc.) as opposed to the athematic optative in *yē/ī* (Lat. *siem, siēs, siet*: *sīmus*, etc., Grk. εἴην: εἶμεν, etc.). Benveniste accepts this thesis and attempts to extend it to explain the origin of the preterit in *ā*. In view of the fact that the inherited optatives in *ye/i*, or *oi* have in later IE languages frequently developed preterit (and, especially, 'imperfect') value, the author assumes a like origin for the Latin *-bam, bās*, etc. and the Irish indic. pret. *-bá*. This theory assumes an extension of this original '*ā*-optative' from thematic to athematic verbs, and the use of the new optative of the verb 'be' as a preterit in periphrastic formations. Such, in brief, is the theory developed by Benveniste. He did not, however, make use of any evidence that might be drawn from the Tocharian forms in *ā* (*a*). It is here that we see these subjunctive and preterit formations in the closest formal relationship e.g. mid. sg. 3 subj. A *klāträ*, B *kalatär*: pret. A *klāt*, B *klāte* (from *käl-* 'bring'); A *pälkātär*, B (act. sg. 3) *pālkam*: A *pälkāt*, B *pälkāte* (from *pälk-* 'see'). Elsewhere I intend to go carefully into the question as to whether or not the Tocharian evidence supports the Trubetzkoy-Benveniste hypothesis of an optative origin for the *ā*-subjunctive and preterit, or whether the view which I advocated in the article referred to above is more reasonable, namely that the subjunctive (optative) use is merely a development from the indicative in *ā*.

However this question need not concern us here. I think few will deny the original identity of the *ā* (*a*)-formations in Tocharian with those of Italic and Celtic. This being the case, we have another feature of the parent speech shared in particular by these three branches of IE.[16]

It is perhaps worthwhile to note here, even for our present purposes, that Tocharian may perhaps strengthen one fundamental assumption of the Trubetzkoy and Benveniste hypothesis, namely that the *a*-formation was the optative formation to thematic indicatives to the exclusion of the thematic optative in *oi* in those languages where it occurred. The optative 'sign' in Tocharian is *ĭ* in both dialects. This is added to the (already characterized) subjunctive stem in the case of the *ā*-subjunctive in B but the *ā* is dropped in A, e.g., to *ār-* 'cease', B act. subj. sg. 3 *āram*, opt. *āroy*, A *āras*, but (mid.) *āritär*, etc. When this sign *ĭ* is added directly to a final palatalizable consonant it effects the usual change, e.g. (subj. 1, 'athematic' subjunctive), to A B *tās-* 'place', A subj. act. sg. 3 tās, pl. 3 tāseñc, opt. mid. sg. 3 tāṣitär, B subj. act. sg. 1 *tāsau*, pl. 3 *tāseṃ*, opt. act. sg. *tāsi*; to A *näk-* 'disappear', B *näk-* 'destroy', subj. 3. sg. A *nkatär*, B *nketär*, opt. A *nśitär*, B *nśitär*, etc.

It seems to me that such regular palatalization would point

to a generalization of the athematic *-ī-* rather than of a monophthongized thematic *-oi-*.

Besides the usual *ā* (*a*)-preterit, Tocharian has also a less usual formation in *ā* (*a*) with palatalization of the preceding consonant. This type is represented by the A act. sg. 1 *klyoṣā*, pl. 1 *klyoṣāmäs*, 3 *klyoṣār* (*klyos-* 'hear'), mid. sg. 3 *pāṣāt*, *wleṣāt* (*pās-* 'keep, observe', *wles-* 'practice'), which serve both as preterits and imperfects,[17] and by the normal imperfect in A when derived directly from the present stem, e.g.: sg. 3 *eṣā* (to *e-* 'give', pres. act. sg. 1 *esam*); *karyā* (*karyeñc* 'they laugh'), *kātäñśā* (*kātäṅkāṣ* 'rises'), etc. In B this formation is of course always preterit, e.g. act. sg. 1 *klyauṣāwa*, pl. 3 *klyauṣāre* (: A *kloṣā*, etc., above), mid. sg. 2 *paṣṣatai* (: A *pāṣāt*, above), etc.

This formation is probably to be connected with verbal stems in *ē* in other IE languages, especially with the non-present stems in *ē* in the Greek second aorist (ἐχάρν, ἐμάνην etc.), the Lithuanian preterit (Lith. *dẽgė*, *šaũkė*, to *dègti* burn', *šaũkti* 'call', etc.).[18] In Italic and Germanic the *ē*-formation is found as a present stem (cf. Lat. *tacēre*: OHG *dagēn*).[19] Thus Tocharian appears in this particular characteristic to part from those branches of IE with which it shows many inherited features from the earliest period.

To summarize: It would appear to me that Tocharian furnishes substantial support to the view that our 'late 19th century' conception of the IE parent language needs to be radically changed in several aspects, and nowhere more radically than in the instance of the verb. For our conception of the verbal categories has been based entirely upon agreements between Greek and Indic.[20] Further, it also appears that Tocharian emerges more and more clearly as a remnant of a very archaic dialect of IE with its earliest close affinities with the dialects of the North and West but with later influential contacts with those of the North and East.

[First published in *Classical Mediaeval and Renaissance Studies* in Honor of *Berthold Louis Ullman*, Vol. I, edited by Charles Henderson, Jr., *Storia e Letteratura, Raccolta di Studi e Testi*, Vol. 93, Roma, 1964, pp. 283-292.]

[1] I am therefore not in agreement with most of the theories presented for various languages in *Evidence for Laryngeals* (Austin 1960). Two notable exceptions are the careful and conservative discussions by H. Hoeningswald for Indo-Iranian and W. Cowgill for Greek. For the most part the assumed reflexes of the various 'laryngeals' are not here subjected to the rigorous testing of the evidence which our neo-grammarian forebears held requisite.

[2] Cf. my discussion in *Indogermanica: Festschrift für Wolfgang Krause* 79.

[3] Cf. Krause-Thomas, *Toch. Elementarbuch* 108; Brugmann, *Grundriss*[2] II, 1.305.

[4] Krause, Μνήμης χάριν, *Gedenkschrift Paul Kretschmer* 189 ff.; Kronasser, *Vgl. Laut- und Formenlehre des Heth.* 125.

[5] Pedersen, *Toch. vom Gesichtspunkt der indoeuropäischen Sprachvergleichung* 43; Kronasser, *op. cit.* 109 ff.

[6] *Toch. Elementarbuch* 162.

[7] Cf. Friedrich, *Heth. Elementarbuch* 1, 26, 88 ff.

[8] For a survey of earlier opinions on the ethnic and linguistic position of Tocharian, cf. S. Feist, *Indo-Germanen und Germanen* (1924) 110 ff.

[9] For further details cf. Friedrich, *op. cit.* 35 f.; Kronasser, *op. cit.* 201 ff.; Sturtevant, *Comp. Gramm.*[2] 146 ff.; Pedersen, *Hitt. und die anderen indoeuropäischen Sprachen* 103 ff.

[10] Cf. Stang, *Das slavische und baltische Verbum* 63 ff.

[11] Cf. Meillet, *Esquisse d'une gram. comp. de l'Arménien classique*[2] 104; Brugmann, *op. cit.* II, 3. 49.

[12] The imperfect in B is of optative origin, but in A it is of the same origin as various preterits (except for the verbs 'be' and 'go' which are original optatives in both dialects). Cf. Lane, *Language* 29 (1953) 278 ff.

[13] Likewise the Hittite ḫi-present (= IE perfect) of the type of 1 sg. *šakḫi*, pl. *šekweni* 'know' (= Goth. *sahw, sēhwum* 'saw') has with great plausibility been drawn into the comparison. Cf. Pedersen, *Hitt. und die anderen indoeur. Sprachen* 81 ff. Sturtevant, *op. cit.* 133. In this connection I might mention in passing that I am not persuaded by many of Kurylowicz's brilliant theories on the origin of the lengthened grade in his *Apophonie* (e.g. for Germanic class IV and V strong verbs, pp. 308 ff.), nor by his explanation of the origin of the *e*- in the Hittite plural forms above in the *Proceedings of the VIII. Congress of Linguists* 288.

[14] The other 'normal' origins of Toch. *ā* are IE *a* and *ə*, cf. A B *āk*- 'lead' (<**ag*-), A *pācar*, B *pācer* 'father' (<**pətar*-), but *a* may also reflect IE *ō* and *ē*. Cf. Krause-Thomas, *Toch. Elementarbuch* 1. 53.

[15] Cf. *Language*, 35 (1959) 179 ff.

[16] The question of the identity of the non-medial-intransitive ('reinpräteritales') *ā*- preterit in Baltic and Slavic (type Lith. *pir̃ko, sùko*, ChSl. *bĭra, tŭka*) is not considered by Benveniste. In any discussion of the origins of the *ā*-preterit as a whole, certainly these must not be ignored. Cf. Stang, *op. cit.* 75 ff., 189 ff.

[17] Cf. Sieg, Siegling und Schulze, *Tocharische Grammatik* 381-2, 386.

[18] Cf. Pedersen, *Tocharisch* 180. On the Baltic and Slavic non-present stem in *ē*, cf. in particular, Stang, *op. cit.* 74 f., 191 f.

[19] In Celtic it is of course impossible to distinguish present stems in *ē* from those in ī.

[20] Cf. also the remarks by Professor Stang *op. cit. Einleitung* 7.

The Tocharian verbal stems in *-tk-*

A curious feature of the Tocharian verb is the number of 'roots' ending in *-tk-*, altogether thirty in both dialects. Nor is the *-tk-* a characteristic of any particular tense or mood stem but goes rather throughout the verbal system, including adjectives and nouns etymologically connected with the verb.

The following list attempts to be complete and it identifies, if possible, the present (indicative), the subjunctive and the preterit formations. The classifications (in Roman numerals) used are those in Krause-Thomas, *Tocharisches Elementarbuch* I (and in the glossary to vol II)[1] except that those presents with nasal infix in dialect A are classified as VII along with the same formation in B. In SSS[2] they were of course VIIb. I regret this difference in classification maintained by the authors. Even though in A these verbs are athematic and in B thematic, they are clearly of the same origin.

1. A *kätk-* 'arise'. Act. pres. sg. 3 *kätäṅkāṣ* VII; subj. sg. 3 *kātkaṣ* V; pret. sg. 3 *kātäk* I.

2. AB *kātk-* 'rejoice'. A act. pres. pl. 2 *kāckäc*, B sg. 3 *kāccäṃ* II; B pret. act. pl. 3 *kaccāre* I. Caus. A mid. pres. sg. 3 *kātkäṣtär*, B *kātkästär*.

3. AB *kätk-* 'cross over'. A act. pres. pl. 3 *ktäṅkeñc*, B sg. 3 *kättaṅkäṃ* VII and *kätkanaṃ* VI; A subj. sg. 3 *katkaṣ*, B *katkaṃ* V; A pret. act. sg. 3 *kcäk*, B *śatka* I. Caus. B act. pres. pple. *śatkäṣṣeñca*; B pret. mid. sg. 2 *śātkatai*, A pple. *śaśätkusāṃ*.

4. B *kärtk-*? Only (caus. ?) pres. act. sg. 3 *kärtkäṣṣäṃ*; vbl. subst. (from pret. pple.) *kekärtkor*.

5. AB *kutk-* 'embody'. B pres. *mid.* pple *kutäṅkmane* VII; B pret. act. pl. 1 *śutkām*, A mid. sg. 3 *kutk[a]t* I. Cf. A. *śtwar-kotkumiṃ* (cf. below).

6. B *klutk-* 'turn' (intrans.). Pres. mid. sg. 3 *kluttaṅkentär* VII. Cf. A caus. act. sg. 3 *lutkäṣṣäm*; A pret. sg. 3 *lyockäs* III. Cf. also A *lotk-*, B *klautk-*, below 23.

7. AB *nätk-* 'support'. B. pres. act. sg. 3 *nättaṅkäṃ* VII and *natknaṃ* VII; subj. 3 *nātkaṃ* V; pret. mid. sg. 2 *ñātkatai* I. Caus. only A inf. *nätkassi* VIII; pret. mid. sg. 3 *nanätkāt* II, pple *ñañitku*.

8. B *pātk-* 'give up, lay aside'. Opt. *pātkoy* V; pret. pple absol. *papātkarmeṃ* *I*.

9. AB *putk-* 'divide'. A pres. act. sg. 3 *putäṅkāṣ*, B pl. 3 *puttaṅkeṃ* VII; A subj. act. sg. 1 *potkam*, B *pautkau* V. Caus. B pres. vbl. adj. *putkäṣṣälya*. Cf. subst. A *potäk* 'hand, paw' (h), 'tax' (?), B *pautke*, *potke* 'tax, tribute'; A *putäk* 'division, quarrel'.

10. AB *pyutk-*. Caus. only 'come about, occur' A pres. act. sg. 3 *pyutkäṣ-äṃ*, B *pyutkäṣṣäṃ*; A pret. act. sg. 3 *papyutäk*, B *pyautka* II, and A *pyockäs* III.

11. AB *prutk-* 'be closed, be shut (up), be filled.' B pres. mid. pple *prutkemane* III; A subj. act. sg. 3 *protkaṣ*, B mid. sg. 3 *prutkātär* V; A pret. act. pl. 3 *protkar*, B *prautkar* I. Caus. A pres. sg. 3 *prutkäs*, B *prutkäṣṣäṃ*; A pret. pl. 3 *paprutkār*, B sg. 3 *prautka* II. Cf. A *protäk*, B *prautke* 'lock, prison'.

12. AB *plätk-* 'come forth'. B pres. mid. pple *plyetkemane* III; subj. sg. 3 *pletkäṃ* I; B pret. pl. 3 *pletkar-c* III, pret. pple A *paplätku*, B *plätku*. Cf. subst. *platkye*.

13. A *plutk-* 'appear'. Caus. only pret. pl. 3 *paplutkār* II and sg. 3 *plockäs* III.

14. AB *märtk-* 'cut (the hair)'. B (subj.) vbl. subst. *markalñe* V; A pret. act. sg. 2 *märtkāṣt*, B mid. sg. 3 *märtkāte* I.

15. B *mutk-* 'strengthen'. B (subj.) inf. dat. *mutkättse-ś* V; pret. pl. 3 *mutkāre* I.

16. B *mlutk-* 'step forth'. Subj. mid. sg. 1 *mlutkāmar* V; pret. pple (?) *mlutku*, *mlucku* I.

17. A *yätk-*?. Cf. vbl. adj. *yätkal*.

18. A *yutk-* 'be sad'. Pres. mid. sg. 2 *yutkatār* III; (subj.) vbl. subst. *yutkālune* V; pret. pple *yutko* I.

19. A *ritk-*, *rätk-*, B *rätk-* 'arise (again)'. B pres. act. pl. *rättaṅkeṃ* VII. Caus. A pres. mid. pple *ritkäsmāṃ* VIII; pret. pple *raritku*, *rarätku* II.

20. AB *rutk-* 'move (away), take off (a garment)'. A pres. mid. sg. 1 *rutäṅkāmār*, B *ruttaṅkemar* VII; B subj. act. 3 *rautkaṃ*, A vbl. subst. *rutkālune* V; A pret. act. pl. 3 *rotkar*, B mid. sg. 3 *rutkāte* I.

21. AB *lātk-* 'cut off'. A pres. act. 3 *lātäṅkāṣ* VII, B *latkanaṃ* VI; B (subj.) inf. *lātkatsi* V; B pret. mid. sg. 2 *lātkātai*, A pple *lālätku* I.

22. AB *litk-* 'fall away, be removed'. A (subj.) vbl. subst. *litkālune* V; pret. pple A *litko*, B *litku* I. Caus. 'remove'. B imperf. sg. 3 *ly(i)tkaṣṣi*; subj. pl. 3 *lyaitkeṃ* II (I?), A pret. pple *lyalyītku*.

23. A *lotk-*, B *klautk-* 'turn, become'. A pres. act. sg. 3 *lotäṅkāṣ* VII, B pres. mid. sg. 3 *klautkoträ* IV; A subj. act. sg. 3 *lotkaṣ*, B sg. 3 *(klau)tkaṃ*, opt. *klautkoy* V; A pret. act. sg. 3 *lotäk*, B. sg. 1 *klautkāwa* I. Cf. subst. A *lotäk*, B *klautke*

24. AB *wätk-* 'separate, decide' (intr.). A pres. mid. sg. 1 *wätkamār* III, B act. sg. 3 *wätkāṣäṃ* IX; A subj. act. sg. 3 *watkāṣ* V, B *wotkäṃ* I; A pret. act. sg. 3 *wtäk*, B sg. 1 *wätkāwa* I. Caus. (1) 'divide, separate' (trans.). A pret. sg. 1 *wackwā*, B sg. 3 *otkasa-me* III. Caus. (2) 'command'. A pres. act. sg. 3 *wätkäṣ*, B impf. act. sg. 3 *watkäṣṣi* IX; A pret. act. sg. 3 *wotäk*, B *yātka* II.

25. A *wkätk-*? Subj. vbl. subst. *wkätkālune* V.

26. A *wrātk-* poss. 'boil, cook' (?). Pres. act. sg. 3 *wrātäṅkāṣ*, mid. pple *wrātäṅkāmāṃ* VII.

27. AB *sätk-* 'spread' (intrans.). A pres. mid. sg. 3 *sätkatär*, B pl. 3 *sätk(e)ntär-ne* III; A pret. act. sg. 3 *stäk*, B pl. 3 *sätkāre*. Caus. A pres. act. pl. 3 *sätkseñc* VIII; A pret. act. pl. 3 *sasätkār-ci* II, B mid. sg. 1 *sätkasamai* III.

28. B *snätk-* 'penetrate, pierce.' Pret. pple *snätku* I.

29. A *snutk-* 'become tired'. Pret. pple *sāsnotku* I.

30. A *spāltk-*, B *spāl(t)k-* 'strive, be zealous'. A pres. mid. pl. 3 *spāltäṅkāntär* VII, B *spalkkaskentär* IX; B pret. mid. sg. 3 *spalkāte* I. Cf. A *spaltäk*, B *spel(t)ke* 'zeal'.

Inasmuch as one gets the impression, from previous discussions of verbal roots ending in tk, that this particular cluster is more or less confined to presents of class VII, the nasal infix class, it is well to present a survey of the actual situation. In the following listings the notation AB means that the same verbs show identical present formations, whereas A or B separately indicates different verbal roots entirely. Cl. II (thematic) AB 1; cl. III (stem vowel A *a* = B *e*) AB 1, A 2, B 2; cl IV (stem vowel A *a*, B *o*) A none, B 1; cl. VI (stem in A *na* or *nā*, B *na*, *ana*) A none, B 3; VII (nasal infix) AB 3, A 5, B 4; cl. VIII (*s*-presents), A 4, B 1. In addition there are altogether four verbs in A and five in B which show 'causative' (cl. IX) presents. Of these this formation only is attested as follows: AB 1, A 1, B 1. But no significance can be attached to this fact. No presents at all are attested for nine roots, one of which occurs in both A and B, and 4 in each of the dialects alone.

The only present classes not represented are, therefore I (athematic), V (stems in *ā*), X (stems in A *nās*, B *nắsk*, *näsk*), XI (stems in A *sis*, B *sask*, *säsk*), and XII (stems in *ññ*). Of these the lack of representation in classes I and V may be purely accidental. The greater number of roots in *tk* by far are of course found in present class VII, where, with the nasal infix, the stem final takes on the remarkable shape *-täṅkā* in A and *-(t)taṅkä/e-* in B.

Little if any significant data arises from an enumeration of the distribution of the roots under discussion among the subjunctive or preterit stem formations. All subjunctives to primary presents ('Grundverba') except two are in *ā* (subj. cl. V). These two exceptions (both in B) belong to the athematic type (cl. I). Likewise all preterits to primary formations clearly or probably belong to the *a/ā* preterit (cl. I). Other attested (primary) preterit formations are classes II and III, where they are all probably to be reckoned as belonging with derivative present formations in *sk* ('Kausativa').

Not only does the cluster *-tk-* go through the entire verbal system and the obvious derivatives of the verbal stem (e.g., A *kācke* and B *katkauña* 'joy': *kātk-* 'rejoice-), but also is found in what appear to be nominal formations which are entirely independent of the derivatives from the verbal root itself. Such are the following: A *lotäk,* B *klautke* 'turn, way, manner' (A *lotk-* B *klautk-* 'turn, become'; A *potäk* 'hand, paw' (? cf. below), B *pautke* 'tax, tribute', A *putäk* 'quarrel' (all: *putk-* 'divide'), A *protäk,* B *prautke* 'prison, lock' (: *prutk-* 'be closed, shut, be full', caus. 'close, shut up, fill');[3] A *spaltäk,* B *spel(t)ke* 'zeal' (: A *spāltk-,* B *spāl(t)k-* 'strive, be zealous').

All the above nouns appear to have the normally characteristic ending of an IE *o*-stem, that is A zero = B *-e* from *-o*: cf. A *kam,* B *keme* (: γόμφος), A *want,* B *yente* (: *uentus*), etc. A number of other words attested only in one of the dialects may be of similar derivation: A *kotäk* in *śtwarkotkum* in 316a 3 . . . *śtwar ñemiṣi śtwar kotkumiṃ* . . . where the last word appears to be the nom. sg. fem. of a possessive adjective in *-um*. The translation "having four jewels (and) four 'forms'" would make sense and hence connection with the verb *kutk-* 'embody' seems probable.[4] Similarly B *wetke* is formally to be related to *wätk-* 'separate, divide', but the sense appears to be adverbial, possibly 'away, off', rather than nominal 'separation' (cf. *TE* II, 243). Formally also A *nātäk* 'master' could be related to *nätk-* 'support' but such a word is always suspect of being borrowed. Less significant would be the possible etymological relationship between B *pletkye* (meaning not certain) and *plätk-* 'advance, come forth', or between B adv. *śatkai, śitkai* 'very' and *kätk-* 'cross over'.

When we turn to an etymological examination of our accumulated materials in *-tk-* we find it to be quite recalcitrant

– even more recalcitrant than we have learned to expect in the case of Tocharian etymology. The usual difficulties of ambiguity of stops and vowels is compounded by the fact that there are two final stops to consider and the probability that between them an intervening vowel has been lost. Nor can we be sure that it may not have been a front vowel since the *t* remains intact (i.e., is not palatalized or assibilated to *c* or *ts*). The syncope might have been earlier than either of these consonant mutations.

However, it would seem probable to me – even certain – that the cluster *-tk-* has nothing to do *per se* with any 'tense' stem formation, present or otherwise. Witness the variety of present classes represented and the number of substantives in *-tk-* apparently not derived from the verbal root itself. This latter situation caused Holger Pedersen to suggest that the formation was denominative in origin.[5] This we shall go into later. But first let us consider the material from the etymological point of view. The order is the same as in the listing above to which reference can be made for identification of forms.

Pedersen (*op. cit.* 171 f.) derives both A *kātk-* 'arise' and AB *kātk-* 'rejoice' from **gʷā-* 'come, go' (in Grk. ἔβην, Skt. *agām,* etc.). The semantic change is possible but not too convincing. However, if the etymology is correct, then both the *t* and the *k* are suffixal and one might compare such derivatives of the root as Skt. *gatu* 'way, place', or Grk. ἀμφισβατέω 'go apart, quarrel', cf. also Arm. *y-otn kam* 'I arise'.

It seems to me that AB *kätk-* may likewise be derived from the same source, i.e., from **gʷə-*. In which case we may compare (for both vocalism and dental suffix) (Grk. βάδην adv. 'step by step', βάδος 'walk', etc. Of course the Greek forms may well represent **gʷm̥-* from the parallel root **gʷem-*.[6]

AB *kutk-* 'embody', except for the possible A **kotäk* in *śtwar-kotkumiṃ* (cf. above), is without internal connections in

Tocharian and the very general nature of the meaning of the verb adds to the natural ambiguity of the phonology. If we assume that **kotäk* means 'shape', as seems possible, we might well be dealing with a denominative verb, which would lend greater precision to our semantic kernel. However there is still no compelling etymology. No doubt the authors of Walde-Pokorny, *Vgl. indog. Wtb.*,[7] had they known the forms, would have listed them under the catch-all root **geu-* 'biegen, krümmen, wölben' (I, pp. 555 ff.) since this radical was set up expressly to bring together forms of the greatest variety of semantic content which had minimally similar phonological shape. But for us here, the only significant conclusion is that the verb may be a denominative.

The two sets of verbal roots given above, B *klutk-*, A *lutk-* and B *klautk-* A *lotk-* (nos. 6 and 23 in the above list), are of course cognate. The loss of the initial *k* in A is no doubt dissimilatory as Pedersen (*op. cit.*, 171) has suggested. The same scholar has likewise suggested that in this instance, too, we are dealing with a denominative verb and that the underlying noun is A *lotäk,* B *klautke* 'turn, way, manner' which likewise shows a double suffix and is to be derived from the root seen in Grk. πολεύω 'turn, go about', Ir. *clo-* 'turn back, defeat' *im-chloud* 'change', *com-chlaim* 'cambio' (cf. Pedersen, *op. cit.* 171 f., and *Vergl. kelt. Gramm.* II, 494, but for the Greek cf. Walde-Pokorny I, 516).

With AB *nätk-* 'hold, support' and subst. B *netke* one is tempted to compare Goth. *nipan* 'aid, support', OIcel. *náð* 'grace, mercy', etc. (for the Germanic group cf. Walde-Pokorny II, 327).[8]

AB *putk-* 'divide' has been compared by Jacobsohn (*OLZ* 1934, p. 212) and K. Schneider (*IF* 57, p. 200) with Lat. *putāre* 'cut' and the derivation has been favorably received by Pedersen (*op.* cit. 171). The etymology is rendered all the more probable if we consider the possibility that the verb is based on the noun A *putäk* 'division' (and secondarily 'quarrel').

The same verbal adjective **pu-tós* may then lie behind the Tocharian forms which appears also to be the source of *putāre* (cf. Walde-Hofmann, *Lat. etym. Wtb.*[2] II, p. 393; Walde-Pokorny, II, p. 12). On the other hand, two other substantives with full grades of root seem also to belong here: A *potäk* usually glossed as 'Pfote, Hand', B *pautke* 'tax, tribute'. The meaning of the latter is of course easily reconciled with that of the verb (i.e., through 'division, share, payment' or the like. This etymology for A *potäk* has however always been in doubt (note the 'vgl.' before the citation of the form in the opposite dialect in *TE* II s. v. v.). The word occurs three times: 455 b 3 //// *k·ra potäk pra*[*v*]*ya*[*y.*] //// where it appears to gloss Skt. *kara*; 6a 6 . . . *śewiṃträ potäk pañwtsi lek yaṣ,* translated by Sieg, *Übersetzungen aus dem Tocharischen* I, p. 9[9] 'er gähnt und macht Miene, die Hand zu strecken'; and 12 b 6-13 a 1 . . . *tmäk säm potäk pañwmāṃ śla śewiñlune lakeyäṣ kā*(*kä*)*tkuräṣ kaśśi yokañi* . . . , trans. (*ibid.* p. 16) 'Sofort erhob er sich von seinem Lager, mit Gähnen die Tatze (?) streckend, und hungrig und durstig . . .'. The translations seem to fit and would agree with the gloss of Skt. *kara* in the sense 'hand'. However it is by no means certain that *kara* 'hand' is intended by this gloss. Another meaning of *kara* is actually 'tax, tribute'. The words are not etymologically related of course: *kara* 'hand' is from *kṛ-* 'do, make', whereas *kara* 'tax, tribute' is from *kṝ-* 'pour out'.[10] On the other hand the use of A *potäk* properly then 'tax, tribute' (= B *pautke*) in the sense of *kara* 'hand' would be almost too slavish a calque to be believed. But there it is. Only in a stereotyped, literary language of translation such as dialect A undoubtedly is, could such a loan translation be possible. The only other possible explanation of *potäk* in the two passages with context cited above would be that we are dealing with an idiom *potäk pañw-* where the meaning 'stretch (oneself)' arises from 'stretch (the body) apart', where *potäk* has a closer semantic affinity with *putk-* 'divide'. But if it really means 'hand, paw', then the meaning could have arisen only by translation of *kara* 'hand' by the word for *kara* 'tax, tribute'.

But with regard to our main purpose in this paper, which is the origin of the *-tk-* cluster, the forms A *potäk*, B *pautke* must be derived from the verbal root, *putk-*, since they show strengthening as, e.g., in the subjunctive (act. sg. 1) A *potkam*, B *pautkau*).

AB *pyutk-* 'come into existence' which occurs only in the 'caus.' form (cf. above) carries the initial *py-* throughout the entire paradigm. Derivation from PIE **bhew-* would seem almost unavoidable as Pedersen has already noted (*ibid.* 288, ftn. 1). However the (secondary) palatalization of *p* to *py* is otherwise unknown in dialect A and is therefore difficult to explain in the present on the basis of a transfer from the aorist ('verschleppte Palatalizierung') since it should not have occurred there in the first place. Such an explanation is of course proper for dialect B and might have been assisted by the need to distinguish the present of this verb from the causative of *putk-* 'divide' since they would otherwise be identical. The only explanation I have to offer for the presence of *py-* in A is the possible influence of the B forms – again brought about by the same need for distinguishing the two verbs. Such an influence however is hardly to be expected even in the instance of a stereotyped liturgical language as A when written by the speakers of the vernacular B. If the derivation is correct then of course both the *t* and *k* are suffixal and the base no doubt the unextended one (as in Grk. φύω, φυτόν, φύσις, etc.) and the verbal adjective **bhu-tós* could be the ultimate source.

The etymology of AB *prutk-* 'be closed, shut up, (be) filled' is much more dubious. The nouns A *protäk*, B *prautke* with their strong vocalism would seem to be derived from the verbal root. The connection with the Slavic group represented by Russ. *peret'* 'shove, press', *zaperet'* 'shut in' is possible (cf. Vasmer, *Russ. etym. Wtb.* II, p. 341). I find no evidence for an extended root form in a dental (cf. Walde-Pokorny II, 666; van Windekens, 99). Of course a verbal adjective **pru-tós* is always a possible starting point.

AB *plätk-* 'come forth' is compared by van Windekens, 97, with Grk. πάλλω 'swing, shake', πελεμίζω 'set in motion'. Semantically more satisfying to me would be the connection with Grk. πελάζω, παλάθω 'approach', πλησίον, Dor. πλᾱτίον adv. 'near, close at hand'.[11] Of course the Tocharian *-t-* need have no direct connection with the Greek dental formations.

Formally A *plutk-* 'appear' can be related to AB *plu-* 'hover', B *plewe* 'vessel' of which the etymology is clear (PIE *plew-* in Lat. *pluit*, Grk. πλέω, etc. Walde-Pokorny II, 94 ff., Pokorny[12] 837) but as is well known almost all this group has the notion of movement through water (or of water) or through the air. Only in Irish do we see a similar (though by no means identical) semantic change, e.g., Ir. *lu-* 'move' (pret. sg. 3 *luis*), *ess-lu-* 'go away'. If this is correct then this is the one instance where a verb in *-tk-* can be connected with another Tocharian verb stem without it. The difficulty is as often that *plutk-* is so poorly attested (cf. above) that a proper notion of the general area of meaning involved is not possible.

A *märtk-*, B *mär(t)k-* is used with A *lap*, B *āśce* 'head' in all complete contexts. Hence the meaning 'cut (the hair)', or 'shave (the head)' seems clear. Van Windekens, 65, compares Skt. *mṛdnā́ti* 'crush', Lat. *mordeo* 'bite'. I should prefer rather the unextended root **mer-* in Skt. *mṛṇā́ti*, OIcel. *merja* 'pound'. Hence both consonants could be considered suffixal. The etymology is of course not too appealing anyway.

B *mutk-* 'strengthen', from the purely formal point of view, may be compared with Grk. ἀμεύσασθαι 'excel', ἀμῡ́νω 'defend' (cf. Walde-Pokorny II, 252 for a collection of materials which, from the semantic point of view, is often quite unconvincing). The trouble as so often is again the dearth of attested forms (cf. above) which makes it impossible to determine the general area of meaning involved. If the etymology is correct then the basis of derivation could easily be **mu-tós*.

B *mlutk-* is translated in *TE* II p. 224 'herauskommen'. This meaning does indeed fit the passage cited (*ce tallārñemeṃ mlutkāmar* 'I shall come out of this misery') which is the only finite verb form attested, but the pret. pple. *mlutku* and *mlucku*, quoted from Filliozat, *Fragments de textes koutchéens de médecine et de magie* p. 67, and 78, both times with *kuñcit* 'sesame', would seem to mean 'crushed', or 'pressed' (cf. *WTG* p. 160, Anm. 1).[13] On the formal side a base *melew-* is required from which a verbal adjective **mlu-tós* would be possible. Such an extension of a root **mel-* beside **melā^x-* (i.e., **meleH-*) in Grk. βλώσκω 'go, come' is of course perfectly in order. However I find no evidence for it outside Tocharian (cf. Walde-Pokorny II, 294).

A *yutk-* 'be sad' is derived by van Windekens, 173, from the root seen in Skt. *yudhyati*, *yodhati* 'fights', Lith. *jùdinti* 'move', Lat. *jubeo* 'set in motion, command'. The derivation has little to commend it from the semantic point of view. On the formal side one objection, if it be an objection, is that the dental is radical. More serious perhaps is the assumption that *dh* between vowels is here retained as *t* (cf. above ftn.[4]). No better semantically would be derivation from **yew-* in Skt. *yuváti* 'joins, etc.', or from **yew-* in Skt. *yuyóti* 'wards off' (cf. Walde-Pokorny I, 201), even though one would then be permitted to assume a verbal adjective **yu-tós* as the eventual source.

A *rätk-* and *ritk-*, B *rätk-* 'arise' is so poorly attested (cf. above) that it is difficult to determine whether the vocalism is properly *i* or *ä*. The authors of *TE* assume (vol. I, p. 49, § 15, Anm. 1) that we are dealing with *i*. If that is the case then the word in all probability is to be derived from the base **er-ey-* seen in Skt. *riṇā́ti* 'let go', Goth. *reisan* 'rise, Grk. ὀρίνω 'set in motion' (Walde-Pokorny I, p. 139 ff.). Another extension of this same root **er-* would appear to be the source of AB *rutk-* 'move away, take away', namely **er-ew-* seen in Skt. *ṛṇóti, ṛṇváti* 'rise, move', Grk. ὄρνυμι 'rouse, move', etc. (*ibid.* 141 f.). Both derivations will allow us to assume the verbal adjectives **ri-tós* and **ru-tós* respectively as the ultimate source.[14]

In a similar fashion an adjective **li-tós* may serve very well as the basis for the derivation of AB *litk-* 'fall away, be removed'. Such a radical is to be noted in Goth, *af-linnan* 'depart', OIcel. *linna* 'leave off, rest', Grk. λιάζομαι 'go aside, recoil, shrink', λίναμαι: τρέπομαι Hesych., etc. (Cf. Walde-Pokorny II 387 ff., with much dubious material).

AB *wätk-* 'decide', caus. 'separate, divide' and 'command' (for distribution of forms, cf. above) has been connected by van Windekens, 159, with Skt. *vadhate* 'strike, beat, destroy' (cf. Walde-Pokorny I, 254 f.), but the etymology is far from convincing, though of course entirely possible from the semantic point of view, although an intermediary 'divide' from 'split' seems entirely absent from the group to which the Sanskrit belongs. B *wetke* probably adverb 'away, off' (rather than noun 'separation'), could not serve as the basis of derivation of the verbal forms.

A *wrätk-* occurs in both places where it is attested in conjunction with *śwāl* 'meat'. K. Schneider (*IF* 57. 200) suggests the meaning 'cook, boil' and would derive from the root seen in Lith *vérdu, vìrti* 'id'. The etymology is very tempting inasmuch as the Lithuanian verb clearly represents a heavy base (*ìr* < *r̥̄*), but the explanation remains obscure. PIE **wrā-*?, but we expect **wr̥̄-*, i.e., **wrA-*. Could this be further evidence in Tocharian for 'uncontracted' sonant + laryngeal? (Cf. W. Winter, *Evidence for Laryngeals* p. 173 f.[15] One hesitates to add to the complexity of the history of the Tocharian vocalism!

AB *sätk-* 'sich ausbreiten' (*TE* II 153, 254) is derived by van Windekens, 111, from the root **sed-* 'sit'. He also 'corrects' the meaning to 's'établir', possibly because of his desired derivation. However an examination of the contexts shows that 'spread', or 'increase' is usually a preferable translation. Of course, even so, derivation from the parallel root **sed-* 'go' (in Skt. *a-sad-* 'go to, reach', *ut-sad-* 'withdraw', ChSl. *choditi* 'go', etc.) is possible. (On the question of the ultimate identity of the two, cf. Walde-Pokorny II, 486).

B *snätk-* 'pierce, penetrate, pervade' could perhaps be related to Ir. *snad*, Welsh *naddu* 'chip, cut' (cf. Walde-Pokorny II, 694) but the comparison is of little or no significance for our purpose here, as well as being quite uncertain from semantic as well as phonological reasons (*dh* > *t*! cf. above, ftn.[4]). On the other hand comparison of A *snotk-* 'become tired' with Grk. νυστάζω 'be drowsy, doze', Lith. *snáudžiu* 'slumber, drowse' is tempting from every point of view. The final dental could be *d* as well as *dh* (cf. Walde-Pokorny II, 697).

The verb A *spāltk-*, B *spāl(t)k-* 'strive, be zeaous', beside the nouns A *spaltäk*, B *spel(t)ke* 'zeal', is ambiguous from the point of view of the vowel. In the instance of the nouns the equation A *a* = B *e* usually indicates PIE *o*. Pedersen (*Zur toch. Sprachgeschichte* 31) makes no mention of the verb and would derive the vocalism of the nouns from *l̥*. This would agree with the development assumed by me in the case of A *talke*, B *telki* 'offering': Goth *dulgs* 'debt'.[16] The etymology which van Windekens, 116, has proposed has little to recommend it, that is, derivation from the root of Skt. *spaṭati*, *spuṭati* 'sauter debout'. The proper, more generic meaning of the Sanskrit words is 'burst (intr.)', caus. 'split open' (cf. OHG *spaltan* 'split', etc. (Walde-Pokorny II, 677 ff.). More tempting perhaps would be comparison with the group of Goth. *spil̥lōn* 'tell', etc., and (without *s*) Grk. ἀπειλέω 'threaten, promise; boast' (cf. *ibid.* II, 676 f.). The basic meaning of the group seems to be 'speak loudly, emphatically', from which the notion of 'be zealous' might arise. In any case, derivation from a verbal adjective **spl̥-tós* seems justified.[17]

I have attempted in the above survey to offer some plausible, or, at worst, merely possible etymologies for most of our materials in the hope that in this fashion the origins of some of the *tk* clusters might become clear. The results have by no means been all I might wish for. However, this much seems to be clearly established, as Holger Pedersen suspected twenty years ago: the *t* and the *k* in all probability belong to different suffixes entirely.[18] Furthermore it would appear that, where there is a plausible etymology, a verbal adjective in *-tos* preceded by a zero grade may be assumed as an ultimate starting point. In fact, several of the attested nouns in A *-täk*, B *-tke* (cf. above) show this vocalism, others show a strong grade (A *o* = B *au*). Indeed all attested primary present formations as well as 'causatives' where the vocalism is not ambiguous show a weak grade root, i.e., in *u* or *i*. Forms in *ä* and *ă̈* are of course of various origins. The former can represent PIE *e* in verbal adjectives from roots of the type CVC (cf. Grk. ζεστός, πεπτός, etc.) and the latter PIE *ə* (cf. Skt. *hitás*, *sthitás*, etc.), though all etymologies involving the roots in *ă̈* given above are most dubious.

If we turn our attention next to the second member of the cluster we are at once forcibly reminded of the various *k*-suffixes widely used throughout Indo-European in secondary derivations of the greatest variety for which the material is conveniently collected by Brugmann in the *Grundriss*[2] II, 1, pp. 473-514. Indeed this suffix is used in Greek in the form -ικός for forming new adjectives from verbal adjectives in -τός, e.g., κριτικός from κριτός, μαθητικός from μαθητός, τιμητικός from τιμητός, etc. To be sure the proper derivation would be *κριτοκός, etc., but apparently the longer form of the suffix in -ικός has been carried over from adjectives like ἱππικός, ἀνδρικός, etc. (Brugmann, *op. cit.* 488, 494). Comparable also are Latin adjectives in *-āticus* from participles in *-ātus* (*donāticus*, *errāticus*, etc.). The connecting vowel *-i-* here need not be considered as original (as Brugmann *op. cit.* 489) since it can represent any weakened short vowel. The Tocharian form of the suffix probably agrees with the Baltic *aka-*, Slavic *oko-* and Germanic *aga-* (or *axa-*) which has been abstracted from the addition of *ko-* to thematic formations (cf. Brugmann *op. cit.* 494). An original intervening front vowel would in all probability remain long enough to palatalize the *t* to *c*.

If this is the correct analysis of the Tocharian *-tk-* cluster then we are dealing with a denominative formation. Hence the 'zero' grades are normal for the primary and 'causative' present systems. The preterit and subjunctive show by analogy, of course, the usual possibilities of gradation for the particular formation.

Pedersen (*Toch.* p. 172 f.) has already suggested a denominative origin for the nasal suffix presents with stems ending in *tk*, e.g., B *kätkanaṃ, natknaṃ* with eventual transfer to the nasal infix class. The transfer was complete in A, partial in B, cf. A pl. 3 *ktäṅkeñc*, B sg. 3 *kättaṅkäṃ* beside *kätkanaṃ* (above), A sg. 3 *lātäṅkāṣ* beside B *latkanaṃ*, etc. Pedersen is certainly correct in considering the nasal suffix formation to be the earlier. However the infix formation was known to him only in dialect A and he considers the reformation to have been perhaps modeled on the *-näs-* class (e.g., pl. 3 *tmäṃsaṃtär*), but this view has little to recommend it. Instead, in my opinion, we are dealing with a simple metathesis of (*t*)*kn* to *tnk* where, in all probability, the *n* was (at least in the beginning) syllabic. In dialect B of course the consonant cluster was frequently lightened by developing a vowel between *k* and *n* (cf. *kätkanaṃ* above). In dialect A the verbs remained athematic (i.e., present stem in *-täṅkā*) in dialect B they became thematic (present stem in *-taṅkä/e-*) by analogy with the inherited nasal infix class (e.g., sg. 3 *piṅkäṃ*, mid. pple *piṅkemane*).

But the particular comparison which Pedersen makes the Germanic denominatives of the type of Goth. *hailnan* 'become well', OIcel. *myrkna* 'become dark' hardly seems to be justified, because only a part of the verbs in *tk* show the nasal formation, though to be sure the major part of them do. Nevertheless it is difficult for me to understand how or where the transfer to other classes could have begun. To me at least the exact history of the various present formations involved here remains obscure, but, with Pedersen, I believe they are ultimately of denominative origin. If there was any particular meaning involved in the beginning (factitive, causative, inchoative, etc.) it is no longer discernible.

As far as the nasal infix into other final clusters is concerned it merely continues a practice carried out more thoroughly in the instance of *-tk-*. This is clear from the comparison of A act. sg. 3 *pältsäṅkāṣ* with B sg. 2 *pälskanat*, or A mid. sg. 3 *mrosäṅkātär* with B *mrausknātär*. One instance of what appears to be a substitution of *sk* for more original *tk* is attested by A *mluskatär* (cl. II) beside B (subj. V) *mlutkāmar* (cf. above), if indeed the two verbs are actually related.

In summary then: The verbal stems in *-tk-* in Tocharian appear to be of denominative origin, possibly starting from a *k*-suffix added to the verbal adjective in *-tós*. They do not seem to reflect any 'k-determinative' of the type seen in Lat. *facio*, *iacio*, or aorists of the type of Grk. ἔθηκα, ἔδωκα. The exact present formation (or formations) involved is uncertain. However the origin of the nasal infix in A- *täṅkā-*, B- *taṅkä/e* is clear: it is a secondary development of the nasal suffix type A *-nā-*, *B -nā-*, *ana-* caused by metathesis of the cluster *tkn* > *tnk*.

[First published in *Journal of the American Oriental Society*, Vol. 85, No. 1, January-March, 1965, pp. 66-73.]

[1] Heidelberg, 1960, 1964. Hereafter abbr. *TE* I, II.

[2] = E. Sieg, E. Siegling und W. Schulze, *Tocharische Grammatik*, Göttingen, 1921.

[3] Only the meaning 'erfüllt sein' for both dialects is given in *TE* II, s.v.v. However SSS p. 453 notes 'scheint dem Skt. *rudh* zu entsprechen. Ebenso B.' W. Krause, *Westtocharische Grammatik* I, p. 263 has 'eingesperrt, erfüllt sein', '*ni-rudh* [= A].'
On account of the meaning of the nouns A *protäk*, B *prautke* and the very frequent corresponding use of the verb (cf. e.g., A . . . *pr(o)tkaṃ prutkāṣ-ñi* 215a5 'may shut me up in prison') it seems to me very probable that the meaning 'be full' is secondary and a mere calque of Skt. *ni- rudh-*.

[4] Cf. SSS p. 233.

[5] *Tocharisch vom Gesichtspunkt der indoeuro. Sprachvergleichung* (Copenhagen, 1941), p. 172. Hereafter abbr. *Toch.*

[6] Of course the comparisons with the Greek forms in *δ* are out of question if W. Winter is correct in his contention (*IF* 67. 16 ff.) that PIE *d* in preconsonantal and intervocalic position is lost. However it is not necessary to assume any particular connection with any of the Greek forms. PIE *g^{w}ə-tós* would do as well. The principal difficulty is reconciling Toch. *ä* with PIE *ə* since the latter usually appears as *á*.

[7] Berlin and Leipzig, 1930-32. Hereafter abbr. Walde-Pokorny.

[8] Van Windekens, *Lexique étymologique des dialectes tokhariens* (Louvain, 1941). Hereafter abr. Van Windekens.

[9] *Abhandlungen d. preuss. Akad. d. Wissensch.* 1943, no. 16.

[10] Böhtlingk-Roth, *Sanskrit-Wörterbuch* (Petersburg 1852-75), s. v. 4. *kara* 3) 'Abgabe, Tribut'.

[11] For the possible relationship between the two Greek groups, cf. Walde-Pokorny II, pp. 53, 57 f.

[12] Indogermanisches etymologisches Wörterbuch I (Bern and Munich, 1959).

[13] = W. Krause, *Westtocharische Grammatik I: Das Verbum* (Heidelberg, 1952).

[14] This derivation seems to me preferable to that of van Windekens p. 105, from base **reud-* in OIcel. *reyta* 'pluck, pick', OE *ā-ryddan* 'plunder, rob'. For these see Walde-Pokorny II, 351 ff.

[15] Photo-printed, University of Texas, Austin, 1960.

[16] Cf. *Language* 14.30, Pedersen, *Toch.* p. 220.

[17] Another possible formal connection would be with the group represented by Lat. *pello* 'drive, strike', but no other forms with '*s*-movable' are attested (cf. Walde-Pokorny II, 57 f.).

[18] Toch. pp. 171 f.

On the Interrelationship of the Tocharian Dialects

A good many years ago now I remarked, in a paper on comparative Tocharian phonology,[1] that the more one observes the similarities between the two dialects, the more forcibly one is struck by their sharp divergences. At that time I did not have at my disposal the texts nor the studies we now have, and comparisons had to be made bit by bit. The only complete ones were E. Sieg, W. Siegling, and W Schulze, *Tocharische Grammatik*,[2] for Tocharian A, and *Tocharische Sprachreste I*.[3] If that was my impression then, how much deeper it has become now! The cleavage between the two dialects is nowhere brought forth more clearly than in the recent *Tocharisches Elementarbuch*, vol. I, of W. Krause and W. Thomas.[4] That is not an inconsiderable merit of this work, though it is, I presume, an unintentional one.

Inasmuch as it is perforce the agreements between the two dialects, rather than their disparities, that are dwelt on in comparative studies, I should imagine that the nonspecialists in the field are used to equating the use of the word dialect in 'Tocharian dialects' with that in 'Slavic, Germanic or Romance dialects', or possibly 'Italic dialects'. To be sure, the divergence of separate languages from one another in any of these 'dialect groups' varies considerably, yet the differences between Tocharian A and Tocharian B are greater than between any two languages of the above groups, especially with regard to morphology, to a lesser extent perhaps in their phonology and vocabulary. But the vocabulary in particular will be the subject of special scrutiny here, for I am sure that many words common to both A and B which have been heretofore taken as cognate are actually the result of extensive borrowings from dialect B into dialect A. In this I am persuaded that Professor Werner Winter's conclusions are largely valid,[5] and in fact I am inclined to go a bit farther than he has. Moreover, the presence of such borrowings is of great importance to our conclusions about the inter-relationship between the two languages.

Let us first, however, summarize briefly the more striking contrasts:

Phonological:

1. A *e* = B *ai* and A *o* = B *au* as the regular reflexes of inherited *i*- and *u*- diphthongs, e.g., A *tre*, B *trai* m. 'three'; A *pekat*, B *paiykāte* 'wrote'; A *klots*, B *klautso* 'ear', A *śol*, B *śaul* 'life', etc.[6]
2. A *a* = B *e* from PIE *o*, e.g., A *ak*, B *ek* 'eye' (Lat. *oculus*); A *kam*, B *keme* 'comb' (Grk. γόμφος), etc.
3. Apocope of final vowels in A which are retained in B, e.g.: A *kam*, B *keme* (PIE *-os*); A *pekat*, B *paiykāte* (PIE-o); A *śäṃ*, B *śana* 'woman, wife' (PIE *-ā*? cf. Grk. γυνή).
4. Also significant here are the results of the accent position as it affects weakening or syncope of medial vowels, especially the interplay of *ä* – *a* and *a* – *ā*. As Professor Winter has pointed out,[7] we have an alternation B *a*/*ä* corresponding to A *ä* or zero, e.g., B *palsko*, gen. *pälskontse*: A *pältsäk*, gen. *pälskes* 'thought'; and B *a* – *ā* corresponds to A *ā* – *a* in many words of three syllables in B but of two in A (where the final has been lost), e.g., B *aknātsa*: A *āknats* 'ignorant', and especially in many verb forms; B *waskāte*: A *wāskat* 'he moved'. While the details of Tocharian accentuation are far from clear in either dialect, and especially so in dialect A as regards 'weak' and 'strong' verb stems, yet these phenomena here referred to make it abundantly clear that the two dialects differed widely in this respect and had differed widely for a considerable period of time – during which the vowel weakenings and the syncope, which were dependent on accent position, had arisen.

Other distinctions in historical phonological development are, it seems to me, less significant of the long period of time during which the two dialects have gone their separate ways. Some others, however, might be mentioned as adding at least to the difficulty of mutual comprehensibility to speakers of the two, though for the most part they would affect merely individual pieces of vocabulary. Examples are: 'palatalization' of w in B; B *yente* = A *want* 'wind', B *yasa* = A *wäs* 'gold', etc.; B *st* = A *ṣt*: B *stām*, A *ṣtām* 'tree', B *kest*, A *kaṣt* 'hunger'; B *ts* = A *ś* by a second palatalization in some categories of forms, e.g., B *tsmentär*, A *śamantär* 'they grow', B *tsälpentär* A *śalpantär* 'they go over, are released', etc. The alternation between *sk* and (palatalized) *ṣṣ* in B corresponds to a simple *s* alternating with *ṣ* in A in *sk* presents, e.g., B sg. 1 *aiskau*, 3 *aiṣṣäṃ*, pl. 1 *aiskem*, 3 *aiskeṃ* but A sg. 1 *esam*, *eṣt*, 3 *eṣ* (*eṣṣ-äṃ*), pl. 3 *eseñc*. Toch. B shows a secondary palatalization of *k*, *p*, *m*, and *ts* to *ky*, *py*, *my*, and *tsy* in certain categories of the causative, e.g., subj. mid *kyānamar*, pret. *kyānawa* to pres. *knastär*, caus. of *kän-* 'happen', beside A subj. act. *knāsam*, (pres. *knāṣtär*). Material of this same type could be cited abundantly, but much of it is significant only insofar as it affects the morphology of the two dialects, as is true, for example, in the last instance.[8]

It is indeed in morphology that the two dialects go most widely asunder. In the plural, where, to be sure, some originally identical formations are found, only rarely do we find cognate words with cognate plural endings, e.g., B *-wa* = A *-u* only in B *ostwa*, A *waṣtu* 'houses', and B *kwarsärwa*, A *kurtsru* (beside extended *kursärwā*), pl. of a measure of distance; B *-nta* = A *-nt* only in B *yärkenta*, A *yärkant* 'honors', and B *pälskonta*, A *pälskant* 'thoughts'. The later ending is for the most part extended by *-u* in Tocharian A: B *wranta*, A *wräntu* 'waters', etc.

Furthermore, in those plurals that distinguish the oblique from the nominative, the former is always in *-ṃ* (i.e., final *n*) in B but in *-s* in A, e.g., B nom. *meñi*, obl. *meñäṃ*, A *mañi*, *mañäs* 'months' (sg. nom. B *meñe*, A *mañ* 'moon, month'). This, it seems to me, is a more fundamental cleavage than the mere disagreement in vocabulary assigned to this or that plural formation, or even more significant than the later independent developments of the same original formation, as, for example, the widespread extension of original endings in A by *-ā* or *-u* (cf. the example above). For here we have in all probability an instance of the extreme divergence in the laws of finals in the two dialects, that is, vowel plus *-ns* becomes *-n* (spelled *ṃ*) in B, but *-s* in A. In other words, the full Proto-Indo-European ending must be postulated for Proto-Tocharian. The distinction is parallel (insofar as the final consonant group is concerned) to the contrast in the development, say, between Skt. *vr̥kān* and Lat. *lupōs*.[9] There are of course two other possible solutions: one, B *-ṃ* and A *-s* result from different sandhi developments, which is improbable, since sandhi seems of little significance in the development of Tocharian; or, two, the endings have entirely different origins, which is of course possible.[10]

With regard to the oblique singular, the two dialects show one agreement, namely the ending *-ṃ* (= final *n*) which in all probability is to be derived from the stem suffix of old *n*-stems after the case endings themselves have been eroded away. The ending is limited to masculine, rational beings in B and for the most part in A where, however, it has been extended to a few feminines. This is of course an important point of agreement between the two dialects and one which has its germ in pre-Tocharian, since it is to be compared with the development of epithets like Lat. *Catō* (*catus*), Grk. Στράβων (στραβός), and, especially, with the weak adjective inflection in Germanic.[11]

Otherwise the oblique singular in A is, with few exceptions, like the nominative, but in B we find a wide assortment of formations. The most striking of these, perhaps, is the ending

-ai or *-yai*, especially for feminines *aśiyai*, nom. *aśiya* 'nun', *mñcuṣkai*, nom. *mñcuṣka* 'princess', *preśyai*, nom. *preśya*, *preściya*, *preśyo* 'time', but there are rarely masculines also e.g., *yerkwantai* 'wheel' (nom. not attested). The only probable example of this type is the (highly irregular) A k_u*le*, to nom. k_u*li* = B *klai*, nom. *klyiye*.

Another important type of singular in B is that which ends in *-e* in the nom. but drops it in the obl., e.g., nom. *riye*, obl. *ri* 'city' (A nom. obl. *ri*), nom. *ytārye*, obl. *ytāri* 'way' (A *ytār*), nom. *arañce*, obl. *arañc* 'heart' (A *āriñc*). The identity of nom. and obl. in A results, of course, from the syncope of the final *-e* which is kept in B.

In dialect B, an archaic relic is found in the distinction of palatalized vs. unpalatalized *t* in nouns of relationship: nom. *pācer*, *procer*, *mācer*, *tkācer*, obl. *pātär*, *protär*, *mātär*, *tkātär*, but A nom.-obl. *pācar*, *pracar*, etc.

However, these and other differences in the nom. and obl. sg. and pl. formations are not so significant for the mutual comprehensibility of the two languages (and that is really what we are talking about here) as is the radical divergence in both the genitive and, especially, in the 'secondary' cases, i.e., those based on the oblique.

In B the regular ending of the gen. sg. of nouns is *-ntse* (*-ṃtse*), but in A it is *-s*. The history of both is disputed and still, to me, uncertain. Moreover, in spite of the many attempts to derive both from a common origin, I am myself not persuaded, although there are many direct correspondences, e.g., B *ñäktentse*: A *ñäktes* 'of a god'; *yäkwentse*: A *yukes* 'of a horse', etc. Such agreements can hardly be considered significant, since the two endings are far and away the most frequent.[12]

Only three gen. sg. formations seem to me to have a claim to being cognate: (1) A B *-i*, e.g., in nouns of relationship A *pācri*, B *pātri*, and in A also extended (as-*y*) to some nouns in *-ā*, *-u* and *-i*, especially Sanskrit loanwords, *ñäkteññāy* 'of a goddess', *upādhyāy* 'of a teacher', *Viṣṇuy*, etc.; (2)

A -(*y*)*āp*, B -*epi*, originally an adjective ending; (3) B -*e*, A zero, in B *lānte*, A *lānt* 'of a king' (nom. B *walo*, A *wäl*), from PIE -*os*. But the first and the last of these are mere relics, and of the second only the final parts A -*p*, B -*pi* are equivalent. Besides, the extension to nouns occurs only in A.

The gen. pl. in B is normally -*ṃts*, less usually -*nts*, or merely -*ts*. In A we have two endings, the regular -*śśi* and the rarer -*is* (only for nouns which have a single nom.-obl. pl. ending), but these show also the alternant -*śśi*. Again any connection between the endings of the two dialects is most dubious (as is also that which has been suggested between -*is* and -*śśi* by deriving the latter from -*s-ts-i*).

With regard to the secondary cases, i.e., those clearly formed by postpositions added to the oblique, there is only one exact agreement, that of the locative A -*aṃ*, B -*ane*, and one other that seems probable, the dative (*TE* 'allative') A -*ac*, B *aś*, -*aśc*. Furthermore, there is not even agreement in the case functions, e.g., A distinguishes formally between an instrumental in -*yo* and a so-called perlative in -*ā* which shares with it the functions of agent and of manner, on the one hand, and usurps the function of the locative on the other. Most of these functions are expressed in B by the suffix -*sa* (usually called instrumental, but perlative in *TE*). On the other hand, B has a special causal suffix in -*ñ* (rare) 'through, on account of', e.g., *läkle-ñ* 'on account of suffering'.

Even more important perhaps than these formal (and functional) differences between the two dialects, is the fact that insofar as we can tell in dialect A the secondary case endings were firmly attached to the preceding oblique case, forming with it a unit in the same way that the various cases are units in any inflectional (or agglutinating) language, but in dialect B the evidence of vowel weakening of *a* to *ä* in the syllable before the accent would indicate that the secondary endings are really still postpositions and do not affect accent position at all, e.g., B nom. *yarke*, gen. sg. *yärkéntse*, inst. sg.

yárke-sa, nom.-obl. pl. *yärkénta*, in contrast to A *yärk*, gen. *yärkes*, inst. *yärk-yo*, pl. *yärkant*, etc. To this extent are the endings to be considered free forms in both languages: in so-called 'group inflection' both secondary and genitive endings may be attached to the final member only of syntactic groups consisting either of nouns or of a noun preceded by attributes: A *śäṃ sewās ckācräśśäl* 'with wife, sons, (and) daughters', B *kektseñ reki palskosa* 'by body, word, (and) thought'. However, this fact hardly makes them free forms any more than the possessive *s* is free in 'the king of England's hat'.[13]

In adjective inflection the two dialects show a great deal more agreement than in the instance of the nouns, though in detail there is great divergence in the frequency of this or that particular formation. In B, for example, the pl. nom. *-ñ*, obl. *-(nä)ṃ* has seen a wide extension; e.g., B *ratre, rätreṃ*, pl. *rätreñ, rätre (nä)ṃ*; fem. *rtarya, rtaryai*, pl. *rätrona*, but A *rtär, rträṃ*, pl. *rtre, rtres*; fem. *rtri, rtäryāṃ*, pl. *rtraṃ* (i.e., like *āṣtär*: B *astare*, pl. *astari*, etc.).

Possibly more significant than other differences would be the divergence in the inflection of the preterit participle. The Indo-European origins of this form seem clear. It is based on the Proto-Indo-European perfect active participle in *-wos/us-*. In dialect B the *s*-stem has been kept throughout the inflection, except for the fem. pl., e.g., masc. sg. nom. *yāmu*, obl. *yāmoṣ*, pl. nom *yāmoṣ*, obl. *yāmoṣäṃ*; fem. sg. nom. *yāmusa*, obl. *yāmusai*, pl. nom.-obl. *yām(u)wa*. But in dialect A the *-nt*-stem has largely taken over, e.g., masc. sg. nom. *yāmu*, obl. *yāmunt*, pl. nom. *yāmuṣ*, obl. *yāmuñcäs*; fem. sg. nom. *yāmus*, obl. *yāmusāṃ*, pl. nom.-obl. *yāmunt*. The reverse has happened in the masc. pl. nom. of the *nt*-stems, e.g., A *ymassuṣ* to *ymassu* (beside B *ymassoñc* to *ymassu*).

That the pronouns, especially the demonstratives, show considerable divergence is not surprising. Even more closely related languages, such as Germanic, show remarkably different forms. Pronouns are always subjected to continual reinforcing by added particles, which shortly become necessary and inseparable parts of the basic stems. One divergence does seem remarkable and possibly old, namely distinction of gender in A masc. *näṣ*, fem. *ñuk*, beside B masc. and fem. *ñäś*, *ñiś* 'I'. Historically all three forms are most unclear, but if we could ever find out what non-Indo-European influence brought about the distinction in gender in A, we might know considerably more about the wanderings and contacts of the 'Tocharians'.

But I must hasten on to the verb. At first glance the verb systems of the two dialects seem deceptively alike, but the longer one studies them, the more one is impressed by the remarkable differences. Possibly the mistaken notion of great similarity is caused by a first quick glance at the present system where many cognate present stem formations do occur, and where especially the *r*-endings of the middle catch the eye. The same illusion trapped early scholars, especially those few who had in their mind's eye the Old Irish deponent conjugation, into suggesting that Tocharian was a Celtic language.

The present middle endings are remarkably identical and do reflect a very significant common Tocharian development retained quite intact in both dialects. However, even a quick glance at the present active endings tells quite another story. Only one single ending here can be identified without equivocation as the same in the two dialects, namely the 2nd pers. sg. *-t*. Elsewhere we see such contrasts as sg. 1 A *-m*, B *-u*, 3 A *-ṣ*, B *-ṃ*, pl. 1 A *-mäs*, B *-m*, 2 A *-c*, B *-cer*, 3 A *-ñc*, B *-ṃ*. Some of these are clear as regards their origin, e.g., sg. 1 A *-m* < *-*mi*, but B *-u* probably from *-ō*, i.e., athematic vs. thematic primary ending; pl. 1 A *-mäs* < *-*mos* plus vowel, B *-m* < *-*me* (or *-*mo*), 3 A *-ñc* < *-*nti*, B *-ṃ* < *-*nt*,[14] i.e., primary endings in A but secondary in B. Such differences must be very old.

Of all the tenses it is the preterit that shows the greatest agreement both in possible stem formations and in endings, not only in the middle but also in the active. In the latter respect only a few are irreconcilable, e.g., active pl. 1 A *-mäs*, B *-m* (as in the present), and in the middle sg. 1 A *-e*, B *-mai*, pl. 2 A *-c*, B *-t*. And ,while it is true that the same original stem formations are readily identifiable in both dialects, the details of development, possibly due to differences in accent, are very different, cf., e.g., (from *tärk-* 'release') act. sg. 3 A *cärk*, B *carka*, pl. 3 A *tarkar*, B *cärkāre*; mid. sg. 3 A **tärkāt*, B *tärkāte*, pl. 3 A **tärkānt*, B *tärkante*. To be noted especially is the regular interchange of *ä/a* in the sg. and pl. active in A, whereas in B the alternation is conditioned by the accent that apparently in such forms falls on the antepenult. In the subjunctive, too, in A we note a regular (but different) alternation (*kälk-* 'go', *kälp-* 'obtain') act. sg. 3 *kalkaṣ*, pl. 3 *kälkeñc*; mid. sg. 3 *kälpātär*, pl. 3 **kälpāntär*. In B, of course, the subjunctive is, to a great extent, independent of the preterit in stem formation, cf. to *tärk-*: act. sg. 3 *tārkaṃ*, pl. 1 *tarkam* (*ā*-subj.); to *kälp-* act. sg. and pl. 3 *kallaṃ* and *källaṃ* (*nā-* subj.; *lpn* > *ll*).

The usual derivation of the subjunctive and the preterit from the same stem in dialect A, as opposed to B, is one of the most marked contrasts between the two. There are, to be sure, many irregularities left in the former, but, as is remarked in SSS, the difference between preterit indicative and the subjunctive is most frequently only a matter of personal endings, 'secondary' in the former, 'primary' in the latter. In dialect B, however, the subjunctive formations show greater variation. In fact, except for two (those in *-i-* and *-ñ-*), all the 'signs' of the subjunctive are found also in the present indicative, and conversely all the present 'signs' except three (*-o-*, *n*-infix, and *-s-*) are found also in the subjunctive.

It is, of course, the *ā*-subjunctive that is the dominant type in both dialects, and apparently increasingly so in A, which is in part due, it would seem, to the formalizing of the relationship between *ā*-subjunctive and *ā*-preterit (see above).

Even more indicative, however, of a long period of independent development of the two dialects is the almost complete divergence in the formation of the imperfect. In dialect B it is based completely on the Proto-Indo-European optative formation in *ī*. The sign *i* (*y*) is normally added to the present stem minus any final vowel, but present stems in *ā* keep the *ā* and form an imperfect in *oy*, e.g., *palkäṃ* 'shines', impf. *palyśi*; *mäsketär* 'is', impf. *mäskitär*; *śuwaṃ* 'eats', impf. and opt. *śuwoy*, etc. In dialect A only two instances of this type of imperfect are found, namely for the verbs 'be' and 'go', respectively sg. 3 *ṣeṣ* and *yeṣ* = B *ṣey*, *ṣai* and *yey*, *yai*. Otherwise in dialect A the regular imperfect is formed from the present stem. This basic and, it would appear, extremely old cleavage between the dialects is possibly of greater significance than would appear to be the case at first glance.

The development optative > imperfect (or preterit) is found sporadically throughout Indo-European, from Indic to Celtic.[15] Its roots are possibly even in the parent speech, i.e., in the use of the optative to signify repetitive or habitual action in the past. Yet, outside of Tocharian, it seems to be particularly characteristic of Iranian, and occurs especially in various Middle Persian dialects, such as Sogdian and Khotanese.

I am inclined to see in the development optative > imperfect in Tocharian the result of long and intimate contact between the speakers of dialect B and those of the northeastern Irianian dialects. On the other hand, if, as I shall undertake to demonstrate later, dialect A was a language of greatly restricted use in both area and function, then it is not surprising that it did not suffer the same influence. Besides, it was at a greater distance from intimate Iranian contacts than was dialect B. The use of the optative of the verbs 'be' and 'go' as imperfects in dialect A can be old. It is not surprising if two highly irregular verbs of this sort should be aberrant in their development from the general run. Or, and this is what I suspect, we may have here evidence of the tremendous influence of dialect B on dialect A throughout the period of its documentation and indeed perhaps long before that.

Of course it is possible that the development optative > imperfect is independent of outside influences, but if so the divergence between A and B is stranger still. For if it is independent, it would seem to me to be necessarily of pre-Tocharian origin and would thus be a development shared in particular with Indo-Iranian, Celtic, and possibly Armenian. On the other hand, Armenian may show the same Iranian influence as Tocharian. The Celtic would then have to be completely independent.

Possibly some of the more significant data for our purposes here are to be gleaned from a comparison of the vocabularies.

Already in the introduction to his *Fragments de textes koutchéens*, 32 ff.,[16] Sylvain Lévi has commented on the independence of the technical vocabulary of Buddhism in the two Tocharian dialects. His list includes such terms as the following:

A	B	Sanskrit
lyalypu	yāmor	= karman
kārme	emprem̩	= satya
klop	lakle	= duḥkha
pñi	yärpo	= puṇya
märkampal	pelaikne	= dharma
śkatampeyum	śkamaiyya	= daśabala
plyaskem̩	ompalskoññe	= dhyāna, samādhi

Such divergences as this are, of course, extremely important, in that they show the independence of the two languages at the time of the earliest translation of Buddhistic works, and therefore, it would seem, the independence of the activities of the Buddhist missions to the two peoples.

Some of the words above, though used in technical Buddhistic formulae, reveal a cleavage of more general and therefore more fundamental nature, e.g., *klop* vs. *lakle*. These appear to be old words in the two languages, though to be sure even their internal etymological connections are to me obscure. For the latter a connection with either *läk-* 'see' or *lyäk-* 'lie' could be defended from the formal but hardly from the semantic point of view. A *klop* seems to have no possible relatives in either dialect. Likewise A *śka-tampeyum*, B *śka-maiyya* show, in their second element, a similar cleavage. A *tampe* 'strength' belongs of course with AB *cämp-* 'be able, can', but so far as I know no cognate form with unpalatalized *t-* exists in B. The form must be very old in A. As for B *maiyya*, it is not only without cognate in A, but is of doubtful connections within Tocharian. Possible would be eventual relation to B *mai-*, A *me-* 'measure', but semantically the etymology is not satisfying.[17] A *plyaskeṃ* and B *ompalskoññe* are probably independent formations from the same root, cf. A *päl(t)sk-* 'think', *pältsäk* 'thought', B *pälsk-*, *palsko*. A *märkam-pal* and B *pelaikne* contain cognate nouns A *pal* = B *pele* 'right, order'. The first part A *märkam-* is still obscure (cf. *sne märklune* = Skt. *ahārya*? SSS 455), and the final part of the B form can be either *yakne* 'way, manner' or possibly *aikne* 'id'.[18]

Other remarkable contrasts that affect the vocabulary are A *wrasom* but B *onolme* for Skt. *jana, bhūta, sattva,* etc.,[19] and the words for 'good' and 'evil'. For the former as an adjective we have nom. sg. m. A *kāsu* but B *kartse* (also fem. sg. nom. *kartsa*, obl. *kartsai*; the rest of the forms are from A *krant* = B *krent-*). As substantives *kāsu* and *kartse* are termini technici 'the good'. While it may be possible to connect B *karts-* with *krent-*, A *kāsu* must stand quite apart.[20]

For 'evil' we have A *omäskeṃ* (adj. and sb.) and *umpar* (adj.) but B *yolo* (adj. and sb.). For the latter Sieg and Siegling suggest (*Sprachreste B* 1.158) 'vielleicht iran. Lehnwort' without further identification, but they no doubt follow Hansen's derivation from Sacian (Khotanese) *yolo,* which might itself be of Turkish origin.[21] The important point here is, for us, the fact that we have a probable late borrowing from an Iranian dialect in B only, not in A.

These technical terms or words in technical use are not the only lexical divergences between the Tocharian dialects. I present here only a partial list. It embraces the greatest variety of terms, names of parts of the body, concrete and abstract nouns of all sorts, descriptive adjectives of all sorts, adverbs, etc.

A	B	
mrāc, lap	āśce	'head'
śāku	matsi	'hair (of the head)'
puskāñ (pl.)	ṣñor	'sinew'
āy, pl. āyäntu	āy, pl. āsta	'bone'
pāccās	saiwai	'right (hand)'
mokone	ktsaitsäññe	'old age'
śwal	mīsa	'meat'
naṣu	waṣamo	'friend'
yäslu	sāṃ	'enemy'
mäśkit	mñcuśke	'prince'
napeṃ	śaumo	'man'
śom	śamaśke	'boy'
yṣaṃ	tsrerme	'fortification ditch'
ṣukṣ-	k$_{u}$ṣai (obl.)	'village'
tsmār	witsako	'root'
niṣpal	waipecce	'property'
sañce	sklok	'doubt'
smale	waike	'falsehood'
sont	nauntai	'street'
kunti	lwāke	'jar'
tsopats (sg.)	orotstse	'large'
śāwe (pl.)		

kupār	kätkre	'deep'
kāpñe	lāre	'dear'
aryu	walke	'long (of time)'
tsru	totka	'little, few'
tāpärk	ñake	'now'
lek	päst, pest	'away, off'[22]
letkār	waiptār	'apart'
oseñi	kästwer	'at night'
ksär	tsoṅkaik	'in the morning'

To this list, which could be greatly lengthened by the inclusion especially of more adverbs, conjunctions, prepositions and postpositions, I might add only a short list of verbs, again without any attempt to be complete. I would draw attention particularly to suppletive stems.

1. A *kälk-*, B *mas-* (sg.), *mit-* (pl.), pret.-subj. stem to AB *i-* 'go'.
2. B *ās-*, inf. and imptv. stem to AB *pär-* (pres.), *kām-* (pret.) 'bring'.
3. A *ken-*, B *kwā-*, *śauk-*, pres. to AB *kāk-*, pret. -subj. 'call'.
4. A *träṅk-* beside B *wesk-*, pres. to AB *weñ-*, pret.-subj. 'speak'.
5. B sg. 3 *ste, star*, pl. 3 *stare, skente*, pres. copula beside AB *nes-*, pres. 'be'.

Besides these suppletive forms may be mentioned here also:
1. A *knān-*, B *aik-* 'know, recognize'. The former is found as a verb stem in A only but has the derivative B *aknātsa* = A *āknats* 'ignorant'. Both dialects have another verb for 'know', *kärs-*.
2. A *kātk*, B *tsäṅk-* 'arise, come into being'.
3. A *pāt* (pret. pl. 3 *pātar*), verb beside noun B *āre* 'plow'.

Interesting and of some importance for our purpose here is the article by O. Hansen to which reference has been made above. Of the fifty-one words submitted as possible borrowings from Iranian, twenty-one are attested in Saca (Khotanese), or on various grounds appear to be for the most part of Saca origin. For thirteen others Hansen assumes a Sogdian source. For the rest he indicates merely a 'middle Iranian' origin.

This 'middle Iranian' origin for all these probable or possible borrowings would perhaps speak against the theory often defended in the past, that Tocharian, and dialect A in particular, was reintroduced in northern and eastern Chinese Turkestan by a return migration of the Tocharians of classical reference, who were established in Tocharistan (Bactria, upper Oxus) before and around the beginning of the Christian era. If this were true, then certainly some of the borrowings should be expected to be of that date and would reflect an earlier Iranian phonology. A fuller investigation of the contacts between the Iranian languages and Tocharian is urgently needed.

In the article entitled 'Lexical Interchange between "Tocharian" A and B', already referred to above,[23] Werner Winter listed some forty words which he considered to be 'certain or possible' borrowings from dialect B into A, including some words of Iranian origin (or transmission). On the other hand, only five words appear to have traveled in the opposite direction, from A to B, and these are by no means as probable as the greater share of the former list. If borrowed, one difficulty with them is that they came into dialect B at a fairly early date – earlier than those from B to A – and consequently suffered phonological changes in B which disguise their origins. On the other hand, many of the first group, those from B into A, appear to be of fairly recent importation.

There seems little to be gained by any attempt to classify the loanwords from a semantic point of view. They include both nouns and adjectives, not to mention adverbs and conjunctions, and range through the most concrete ('fruit' *oko*, 'knife' *yepe*) to the most abstract ('best' *śpālmeṃ*, 'annoyance' *krāso*). In this regard they are to be contrasted with the borrowings from Iranian which are to a great extent technical if not always Buddhistic: A *āmāś*, B *amāc* 'minister', A *aśi*, B *aśiya* 'nun', A *käṣṣi*, B *käṣṣi* 'teacher', A *ṣāmaṃ*, B *ṣamāne* 'monk', etc.

Professor Winter has also suggested that certain suffixes were borrowed by dialect A from B, namely the adjective suffix *-assu*, e.g., in *tuṅkassu* 'loving' (*tuṅk* 'love'), *śolassu* 'āyuṣmant' (*śol* 'life'), cf. B *täṅkassu*, *śaulassu* with the same meaning. The original form in A was probably *-su*, as in *kipsu* from *kip* 'shame'. A second suffix which might be borrowed, according to Winter, is the abstract formation *-rñe* (e.g., *ekrorñe* from *ekro* 'sick', *tālorñe* from *tālo* 'miserable', etc.). One particular form AB *ykorñe* (: AB *yäk-* 'be negligent') may actually be borrowed in toto.[24] The proper suffix in A is simply *-ne*, cf. *pāpṣune*: B *papāṣṣorñe* (A *pās-*, B *pāsk-* 'observe').

In my opinion, Professor Winter has by no means exhausted the possible list of borrowings from dialect B by dialect A, but for the most part other words are merely suspect and there is no way to prove by their phonology or otherwise that they are not cognate. Indeed it appears to me that, in view of the wide divergence between the two dialects in most other respects, too exact a similarity between forms in the two dialects make such forms the object of immediate suspicion. The influence of dialect B upon dialect A in vocabulary is far greater than we have heretofore suspected or, indeed, than we shall ever be able to prove. The reason for my suspicions will be made clear in a moment.

Of particular interest are some words of Iranian origin of which dialect B has been the transmitter. Professor Winter lists AB *käṣṣi* 'teacher' and A *āmāṃ*, B *amāṃ*, 'pride' from Hansen's list. I believe we may include a few others: A *āmāś*, B *amāc* 'minister' (Saka *āmāca*), A *āśari*, B *aśari* 'teacher' (Saka *āśiri* < Skt. *ācārya*), and perhaps A *kāṣār*, *kāṣāri*, B *kaṣār* '*kāṣāya*, 'yellow-red monk's dress', cf. *kaṣara* in Krorainian Prakrit.[25] In fact it is possible, even likely, that the greater share of the later Buddhist technical vocabulary common to the two dialects, and of Iranian origin, has been transmitted to A by B.

The transmittal of this common technical Buddhist vocabulary of Iranian origin is, like the other terms borrowed by A from B, of fairly recent date. It is to be contrasted with those Buddhist terms mentioned above which show such a remarkable divergence. Sylvain Lévi has, in the discussion referred to above, suggested a most plausible explanation.[26]

The original Buddhist missions among the Tocharians were of Iranian origin. Later came a more direct influence from India. This latter effort affected the region of Kucha more deeply than it did the more distant Karashar-Turfan territory, and overlaid the more original Iranian influence with later, more direct borrowings from Buddhistic Sanskrit. A particularly important form for Lévi is A *Metrak* 'Maitreya', which is preserved in its Iranian form. In dialect B the corresponding *Maitrāk* occurs once (74bl = T III. Š 65.2). Otherwise the more direct *Maitreye* (Skt. *Maitreya*) is regular. In fact the name of the Buddha itself shows the later (or at least the continual) influence of Sanskrit in dialect B as opposed to A: B *pudñäkte* (*pañäkte* in prose) as opposed to the earlier form in A *ptāñkät*.

However, Lévi does not exploit his evidence further in any attempt to explain the anomalous distribution of the manuscript remains of the two dialects: A only in the east, Karashar-Turfan, but B both in the west and the east, Kucha-Turfan. In an early discussion he did prove beyond doubt that dialect B was the spoken language of the region of Kucha in the earlier part of the second half of the first millennium A.D.[27] No one has ever since, to my knowledge, attempted to dispute that fact. But there is no evidence that I know of which forces us to think that either dialect was a vernacular language of the time, spoken by the native population of the eastern area where the manuscripts of both A and B are found.

The solution is a simple one. At the time when the extant materials in dialect A were written it was purely a liturgical language in the monasteries of the east, and had been so preserved for several centuries at least. To what extent it was also a spoken religious language in the same circles, I shall not venture to say, but it had long since ceased to be a vernacular. Any one of several languages, or indeed several at the same time, could have been used as vernaculars in the region, though some form of Turkish was no doubt in the ascendancy. But the spoken language of the earlier Indo-European-speaking inhabitants had been lost. And no wonder. From the first two centuries preceding the Christian era down through the first six hundred years A.D. the Turfan oasis had been the object of continuous struggles between the Chinese and the various barbarian hordes from the north – the Hiung-nu, the Avars, the Turks, and probably a dozen other tribes related or unrelated ethnically and linguistically to these, whose names alone are recorded in the Chinese annals. It is possible that dialect A was at one time the spoken vernacular of the Turfan region alone, and not even of Karashar to the west. It could have been brought there by monks merely in its capacity as a written language for use in the monasteries. But there is no proof either way.[28]

On the other hand, the region of Kucha, better protected from the barbarians by the mountains to the north and farther from China, was better able to maintain its independence than Turfan or even Karashar. Besides, it had the latter as a buffer state to its east, to bear the brunt of the Chinese-barbarian tug-of-war for dominance over the cities along the caravan routes between east and west. Kucha itself was the center of an early and flourishing Buddhist monastery culture which came more and more under direct Indian influence from the time of the famous scholar Kumārajīva (A.D.

344-413), son of an Indian father with a Kuchean princess as mother. The article by Lévi referred to above[29] has collected for us from the Chinese documents the references to Kucha. The picture one gets here contrasts sharply with the history of Turfan, especially from the time of Kumārajīva until the end of the eighth century. Not the least significant of these accounts is that of the famous Chinese pilgrim, Hiuen-Tsang, who passed through Kucha in 630. Just previous to his arrival in Kucha, Hiuen-Tsang had passed through Turfan and Karashar, and his account leaves no doubt about the difference in political affairs which obtained in the east. The king of Turfan, K'iu Wen-t'ai, was holding his power only by walking a tightrope between the Chinese on the one hand and the T'u-kiue (Turks) on the other, and, immediately after the departure of Hiuen-Tsang, he allied himself with the latter against the former to invade Yen-k'i (Karashar).[30] The differences in political conditions that prevailed in Kucha and Turfan were clearly such as might lend credence to my view that, whereas Tocharian B was clearly the vernacular of a comparatively rich and flourishing culture, its sister dialect in the east, Tocharian A, might well have ceased to be a spoken language. The population using it was subjected continuously to the conquest of the Chinese or of the barbarians, and received sporadic infusions from the hordes of the latter, which were never given time for assimilation to the native language before a new invader appeared on the horizon.

The presence of documents in dialect B in the east, from Karashar to Turfan, does not mean that it had supplanted dialect A in that area in the period under question. Rather, its presence there is indicative of the vigor of the Buddhist culture of the west which had expanded into the monasteries of the east as a second, if not a competing, language for religious use – possibly, indeed, as the spoken language of everyday use in the monasteries alongside the traditional liturgical language of this area, dialect A.

That this was the true relationship between the two languages is not only clearly possible from the historical events that have been so hastily summarized, but it is made even extremely plausible by certain facts about the use of the languages themselves.

As we have already seen, Lévi's conclusion that dialect B was the vernacular language of Kucha has never been questioned. That it was also the monastery vernacular in the east seems to me the logical conclusion from the content of some of the manuscripts found in the region. For example, the great manuscript dealing chiefly with various kings of Kucha, especially with Suvarṇapuṣpa, comes from Murtuq (*Sprachreste B* 2, nos. 415-421), as does also a more fragmentary one in which King Kanaṣka is mentioned (*ibid.*, nos. 422-427). It is reasonable that the author would use his own vernacular language in the writing of history. Or perhaps more to the point, if dialect A had been the vernacular at this time in this region, certainly history relating the events of another region would have been composed in it. Another clear bit of evidence pointing in the same direction is that dialect B appears to have been the language for instruction in Sanskrit. Cf. B no. 550 (= T II. S 01), one side of which gives the paradigm of Skt. *anaḍvah-*, and the other of *suhaviṣ-*, with translation in Tocharian B. The signature indicates that this text was found at Sängim near Turfan.

Another bit of similar evidence, but not so clear perhaps, is to be deduced from B no. 605 (= T III. Š 75.2) from Sorčuq (region of Karashar). This complete manuscript leaf has on the recto an exercise in writing ligatures, and ends with the sentence in dialect A: *säs śäkwepint amok piktsi papyutäk* 'This twelfth art brought writing about (?)'. On the reverse side at the lower right-hand corner we read, also in dialect A: *cesäs amokäs toṅkitsā [e]l wäs* 'These arts Tonkitsā gave as a gift'. Subsequently[31] the empty space on the reverse side has been filled with a text in dialect B, which begins 'Since (?)

Darmachandra commanded to write the 'arts' in the desire (of obtaining) the dignity of a Buddha', continues with pious wishes and praise for the advantages of learning and practicing writing, and ends 'all who learn this may become Buddha'.[32]

Two Tocharian A manuscripts (*Sprachreste I A*, nos. 251 and 372) have inscriptions containing B words on the recto which is otherwise blank. No 251*a*: [*p*]*rathama pärweṣṣe kāsu tākis sa*[*n* . . .], where B *pärweṣṣe* 'first' (translating Skt. *prathama*) is followed by A *kāsu tākiṣ* 'good may be' (I shall not attempt to complete the following word); no. 372*a*: *rweṣṣe kartse tāko*, which is entirely in dialect B and may be completed after the preceding to read (*pä*)rweṣṣe *kartse tāko*(*y*). Both inscriptions appear to be the opening phrases (the former partly, the latter perhaps entirely, in dialect B) to works in dialect A – exactly what might be expected if the prevalent written language is the former, and the latter an old 'dead' language of limited use.

But possibly the most significant of all is *Sprachreste I A*, no. 394, from Sängim. The text itself is entirely in dialect A, but it has nineteen glosses in dialect B and two in Uigur. The last two glosses appear to be in a different hand from those in Tocharian B, though it is of course impossible to tell for certain from the facsimile.[33] It should be abundantly clear that we are dealing with the glossing of a Tocharian A text by a newcomer whose monastery language, at least, was dialect B, and to whom the 'old' monastery language of the area was not familiar. His own native speech may have been Turkish.

The facts of language use, insofar as they can be judged, lead us then to conclude that dialect B, the native vernacular of the west, the Kucha region, was also a monastery vernacular in the east, in the region Karashar-Turfan. It was also a language of fairly recent importation, at least later than some of the extant documents in dialect A, witness the B glosses and the added B text on A manuscripts discussed above.

Other facts about the two languages themselves lend further

support to the same view and, at the same time, indicate that dialect A, if not a dead language, actually was a petrified one. This is indicated by the extreme regularity of the language both in form, and, in general, in orthography, as against B. The latter shows extreme irregularities that may not be entirely attributable to orthographical variation alone or even to differences of chronology in the composition of the documents themselves, though this is in my opinion largely to blame. Professor Winter, however, believes that a considerable part of this variety of form must be attributed to dialectal differences within Tocharian B, and has attempted to show that three main dialects are to be distinguished: a western dialect, exemplified especially by the MQ (Ming- Öy Qizil) texts (near Kucha), a central dialect especially represented by Š (Šorčuq near Karashar), and an eastern dialect to which belong the S, M, D, and T texts (Sängim, Murtuq, Xočo, and Toyoq, respectively, in the Turfan area).[34] A great many of his arguments, particularly as regards phonology, are rather convincing, but those that seek to establish formal differences are less so. (There are only two of the latter: fem. pl. of gerundives in *-llona* in the west vs. *-lyana* in the east, and the substantive verb pl. 3 *skente* in the west vs. *stare* in the east). In my opinion there is too much chance of accidental omission of one form or the other in the manuscripts from different areas.

But in any case, irregularity of form, be it purely a scribal matter or a reflection of dialectal difference, is exactly what we would expect of a living, spoken language. Furthermore, and this is most important, the significant direction of lexical borrowing is, so far as can be determined, from B to A. Again this is what one would expect in the instance of scribes whose old liturgical language was the latter, but who have been surrounded and overwhelmed, as it were, by missionaries from the west, who not only write but speak another language whose similarities in the lexicon are just great enough to cause confusion. The morphologies of the two languages are, however, sufficiently different to keep them apart. As we all know, this is exactly what happens to the immigrants' language in America, though here to be sure it is the 'invaders' who are in the minority.

Yet another point: I have spoken above about the extreme irregularity of both script and spelling in dialect B[35] as opposed to A. Professor Winter has already emphasized, within the B texts, the regularity of those from Šorčuq (in the Karashar region), to which he gives the name 'Central dialect'. The form of writing dominant in these texts is to be contrasted with that found especially in the west at the Ming-Öy Qizil site. Winter suggests that a special sort of ductus was developed at Šorčuq, and that the scriptorium here possessed great prestige, so that its influence was felt later back at the 'home site' to the west, resulting in texts at Ming-Öy Qizil which show a mixture of both the 'old' ductus native there and the 'new' ductus of Šorčuq.

Let us examine the situation with regard to ascertaining if similar, though of course less striking, differences in writing and of orthography exist there in the case of A.

The greater share of the A manuscripts in *Sprachreste I* come from Šorčuq, nos. 1-383, in fact, and of these all but nine (374-383) are from one site, the so-called 'Stadthöhle'. The others, 384-467, come from the Turfan area: 384-393 from near Murtuq, 394-428 from Sängim, and 429-467 from Xočo.

Unfortunately, the editors of *Sprachreste I* (A texts) did not inform us about the appearance of the writing in any great detail, as they did in the instance of the B texts in *Sprachreste* B, and in the *Tafeln* part of *Sprachreste I* they chose for photography only the better preserved fragments, and of the 103 thus chosen all but seven are from Šorčuq. Of these seven, three are from Sängim and four from Murtuq.

However, the editors do make a few pertinent remarks. For example, as regards the bilingual nos. 384-386 from

Murtuq, they say 'Die Schrift is ungelenk und ihr Duktus scheint einer späteren Zeit anzugehören', and 'das Tocharische weist häufige Unregelmässigkeiten in der Ortographie auf'. (*Sprachreste I*. 212). These pieces are fortunately among those reproduced in the *Tafeln* (pp. 60, 61, 62). Instances of misspellings are clearly *mälskes* for *pälskes* (384b1), where the preceding word is *cam* and the following *āśāwesuneyä* for *āśāwesuneyo* (? 384b1-2); *kuyolte* for *kuyalte* (384b2); *pälkāluneyā* for *pälskāluneyäṣ* (385b3); and many others of similar sort. The Sanskrit words are also quite often corrupt. This situation leads me to suggest that it is a copy of a more original manuscript by a person not adept either in using the 'standard' ductus nor in the dialect he was writing. That he was not an Indian seems clear from the type of error he makes in the Sanskrit. That he was more familiar with dialect B would seem to be deduced from his use of the word *tsārwo* 'joy'. This word occurs twice here, and here only in A texts. It is clearly borrowed from B.[36]

This would seem to be true also in the case of two manuscripts from Šorčuq, nos. 219-238, and 239-242, both containing fragments of the *Maitreyāvadānavyākaraṅa*. Here we find such orthographical peculiarities as the frequent use of *ś̱a* for the more usual *śä* of A texts (cf. the editors' note 107), and also the very common writing of *ī* and *ū* for *i* and *u* where A normally prefers to write the latter, e.g., *käṣṣī* 221 b 3, 7 and often; *kākmūräṣ* 220 b 5, *lyalypūräṣ* 221 a 3, 6, *kārmetsūnentu* 221 b 4, etc. Most significant of all, however, are the spellings *lāñc* (222 a 2) for *lāñś* 'kings' and *krañc* (230 b 5 and 242 a 4) for *krañś* pl. m. of *kāsu* 'good'. These are to be compared at once with B *lāñc* and *kreñc* which are the regular forms. So far as I know these spellings occur only here.[37]

In this connection it seems possible to met that the variant spellings in B *lāś* (111 a 5 = TII. S 51.10) for *lāñc, kreś* (107 b 3 = TII. S 54) for *kreñc,* and other instances of the spelling *-ś* for *-ñc* or *-c*, for which I do not have exact reference, if they occur only in manuscripts of eastern (Karashar-Turfan) origin, are owing to the influence of A. Against this interpretation is, of course, the spelling of *epyac* as *epyaś* (330 b 5), where the corresponding form in dialect A also has c: *opyac.*

That dialect A was not a spoken language in the Turfan area seems to be deduced also from the use of extensive glossing of some B texts from the east by Turkish words, cf. for example *Sprachreste B* 2, nos. 324 (= TIII. M 169.14), 325 (= TIII. M 146.3), 328 (= TII. S 52.3), 329 (= TII. S 38.1), and especially 330 (= TII. S 48.1) and 331 (= TII. S 57.1). So far as I know there is no extensive glossing of A texts in Turkish (cf. the A text no. 394 with nineteen B glosses and two in Uigur mentioned above), nor is there any glossing of B texts by A words. Again this supports my suspicion that, as a vernacular language of the area, A had been long since replaced by the language (or languages) of its invaders. The convert to the new Buddhist missionary effort from the west spoke in this instance Turkish, not Tocharian.

To sum up: An examination of the languages themselves, their phonology, their morphology, indicates that the two Tocharian dialects A and B have gone through a long period of independent development; how long is of course guesswork, but it might be anywhere from five hundred to a thousand years, certainly not less than five hundred. They are, in my estimation, no longer mutually intelligible.

The vocabularies, too, diverge to a certain extent, especially in Buddhist technical terms. Dialect A seems to preserve an older stratum which shows decided Iranian influence alongside a newer one of more immediate Indian origin. The Buddhist vocabulary of dialect B, on the other hand, shows less Old Iranian influence and more Indian and later Iranian.

With regard to the reciprocal influence between the two dialects in matters of vocabulary, B has been the giver, A the receiver. In matters of orthography the reverse seems true. The orthography of the B MSS is more regular at Šorčuq (near Karashar), where the influence of dialect A could be felt most strongly.[38] Indeed, farther to the east, at Sangim at least, the writers of MSS in dialect B have even gone so far as to borrow some very definite spellings from A, namely *-ś* for *-c* and *-ñc* (cf. above). Such forms as *lāś* or *kreś* are not to be considered borrowings. The instances where A texts show B orthographical characteristics (e.g., *śa* for usual *śä* and fluctuating spelling *ī/i* and *ū/u*, cf above) are to be explained as because of the copying of an A text by a person more used to writing B than A.

Where both dialects appear in the same texts, the material in B seems clearly to be the intruder. The language of instruction, insofar as we have evidence, was clearly B. B texts are glossed by the vernacular of the region, Turkish, not Tocharian A.

So far only oblique reference has been made to the problem of the name 'Tocharian'. To me it is not a matter of great importance, though I have never been convinced that the speakers of either dialect could be identified in any way with the Tocharians of classical antiquity. Most of the discussions of this issue, pro or con, have, it seems to me, argued *de parti déja pris*. I am inclined to agree with W. B. Henning when he says: 'The tendency to confuse different names with little or no regard to time and space is as prominent in recent contributions to the 'Tokharian' problem as it was in the earlier ones . . .'[39]

The facts about the two dialects, both as regards their form and their use, and the deductions I have made from these facts, in no way support the thesis that either dialect is related to, much less a descendant of, the language of the historical Tocharians. Indeed, everything argues against it, especially against the view that dialect A represents a later migration from Tocharistan back to the area where the documents are found.[40]

Rather it had been at one time the native language of the

region of Turfan, if not also of Karashar, but was no longer at the period of documentation. The vernacular was another language or other languages, one of which was Turkish. Dialect A is preserved merely in a fixed written form as the language of a conservative Buddhistic culture. But even as such its use was giving way in the monasteries to that of the vigorous missions from the west who not only wrote but spoke in dialect B.[41]

(*Participants in the discussion following the conference presentation of the first version of this paper: Marku, Welmers, Collinder, Winter, Emeneau, Birnbaum.*)

[First published in *The Ancient Indo-European Dialects*, University of California Press, Berkeley, California, 1966, pp. 213-233].

[1] *Lg.* 14.20-38 (1938).

[2] Göttingen, 1931. Hereinafter abbreviated SSS.

[3] *Tocharische Sprachreste I. Die Texte. A. Transcription. B. Tafeln* (Berlin and Leipzig, 1921). Abbreviated as *Sprachreste I.*

[4] Heidelberg, 1960. Hereinafter abbreviated *TE.*

[5] 'Lexical Interchange between "Tocharian" A and B', *JAOS* 81.271-280 (1961).

[6] Further examples of all these equations are available in *TE* 50 ff.

[7] *Loc. cit.* 271.

[8] For further similar data, see *TE* 61-71.

[9] See *TE* 128.

[10] The derivation of the A ending *-s* from the *s*-stem, after loss of ending, might be possible.

[11] *TE* 108 f.

[12] Reference to discussions in *TE* 103 n, and 104 Anm.

[13] Further examples of group inflection in *TE* 91 f.

[14] The word for 'twenty' B *ikäṃ*, beside A *wiki*, poses a problem here. In my opinion neither form is derived directly from **wigenti*, though to be sure the A form may be compared with the 'short' pl. 3 act. pres. A *-i* beside *-iñc*, e.g., *tränki*: *tränkiñc* (cf. SSS 326 f.).

[15] For a general statement with bibliography, see W. Couvreur, *BSL* 39.247 f. (1938); E. Benveniste, *BSL* 47.17 f. (1951). Special discussions of the development in different languages are to be found in: F. Edgerton, *Buddhist Hybrid Sanskrit Grammar* 1.161 f.; J. A. Kerns, 'The Imperfect in Armenian and Irish', *Lg.* 15.20-33 (1939); Krause, 'The Imperfect in British and Kuchean', *Journal of Celtic Studies* 1.24 ff. (1949-50).

[16] Paris, 1933.

[17] Another etymology in A. J. van Windekens, *Lexique étymologique des dialectes tokhariens* 60 f. (Louvain, 1941).

[18] Cf. SSS 248; *Toch. Sprachreste. Sprache B. Heft* 1: *Die Udānālaṅkāra-Fragmente,* 100 (Göttingen, 1949). Hereinafter abbreviated *Sprachreste B.*

[19] Lévi, *loc. cit.*, lists A *śoṣi* = B *onolme*. But the B equivalent is rather *śaiṣṣe* = Skt. *loka.*

[20] Winter, privately, mentions the possibility of a connection between A *kāsu* 'good' and B *kāswo* 'leprosy'. The phonetic equivalence is impeccable.

[21] O. Hansen, 'Toch.-iran. Beziehungen', *ZDMG* 94.162 (1940).

[22] Beside the cognate preverbs in much the same use A *lo*, B *lau* (rare): A *lok*, B *lauke* adv. = Skt. *dūra.*

[23] Note 5.

[24] For the forms, see SSS 20 f.

[25] T. Burrow, *The Language of the Kharoṣṭhi Documents from Chinese Turkestan* (Cambridge, 1937); and 'Tocharian Elements in the Kharoṣṭhi Documents from Chinese Turkestan', *JRAS* 667-675 (1935). In view of the meager and doubtful nature of 'Tocharian' remains in these materials, I have not considered it of any use to attempt to place them dialectally alongside Toch. A and B.

[26] Cf. note 16, above.

[27] *Journal asiatique* 1913:2.311 ff.

[28] For a detailed account with reference to the Chinese sources, see especially the study by W. Fuchs, 'Das Turfangebiet. Seine äusseren Geschicke bis in die T'angzeit', *Ostasiatische Zeitschrift* 13.124-166 (1926). A briefer account will be found in Lévi's discussion in his *Fragments de textes koutchéens* (above, note 16), 8 ff.

[29] See note 27.

[30] Fuchs, op. cit. 148; Lévi, op. cit. 18.

[31] 'Nachträglich', so Sieg and Siegling, in prefatory remarks to B no. 605.

[32] Sieg and Siegling, *Sprachreste I A*, introd. v n. 2, cite as occurring in two other B MSS similar formulae in dialect A: *säs trit amok* and *säs pänt amok pyockäs piktsi*. These I have not been able to identify, in spite of the fact that the editors indicate that the MSS in which they occur have been arranged with the B materials for eventual publication.

[33] *Sprachreste I B (Tafeln)* 57.

[34] 'A Linguistic Classification of 'Tocharian B' Texts', *JAOS* 75.216-225 (1955); 'Zur Dialektgliederung von 'Tocharisch' B', *KZ* 75.233-237 (1959).

[35] Above, note 34.

[36] Cf. Winter, *JAOS* 81.274 (1961).

[37] Cf. SSS 100, 145. Winter suggests (privately) that the analogy of the obl. pl. *läñcas, krañcas* would easily lead to the reformation of these nom. pls., and would likewise (with P. Poucha, *Thesaurus Linguae Tocharicae Dialecti A* 62 [Prague, 1955]) complete *kra[ñc]^{ä}* at 342b4.

[38] Cf. Krause, *Hdb. der Orientalistik* 4.3. *Tocharisch* 7 (bottom); Winter, *JAOS* 75.225; both, of course, without the deduction of any orthographical influence of A on B as proposed here.

[39] *Asia Major, N. S.* 1.159 (1949-1950).

[40] So Sieg and Siegling, *Sprachreste I A*, introd. v, and supported by Pelliot in 'Tokharien et koutchéen', *Journal asiatique* 224.62 ff. (1934). However, the view was later abandoned by Sieg in 'Und dennoch 'Tocharisch',' *SBBAW, Phil.-hist. Kl.* No. XVII (1937), where he

returned to the view that 'Tocharian' A was the native language of the eastern region in particular of the realm Agni (= Chinese Yen-k'i), i.e., Karashar. To my knowledge Sieg never abandoned the opinion that Tocharian was the correct name for both dialects, and that the speakers were to be identified with the 'Tokharoi'.

41 The article by Winter, 'Tocharians and Turks', *UAS* 23.239-251 (1963), appeared too late for any careful evaluation for the purposes of this paper.

Part II

Studies in Honor of George Sherman Lane

The Development of Proto-Algonkian *-awe-

Mary R. Haas
University of California, Berkeley

1. There is a close relationship between comparative Algonkian and comparative Indo-European studies, a fact which is perhaps not as well known to present-day Indo-Europeanists as it might be. The reason for this is that the foundations of comparative Algonkian were laid by two highly trained Indo-Europeanists, Truman Michelson and Leonard Bloomfield. Michelson's writings, though of great importance to the specialist, are too diffuse to be appreciated by the nonspecialist. Bloomfield's principal papers, on the other hand, are not only indispensable to the specialist but can also be read with interest by the comparativist in other fields.

I suspect that the greatest triumph of Bloomfield's life, in his own estimation, was his irrefutable demonstration that the same rigorous methods that had been applied with such success to the written Indo-European languages are equally applicable to nonliterary languages like those of the Algonkian family. It was highly important that such a demonstration be made. Basking in the wealth and diversity of the ancient and modern literary documents at their disposal, Indo-European scholars were usually not a little contemptuous of unwritten languages; many even doubted that the 'comparative method' could be applied if ancient literary records were unavailable. But Bloomfield recognized with characteristic clear-headedness that 'a principle such as the regularity of phonetic change' was either applicable to all languages, unwritten as well as written, or it was an illusion, or worse, 'an error'.[1] It is significant that his first scholarly article in the then new journal *Language*[2] was 'On the Sound System of

Central Algonquian'.[3] It is here that he demonstrates beyond a doubt that the comparative method 'works' just as effectively with a group of related contemporary nonliterary languages as it does with a group of related literary languages. Indeed it sometimes works even better, since much 'fuss and trouble'[4] can be avoided if the comparativist has available phonetically accurate, well-analyzed data on each of the languages he is comparing. 'All historical study of language is based upon comparison of two or more sets of descriptive data. It can be only as accurate and only as complete as these data permit it to be'.[5]

At the time Bloomfield entered the field of comparative Algonkian there was already a plethora of material on the languages of this family, the most widespread in aboriginal North America. It was perfectly clear from this material that the languages are genetically related in the same way and with a similar degree of diversity as the Germanic languages, the subgroup of Indo-European that Bloomfield knew most intimately. But there was one drawback. Most of the material was phonetically inaccurate and poorly analyzed. It would be extremely difficult for an Algonkianist to achieve the degree of rigor needed to convince the Indo-Europeanists if he placed too much reliance on the kind of material that was then available.

Bloomfield met the problem head-on. Turning his back on Trumbull's *Natick Dictionary*[6] (compiled from Eliot's seventeenth century translation of the Bible), Father Rasles's Abnaki dictionary[7] (begun in 1691), and on Zeisberger's Delaware materials[8] – the three languages that Pickering[9] a century earlier had considered suitable for laying the foundations of Algonkian studies – he concentrated on four languages of the Central group, Fox, Cree, Menomini, and Ojibwa. Insofar as possible he relied only on his own materials. At the time the 'Sound System' was written he had only Menomini and some Cree of his own, but by the time his fuller statement, 'Algonquian',[10] was written he had his own full materials on

Cree and a considerable amount of Ojibwa. Only Fox was left aside. For this he had made his own restatement of the language on the basis of materials compiled by William Jones,[11] a native speaker of the language, and he seems to have considered this adequate.[12]

It is abundantly clear now that he succeeded far better than he expected but probably not quite in the way he might have wished, and this for two reasons. In the first place, his own book *Language*,[13] though neatly balanced in its attention to both descriptive linguistics and comparative linguistics, became the 'Bible' of a whole generation of descriptivists and was largely ignored by comparativists. During the 1940s and early 1950s the descriptivists developed and promulgated a strong ahistorical bias, and the few students who had been attracted to the study of Algonkian languages turned their backs on historical work, concentrating exclusively on description. In the second place, his 'Algonquian', which should have been the springboard for an expansion in historical studies of Algonkian languages became instead a 'frozen' model beyond which it was unnecessary to go.

There are signs that a new era of Algonkian studies is about to begin. The extreme ahistoricism of the post-Bloomfieldians is gradually giving way to a more balanced point of view and the attention of younger scholars is no longer riveted to the synchronic side of language to the exclusion of the diachronic. Many inviting tasks await the interested scholar. Since Bloomfield limited himself to four languages, one of these tasks is the testing of his reconstructions against various other languages not utilized by him. In many instances his reconstructions appear adequate to explain the development in all known Algonkian languages. In other instances major or minor revisions may be necessary.

2. The remainder of this paper is devoted to the presentation of a revision of certain reconstructions containing **a·*, or

which may appear to require **a·*, on the basis of FCMO (Fox, Cree, Menomini, and Ojibwa), the chief languages utilized by Bloomfield. If he lacked forms in some of the languages, or had for some reason rejected them, he sometimes made reconstructions on the basis of two languages. It seems he was particularly likely to do this if one of the two was Fox. Using only Fox *ni·na·na* and Cree *niya·n,* he set up PA **ni·la·na* 'we excl.' (no. 339).[14] This does not even account for Ojibwa *ni·nawi,* which he presumably rejected. In Table 1, lefthand column, a new reconstruction **ni·lawena·n-* is set up.[15] This 'explains' not only Fox and Cree but also a Cree alternant and Ojibwa as well as various other languages not used by Bloomfield. In 'Notes on the Fox language' Bloomfield shows that *-awe-* contracts to *-a·-* in Fox,[16] but he does not make use of the rule in reconstructing Proto-Algonkian.

Table 1. The PA words for 'we excl.' and 'we incl.'

PA	*n i· l a w e n a·n-	*k i· l a w e n a·n(a w)-
C	n i· y a· n	k i· y a n a·n a w
C^{a}	n i y a n â n	k i y â n o w
B	n i st ú n à n	ksi st ú n ù n
F	n i· n a· n a	
K		k i· n a n a
Mi	n i l o n a	k i l o n a
D	n i· l u· n a	k i· l u· n a
Ab	n i o n a	g i o n a
Nt	n een a w u n	k een a w u n
Ps	n i l o n	k i l o n
eO	n i· n a w i	k i· n a w i
M-P		g i· y a w

Table 1 makes it clear that PA **awe* is *awə* (*awu*) in Natick, *awi* in Ojibwa (but *a·* before a consonant cluster) and has contracted elsewhere to give Fox, Cree *a·*, Delaware *u·*, Miami, Abnaki, Passamaquoddy *o,* Blackfoot *u.* In Table 1, righthand column, the forms which reconstruct to *ki·lawena·n (aw)- 'we incl.' are shown. Here we have additional evidence for *awe in Mohegan-Pequot.

The new reconstructions are not only phonologically adequate but also morphologically adequate. In noun forms containing reference to a first person plural possessor Bloomfield sets up a suffix *-ena·n-[17] which is used in combination with the appropriate personal pronominal prefixes, *ne- (first person singular) and *ke- (second person singular), giving *ne- . . . -ena·n- 'our excl.' and *ke- . . . -ena·n- 'our incl.' It has not been previously shown that *-ena·n- was also present in the appropriate Proto-Algonkian pronouns. It is also clear that the new reconstructions imply a pronominal base *-i·law- instead of *-i·l-, as set up by Bloomfield. But his *ni·la 'I' (no. 337) as well as *ki·la 'thou' (implied by *ni·la) appear also to be truncated reconstructions when compared with Blackfoot (Table 2).

Table 2. The PA words for 'I' and 'thou'

PA	*n i· l a wa	*k i· l a wa
B	n i st ó a	k i st ó a
F	n i· n a	
K	n i· n a	k i· n a
C	n i y a	k i y a
M	n e n a-	k e n a-
	n e n ɛ-	k e n ɛ-
	n e n ɛ w-	k e n ɛ w-
eO	n i·(n)	k i·(n)
Mi	n i l a	k i l a
D	n i·	k i·
Ab	n i á	g i á
Pn	n ə́ y a	k ə́ y a
Mc	n i· n	g i· l

Fox and Kickapoo have no long vowels in final position; hence the final vowel is shorted from earlier *a· (and then either interpreted as -a, the animate singular suffix, or replaced by it). The three allomorphs of Menomini pose a problem. Bloomfield cuts *-a*, *-ɛ*, and *-ɛ-w-* uniquely in the pronouns and indicates that *-ɛ-w-* occurs in the quotative only.[18] I suspect, however, that *w* is part of the old stem even though the variation of *ɛ* and *a* in the three allomorphs remains unexplained. Abnaki *á* can be < **awa*, **a·wa*, or **e·wa*. The second *n* in the Micmac word is the result of assimilation; contrast *gi·l* 'you'.

3. Since the most accurate Algonkian reconstructions have been made on the basis of FCMO or some combination of these, it is common to compare some other single language with these sometimes limited reconstructions. As a general rule FCMO **a·* corresponds to Natick *on*, *om*, etc. (English orthography), Penobscot *ɔ*, Abnaki *ɔ̃*,[19] e.g. FCMO **wa·pi* 'white': Nt *wo'mpi*, Pn *wɔ̀pi*, Ab *wɔ̃b-* (stem); FCMO **weθa·kw-* 'evening; yesterday'; Nt *wunnonkoo oo k*, Pn *wə̀lɔkwe* 'yesterday', Ab *olɔ̃́gwiwí* 'in the evening'. But sometimes FCMO **a·* corresponds to Nt *au* (English orthography), Pn, Ab *o*, e.g. FCMO **wi·ya·hsi* 'flesh, meat': Nt *wiyaus*, Pn *wə̀yohs*, Ab *wiós*.[20] A revised reconstruction PA *wi·yawehsi (Table 3) removes the difficulty and at the same time shows **awe* represented by *a·* not only in Fox and Cree, but also in Ojibwa where it is regular before a consonant cluster. The new reconstruction also provides us with an etymology, viz. **-i·yaw-* 'body' (Table 4, lefthand column) + *-ehs*, diminutive suffix. It is also not surprising that some of the inflected forms of **-i·yaw-* show contraction of **awe* to *a·* (see Table 4, middle and righthand columns). 'Our incl. body' contains **ke-* . . . *-ena·n-*, the regular inflectional elements already discussed, and 'your pl. body' contains **ke-* . . . *-ewa·w-*, the regular inflection for second person plural possessor. This is clearly shown by the Ojibwa and Cheyenne forms which lack the contractions characteristic of Fox. Cheyenne vowels have shifted counter-clockwise; hence **i*, *o* > *e*, **e* > *a*, **a* > *o*. In addition **y* > Ch *t*.

Table 3. The PA word for 'meat, flesh'

PA	*w i· y a w e h s i	D	w i y u · s
F	o w i· y a · s i	Nt	w e y au s
C	w i· y a · s	Pn	w ə y o h s
eO	w i· y a · s s	Ab	w i ó s
Sh	w i y a w ? θ i	Mc	w e oo s
Mi	w i o s s i		

4. The broad outline needed for the reconstruction of Proto-Algonkian forms is already fairly well-known. The remaining problems will yield only to painstaking attention to details, especially those involving contraction. In many cases more accurate analysis of the individual languages is urgently needed; in particular the methods of internal reconstruction need to be applied. At the same time more attention to the careful comparison of a large number of languages will yield many new insights both in regard to the protolanguage and also in regard to the historical development of the daughter languages. The present paper has provided some examples which show the nature of the kinds of interesting problems that still await final solution.

Table 4. The PA words for 'my body', 'our incl. body', 'your pl. body'

PA	*n i· y a w i	*k i· y a w e n a·n i	*k i· y a w e w a·w i
F	n i· y a w	k i· y a · n a·n i	k i· y a · w a·w i
M	n e· y a w		k e· y o · w a·w-
O	n i· y a w	k i (y) a w i n â n	k i (y) a w i w a
Ch	n e t o v	e t o v a n	e t o v e v o

[1] Leonard Bloomfield, 'On the sound system of Central Algonquian', Lg. 1.130-56 (1925).

[2] He also wrote the introductory article, 'Why a linguistic society?', Lg. 1-5 (1925), but this was a justification and a programme, not a scholarly article.

[3] Lg. 1.130-56 (1925).

[4] 'The fuss and trouble behind my note in Language (Vol. 4, pp. 99-100; 1928) would have been avoided if I had listened to O [Ojibwa] . . . ', Bloomfield, 'Algonquian' in Harry Hoijer and others, Linguistic structures of native America, VFPA 6.85-129 (1945); see footnote 10, p. 88.

[5] Bloomfield, *Language*, New York (1933), p. 19.

[6] James Hammond Trumbull, *Natick dictionary*, Bulletin, Bureau of American Ethnology no. 25 (1903), Washington, D.C.

[7] Father Sebastian Rasles, *A dictionary of the Abnaki language*, Memoirs, American Academy of Arts and Sciences 1.370-574 (1833). This contains an introductory memoir and notes by John Pickering.

[8] David Zeisberger, *Indian dictionary*, Cambridge, 1887. This dictionary is quadrilingual, English, German, Iroquois (Onandaga), and Algonquin (Delaware).

[9] John Pickering, Introductory memoir in Rasles, op. cit., p. 374.

[10] See footnote 4.

[11] Leonard Bloomfield, 'Notes on the Fox language', IJAL 3.219-232 (1925), 4.181.219 (1927).

[12] Actually it is not. A thorough reworking of Fox based on new field work is urgently needed.

[13] New York, 1933.

[14] The reconstructions in 'Algonquian' are numbered consecutively and are easily located by means of their respective numbers which are quoted after them.

[15] The languages used in the table are abbreviated as follows: Ab, Abnaki; B, Blackfoot; C, Cree; C[a], an alternant form of Cree; Ch, Cheyenne; D, Delaware; F, Fox; K, Kickapoo; M, Menomini; Mc, Micmac; Mi, Miami; M-P, Mohegan-Pequot; O, Ojibwa; eO, Eastern Ojibwa; Nt, Natick; Pn, Penobscot; Ps, Passamaquoddy; Sh, Shawnee. The forms quoted are taken from the following works: R. R. Bishop Baraga, *A dictionary of the Otchipwe language*[2], Montreal, 1878; Leonard Bloomfield, 'Algonquian' (footnote 4); id. *Eastern Ojibwa*, Ann Arbor, 1957; id. *The Menomini language*, New Haven and London, 1962; Gordon Day, 'A St. Francis Abenaki vocabulary,' IJAL 30.371-92, 1964; Mary R. Haas, Passamaquoddy word list, Ms.; Le Rév. Père Alb. Lacombe, *Dictionnaire de la*

langue des Cris, Montreal, 1874; Le Rev. Père Pacifique, *Leçons grammaticales théoriques et pratiques de la langue Micmaque*, Sainte-Anne de Ristigouche, P. Q., 1939; Douglas Parks, Kickapoo word list, Ms.; Rev. Rodolphe Petter, *English-Cheyenne dictionary*, Kettle Falls, 1913-15; Frank T. Siebert, Penobscot notes, Ms.; Frank G. Speck, 'Native tribes and dialects of Connecticut, a Mohegan-Pequot diary', 43rd Annual Report of the Bureau of American Ethnology, pp. 199-288, Washington, D. C., 1928; Trumbull (footnote 6); C. C. Uhlenbeck and R. H. van Gulick, *An English-Blackfoot vocabulary*, VKAW, n.s. 29.4.1-261, 1930; Charles F. Voegelin, *Shawnee stems and the Jacob P. Dunn Miami dictionary*, Indiana Historical Society, Prehistory Research Series, 1.63-108, 135-167, 289-341, 409-478, 1937-40; id., 'Delaware, an Eastern Algonquian language', in Harry Hoijer and others (footnote 4).

[16] P. 227.

[17] 'Algonquian', p. 96.

[18] *Menomini grammar*, p. 195.

[19] Reasons for preferring an indication like FCMO for limited reconstructions are set forth in my paper 'Wiyot-Yurok-Algonkian and problems of comparative Algonkian', IJAL 32.101-7, 1966.

[20] Delaware is partly like FCMO and partly like the Eastern languages quoted; thus FCMO **a·* (of the first type), D *a·*, Pn *ɔ*, but FCMO **a·* (of the second type), D *u·*, Pn *o*.

On some Troublesome Indo-European Initials

Eric P. Hamp
University of Chicago

I. The Germanic word for 'day' has long remained without a clear etymological solution. If I do not succeed in convincing my friend George Lane that I have a clear solution – for the standards that we all admire in him do not accept arguments without stern and searching critical assay – I hope at least to raise some considerations that have, I think, been underattended to in the past, and to suggest some avenues of thought that may lead to new solutions.

There seem to be just two serious theories concerning the genesis of **dagaz*: A derivation from the root **dheg*^{w}*h*- 'burn' with a meaning associated with the notion of heat and the sun, and an equation with Sanskrit *áhar/áhn*- 'day'. It is usual to reject the first, increasingly in recent time, on phonetic grounds. Competent authorities have favored the second, but either with unconvincing ad hoc supporting arguments, or simply with an admission that there is no direct way to account for the failure of agreement in the initials.

Walde-Pokorny 1.849 has set forth, it seems to me, essentially the right line of reasoning, and touches on the important matters dealt with up to then, while citing earlier literature. Due reference is made to the heteroclitic *r/n* match found in the Sanskrit noun. It is properly pointed out that the Germanic velar excludes the labio-velar in **dheg*^{w}*h*-. The likelihood of considering some vaguely formulated and unparalleled prefixation, or of positing a simplification of Schwundstufe *dgh*-, are ruled out. The main flaw in their account is the willingness to entertain a cross of some earlier phonetically regular form with **daʒwaz*. This simply begs the question by insisting on dragging in **dheg^wh-*, as I shall show below. This impossible cross, or contamination, is merely repeated by Pokorny, *IEW* 7.

Actually, the willingness one finds to consider seriously a derivation of **dagaz* from a root with a labio-velar is nothing short of surprising, and has an interest all its own, when one reflects upon it. It would be mournful to list the dictionaries of some respectable currency that actually give serious attention to this suggested source. No doubt this must reflect the delay in general recognition by Indo-Europeanists of the regular reflexes of the labio-velar aspirate in Germanic. This was surely aided by the paucity of clear etyma showing this feature and represented in Germanic; by the fact that in such an etymon as ON *gunnr* 'battle', before the rounded vowel (i.e. with the feature [+flat] simply reassigned to the following vowel segment), the reflex is in fact *g*; by the possibility of allotting, against most of the IE evidence, a word such as *warm* to **u̯*; and perhaps even by the fact that within West Germanic only OFrisian shows a distinctive reflex in the vocalism of a word such as *sionga* 'sing'. But if, as we must, we look for maximal regularities, we must insist on rejecting a result that is not **dawaz*, or the like, as a descendant of **dhog^wh-*. Such a phonetic consideration is normally a strong deterrent to propounding etymologies, in the absence of persuasive grounds for contamination from a known source. But, as we shall see, I think there are other corroborative, and perhaps even stronger, grounds for laying this ghost to rest.

First, however, we must clarify a detail of the stem-formation. Entia non multiplicanda sunt. Mayrhofer *KEWAi* 1.68 favors the Germanic-Indic equation because the range of stem-formation agrees; I think he is right, but I think his grounds are unnecessarily proliferated. ONorse shows two variant forms, both with the same meaning and both neuter, *dǿgn* and *dǿgr*, the latter being the more usual, and OE has *dógor* 'day'. Sanskrit *áhar/áhn-* is surely heteroclite, and

Avestan *azan*-offers partial support while clarifying the consonantal phonology in an important way. However, Mayrhofer wants to include as well the third attested stem-shape in Skt. *ahas*- and place this alongside claimed remnants of an *s*-stem in Germanic. In this fashion he would see a triple agreement founded on an *r*/*n*/*s* alternation. Such an agreement would be striking, and probative for a single etymology, but it would represent a gain at considerable cost in our formulation of IE noun patterns. In the first place, there is no need to regard the Sanskrit *s*-stem as old; it is, moreover, a rare variant. There is no difficulty in regarding this *s*-stem as a sandhi back-formation within Sanskrit based on the old *r*-variant; the phonetic realizations of these two underlying forms would overlap under well known conditions. Feist[3] 113 makes OE *dógor* an old *-*s*-, but this is gratuitous. Pokorny *IEW* 7 has the whole Germanic *o*-stem from a neuter *-*es*-, but that is flatly outrageous. The only shred of seeming support from Germanic is the Gothic name of which one writing is Δαγίσ-Θεος. Feist also leans on this, doubtful and isolated though it is. Even granting that we identify and assign its elements correctly, we can still make this a compound with a genitive first element. With this, our *s*-stem vanishes, and we are left with a well understood **r*/*n*-stem in both Indo-Iranian and Germanic. Furthermore, Mayrhofer in his account neglects to point out the important duality of stem *within* Norse. Thus, while we have no triple correspondence, we have a more powerful double correspondence of known status. In the case of such a stem formation, this agreement is a cardinal point in the argument.

In this manner, while trimming Mayrhofer's argument on the stem formation, we have at the same time reached an interesting negative morphological reason for rejecting the root 'burn'. These Germanic words are not a congeries of miscellaneous noun derivatives from some productive verb base in immediate pre-Germanic time; i.e., we do not have something like τόμος ~ τομός. For we have just made it probable, as we shall elaborate below using the sense of these words to support our argument, that the Germanic forms all stem from a single well known IE noun type that would not arise as a productive derivative from a verb base; in fact, in Germanic the *r/n* stems are as moribund as can be, and this must form the starting point of our morphological understanding of these words.[1] We are looking at some old noun somewhat on the order of *sun* or *fire* or *water*.

Let us now consider the meanings of these words, a matter which has strangely escaped careful incorporation in these etymological claims. Meaning is notoriously hazardous to handle; but no etymology can be seriously considered if it fails to show a putative match among the known semantic features of the forms in question and a hypothetical route for getting from a presumed reconstructed bundle of semantic features (doubtless incomplete) to the observed features in the attested forms.

The Sanskrit meanings are not particularly revealing, no more so than Eng. *day*. Stchoupak-Nitti-Renou records such informative collocations as: *a.a.* de jour en jour, °*divam* id., °*gaṇa* m. série de jours, °*āgama* m. venue de jour, °*pati*- m. soleil, °*niça*- nt. jour et nuit, *aho-rātra*- m. jour et nuit, période de 24 heures. Here we clearly have 'day' in the sense of time-unit and of time-of-sunlight.

It is the Norse evidence that we must inspect closely, not merely for the absolute meanings that it shows, but – more important – because it is here that the greatest set of oppositions in lexemes is found. The continuations of Gmc. **dagaz* may mean either 'daylight' or '1/7 of a week'. But *dǿgr* (Norwegian *døger*) and *dǿgn* meant '12 hours of the day or night'. The latter is continued in East Scandinavian as Swedish *dygn* and Danish *døgn* '24 hours'. Note that this closely time-bound meaning attaches precisely to the remnants of the old heteroclite. Moreover, *dagr* has other meanings in locutions which are frozen and therefore old. An early use is for 'gathering' or 'meeting' (*rigsdag*, no matter where in the Germanic world this grew up); this might be rationalized as derived from 'time, appointment (for a meeting)'. A Danish phrase *ha' fred og gode dage* is reshaped to make semi-sense from ODan. *i frid oc dage*; the sense of 'peace, quiet' here can be explained as earlier 'time, leisure'. Underlying all this is an old term referring somehow to 'time, time-unit, lapse of time'. Feist accepts the meaning for Germanic 'Zeit, wo die Sonne brennt'. There is no reasonable way of getting economically to the observed meanings from the notion 'burn'.

**dhegʷh-* must be rejected on phonetic, morphological, and semantic grounds.

With the way thus cleared, how now are we to interpret the vocalisms? In the abstract, we may envisage either a long normal grade with schwa in **dagaz*, or IE **a* or **o* with Dehnstufe in *dǿgr/n* etc. The Indo-Iranian seems to rule out schwa. So, in terms of traditional Germanic orthography we have **dagaz, dōgr/n-* < **dVg-, dV̄g(r/n)*. How are we to view this vrddhi? It is not likely to be original with the *r/n*-formation; though note Gk. ἧπαρ. The ablaut of these nouns is still not settled. Burrow, *The Sanskrit Language* 221, notes that the Sanskrit accent in *áhar* had become fixed; this noun may well have been on its way to being regularized, apart from Germanic tendencies to carry such tendencies to their term. This would help explain the rapid displacement by the productive *o*-stem in a more specific way than on general grounds. As I see it, the key lies in Goth. *-dogs* (*fidurdogs*). This is a normal vrddhi adjective; Schulze KZ 40.404 has compared it to *çatá-çārada-* (misspelt by Feist). If the old *r/n* noun referred always to 'time-unit', while the *o*-stem came to mean 'daylight', the time word quite naturally picked up the ablaut typical of these vrddhi compounds referring to time-spans measured by days. Thus the old ablaut gets frozen in the newer stem-type.

I therefore derive all the Germanic forms from a single noun **dhaĝh-r/n-* 'time unit, or span, of short extent'.

Now we come to the initial. Wackernagel *AiGr* 1.263, in discussing 'tear' (see below) simply refers to early attempts to explain by loss or by unmotivated prefixation. Needless to say we must have a context or condition for such happenings; and a prefix without syntax and cognates is nothing at all. If Indo-Iranian had lost its initial, then we must search for a cognate to match Germanic; this search has now gone on for a good century. If we can find a source for the Germanic initial, then we have a match immediately. The direction of enquiry is clear.

There are certain cases where we can be perfectly sure that earlier media plus laryngeal gave the reflex of an aspirate: *ahám, maha-, duhitr-*. These are admittedly palatals and velars, but Kuiper has also adduced (*IIJ* 1.91, 1957) *sadhás-*: *sēdēs*. Puhvel has remarked (Lg. 35.647-9, 1959) in reviewing such cases that 'no good evidence that a cross-IE normal aspirate derives its origin from a cluster of media + laryngeal' is to be found. But for one thing, our case is an initial – an instance spanning juncture, if you like. Secondly, we are hardly dealing in numbers that permit statistical statements. I submit, then, that this neuter noun in situations of concord (perhaps accusatives of time) was once e.g. **tod Háĝhr*, pronounced something like [todháĝhr̥], and that pre-Germanic reinterpreted this as **tod dháĝhr*. The nature of the laryngeal, and hence of the vowel, remains for the moment ambiguous.

Unless we can find a match for our word, this rests as pure speculation – though, I would claim, reasonable and motivated speculation. Now, there is an Albanian word that has never been explained, *herë* 'time, Mal'. Meyer *Etym. Wb.* 151 derives it from Lat. *hōra* ('mit *ē* = *ō* wie sonst'), and this has been uncritically handed down. But when after Cicero was a Latin *h* heard in Illyria or Dacia? In my essay in *Evidence for Laryngeals* I hope to have shown preliminarily that Alb. *h-*

continues specifically an *a*-coloring $*H$. Medial inter-voiced stop is regularly lost in Albanian. The rest is routine Albanian morphology: If we may start with *o*-grade, $*H_a o\acute{g}hr$ had a plural $*Ho\acute{g}(h)r\bar{a}$, which on loss of final sibilants became a feminine singular or plural; then with the well documented Albanian predilection for Dehnstufe, $*H\bar{o}\acute{g}r\bar{a}$ > *herë*.

It may be considered a weakness of the proposed Albanian formulation that we must posit an *o*-grade $*H_a o\acute{g}hr$. (It is, of course, circularly possible that the Germanic and Indo-Iranian represent *o*-grade also.) However, as I have shown elsewhere, Alb. *ujë* 'water' can be derived only from **udriā*; this would tend to indicate that the *r*-form of such nouns could take over the total function of the old alternation, and that in ablaut and derivation what we see of such nouns in Albanian as far back as we can reach is already somewhat removed from the classically reconstructed shapes that the older IE languages give us.

Provisionally, I suggest that the earliest reachable form for Germanic **dagaz* is $*H_a\acute{e}\acute{g}hr$ or $*H_a o\acute{g}hr$-. If the *r*-forms were always in an ablaut grade other than zero in the second syllable, as Indo-Iranian and Germanic easily suggest, the first-syllable ablaut in the pre-Albanian shape would be supported by the fact that, as in *ujë*, the zero-grade of the *r*-element betrays a derived formation.

II. I have already tried, *PBB* (Tübingen) 81.263 ff, 1960, to show that the multiplicity of forms for 'Träne' in IE, especially those of Germanic, can be reduced not merely to a small number of forms (two), but to a pair that must have coexisted in IE related by a known suffix formation (*r/n*) that induced in this noun a simple dissimilation which led to the pair of alternates. That is, we start from a synchronic IE **dak̂ru* ~ *drak̂ur/n-*, from a pre-IE **drak̂ru(-r/n-)*.

Szemerényi (*IE Numerals* 102) has meantime improved the regularity of formulation for the descendant Germanic forms by suggesting that in OHG and OSax the change **traxur/n-* > **traxar/n-* is a regular phonetic one, and not suffix substitution (which is the same as saying ablaut analogy), paralleled in **texun* > **texan* '10'. But this still leaves the notorious set Skt. *áśru-*, Avest. *asru-*, Lith. *ašarà*, Toch. A (East Toch.) *ākär*, pl. *akrūna*, pl. f. *ākrunt* unexplained; their antecedent **áḱru-* must be placed beside the two alternants already mentioned.[2]

I propose that we may now see in **áḱru* a form developed within the IE period by misdivision of the neuter **dáḱru*, analogously to, but in the opposite direction from, the process just outlined for **dagaz*. That is, **tod dáḱru*, often heard as *[*todàḱru*], was misdivided as **tod áḱru*.

How could this happen, and why did it not happen often to neuters in **d-*?[3] We may suppose that *-*d*+*d-* over juncture was either long [d:] or simple [d] in IE; what kept it from being interpreted as phonological /dd/, or /d-d/ over morphological boundary within a word, was the fact that it was not [dzd]. Normally, speakers automatically restored such auditory instances to their underlying form in *d-*, on hearing them. In this they could be guided by the form in all other contexts. But in the word in question there was already room for indecision, since two alternate initials already existed in the language: **dr-* and **d-*. Such an alternation was already an anomaly. We may say, then, that some speakers (dialects), with no loss in economy, substituted a new anomalous alternation **dr-* ~ zero. This may point to the fact that synchronically at that time **dáḱru* was used in the nominative-accusative, and **drakur/n-* in the oblique cases.

[1] But Greek did show a limited number of derivatives from verb bases; see Chantraine *Formation* 218.

[2] Petersson *Heteroklisie* 196 was on the right track, but missed the detail of the suffixes; and his view rules out any clarification of *áḱru.

[3] K. Schneider IF 57.203, 1940, with Sprachübertragungen oder Sprachmischungen merely substitutes names for ignorance, with no explanation.

Hittite *udatis*

E. Adelaide Hahn

Hunter College of the City University of New York

The *locus classicus* for the use of Hittite *udatis* is a document[1] in which Queen Puduhepas promises certain gifts for five years to the goddess Lelwanis in exchange for the life and health of her husband, King Hattusilis III, who reigned early in the thirteenth century. Lelwanis is identified by Goetze (*ANET* 393 fn. 4) as Ishtar, the patron goddess of the royal couple. This document was published in 1949 by E. Laroche (*RA* 43.55-78) under the title 'Le voeu de Puduhepa'; and again, in considerably augmented form, in 1965, by Heinrich Otten and Vladimir Souček under the title *Das Gelübde der Königin Puduḫepa an die Göttin Lelwani* (Wiesbaden).[2]

Pud. is not only a valuable source for the student of language, but also a document of such human interest that I cannot resist saying a few words about it from the philological rather than the linguistic viewpoint. Puduhepas promises Lelwanis not only offerings of animals such as sheep and goats, and various gifts of gold and silver including a number characterized as 'days and nights', 'months', and 'years' (whatever that may mean), but also about a hundred persons, who are presumably to serve as temple-attendants of one sort or another. Fifty of these are grouped into nine 'houses', evidently households or families, each with its own head;[3] and Puduhepas[4] takes considerable pains in the assignment of individuals to these houses. Thus she evidently tries to keep relatives together; e.g., one woman is accompanied by a son and a daughter (1.10-11), another by her brother's daughter (1.59-60), another by her brother-in-law's daughter (1.61-62). A girl named Titais is given to Apallus as a wife, and her (presumably younger) brother, a boy named Tatilis, is given to Apallus as a ward (1.51-53). One poor little waif named Palluwas, who apparently has no one belonging to him,[5] is similarly given to a designated woman to bring up (1.63-64). Indeed, boys and girls and infants[6] are always specially provided for. Puduhepas in her distribution takes cognizance of sex as well as of age: though there is one house without a male (3.34), she usually tries to provide an adult male addition to a house that would otherwise be all women and children (3.27-28, 30-31), and she similarly provides a lone female[7] for a house with a superabundance of males (3.37-38). She is evidently concerned with the well-being of her personnel: she promises investigation of a house plagued by illness (3.41-42), and of another visited by death (3.47-48). Any good Samaritan who has provided a needy colleague with grain is to be repaid when the harvest comes; Mumulantis – whoever he is – is to see to this (3.53-57). The names are a fruitful source of study in their own right.[8] Some are of interest as ethnica. Some, especially in the stem-form, sound like Lallnamen: we meet numerous females called *Mamma,* likewise a man *Kukku,* and two boys *Dudu* and *Tuttu.*

Now to turn to strictly linguistic matters. The document is as poor in art or skill as it is rich in human interest; it is syntactically a hodge-podge. For this very reason, its almost complete consistency in one respect is all the more noteworthy. This is the form in which the names are recorded.[9] When the name is used in complete isolation as an item in a list, it has the nominative case-ending, *-as, -is,* or *-us*; the person is simply referred to as *Abbas* (1.10), *Mammas* (1.13), etc.[10] But when, as frequently happens, some additional information is given as to the age and sex of the person involved, or as to his or her kinship with another person previously named, then we find not simply '1 girl nursing, Mammas', or '1 daughter of her, Mammas', but '1 girl nursing, Mammas *her name* (1.65), or '1 daughter of her, Mammas *her name* (2.2b).[11] 'His name' or 'her name', in Hittite *laman-set,* is invariably here, as almost invariably everywhere in Hittite, written in Akkadian, *ŠUM-ŠU*.[12] And when *ŠUM-ŠU* is present, the name preceding it is written in the stem-form, ending in *-a, -i,* or *-u*.[13] Presumably the same distinction holds good when the name is used not in syntactic isolation but as the subject or object of a verb;[14] we would expect the stem-form with *ŠUM-ŠU,* the nominative or accusative case without it. But as it happens, all the names combined with a verb[15] are, with one exception,[16] followed by *ŠUM-ŠU,* and are therefore in the uninflected form.

Now, what are these endingless forms that I have been calling stem-forms?

One explanation may be that they are Akkadian. We always find such forms in the formulaic introductions to historical documents, which are regularly written in Akkadian; and Sturtevant, *Chr.* 84, holds that 'the proper names, even if they are elsewhere declined in the Hittite fashion, are here treated as indeclinables, as is usual with Akkadian proper names'.[17] Then I would suggest that the use of the Akkadian form in *Pud.* may be due to the juxtaposition of the Akkadian *ŠUM,* which might well have been responsible for the presence of an Akkadian form before it as well as after it (Akkadian *ŠU* for Hittite *set* 'his' or 'her'[18]). Similarly in the folk-tales and the epics, proper names in the genitive and dative can be written either in the Hittite inflected case-form, or in the uninflected, unquestionably Akkadian, form with an Akkadian preposition: e.g., genitive *Keššiyaš* (*KUB* 17.1.2.7) and dative *Keššiya KUB* 33.121.2.12), vs. *ŠA ᴰANU* 'of Anus' (*KUB* 33.120.1.26), *ANA KEŠŠI* 'to Kessis' (*KUB* 33.121.2.9), *ITTI APPU* 'with Appus' (*KUB* 24.8.1.30).[19] A Sumerian ideogram may also induce the writing of a neighboring form in Akkadian.[20] I have noted that this is specially likely to occur in the folk-tales and epics with an ideogram denoting kinship, in combination with which an uninflected form is readily interpreted as a genitive even though unmarked as such by either Akkadian preposition or Hittite case-ending. Thus we meet AMA KEŠŠI 'Kessis' mother' (*Bo* 4473.2.2), *DAM APPU* 'Appus' wife' (*KUB* 24.8.3.3), *DUMU* ᴰ*KUMARBI* 'Kumarbis' son' (*KUB* 17.7.3.9).[21]

However, I would venture to suggest a different explanation for the endingless forms in question, and that is that they are really neuter nominative-accusatives used as adjectives in agreement with the Hittite *laman* represented by Akkadian *ŠUM*. In a monograph probably to be entitled *Naming-Constructions in Some Indo-European Languages*, to which I am engaged in putting the finishing touches at the moment of writing this article, I suggest that the so-called, and justly-called, 'Greek accusative' 'in name'[22] was developed from a misunderstood nominative-accusative in partitive apposition with the noun designating the possessor of the name, which in early Greek, and always, so far as I know, in other Indo-European languages, including Sanskrit (where *nāma* has often been compared with Greek *onoma*[23]), is met only in the nominative and accusative. Partitive apposition is very common in early Greek (as well as in Hittite), and its use in connection with the relation of the name to its owner is not at all surprising in view of the extremely important part that was assigned to the name in primitive myth and folk-lore. As for the word denoting the name itself, that must have served as an appositive to *both* the other nouns. Thus the early construction would have been *homo nomen Iulius* or *hominem nomen Iulium*,[24] and only in the course of time would the appositive *nomen* in agreement with *homo* or *hominem* have developed into an accusative of specification.[25] The close relationship existing among the three words seems to me to be pointed up by the fact that in a passage where *homo* and *nomen* are in different cases, *Iulius*, while logically belonging to *nomen*, is not infrequently attracted into the case of *homo*: thus, Sanskrit can say *homo habet nomen IULIUS* (e.g. *RV*

2.37.2) instead of *homo habet nomen IULIUM*; and Latin can say *homini est nomen IULIO* (e.g. Plautus, *Men.* 1096) instead of *homini est nomen IULIUS*, and *homini faciunt nomen IULIO* (e.g. Plautus, *Men.* 77) instead of *homini faciunt nomen IULIUM*.

There is a clear case of attraction not of case but of gender[26] in Sanskrit, *RV* 6.66.1 vapur nu tac cikituse cid astu samenam nāma dhenu patyamānam 'now that (thing) [i.e. creature] possessing the same name cow [the same bovine, or milk-giving, name] shall be a wonder to the wise'.[27] A similar construction existed in early Latin, if we are to believe Gellius 15.29: Verba Pisonis haec sunt: *L. Tarquinium, . . . quia Tarquinio nomine esset, metuere* . . . Quia *Tarquinio* inquit *nomine esset*, hoc proinde est, tamquam si ego dicam, *mihi nomen est Iulium* 'These are Piso's words: 'They feared Lucius Tarquinius, because he was of the Tarquinian name.' That he said, 'he was of the Tarquinian name,' this is just as if I were to say, 'I have the Julian name'.' Gellius is obviously, and doubtless correctly, interpreting *Tarquinio* as an adjective in agreement with *nomine*, just as I am interpreting *dhenu* in the Sanskrit passage as an adjective in agreement with *nāma*.[28]

It seems to me that we have a very close parallel to the Sanskrit and Old Latin in several Hittite passages from the Story of Appus (*KUB* 24.8), where we hear of two brothers called 'Bad' and 'Good' being given respectively *ḪUL-lu ŠUM-an* or *laman* (3.7 and 10) and NÍG.SI.SÁ-*an ŠUM-an* (3.14 and 16),[29] which certainly seem to mean 'a bad name' and 'a good name'. Güterbock (*JAOS* 65.250 fn. 15) envisages this possibility, but dismisses it,[30] and concludes (ib. 250) that in ḪUL-*lu* and NÍG.SI.SÁ-*an* we have stem-forms.[31] But I believe, as I have already indicated, that there is a possibility of their being nominative-accusative neuter adjectives, and the same would apply also to the vowel-stems in *-i* and *-u* (*Šintalimini*, *Ullikummi*, *Appu*) cited elsewhere (250) by

Güterbock, and also to those in *-a*, *-i*, and *-u* occurring in *Pud.*[32] One of these forms is *Udati*, which, after this long preamble, we are at last ready to discuss.

Udati(*s*) occurs eleven times in *Pud.*[33] The passages are as follows, those starred being in newly-discovered fragments, and therefore included only by OS, not by Laroche.

1. 1.58 1 SAL-*TUM* ᶠ*Ú-ta-ti Pí-ta-ga-at-ti-e-ni* [*ŠUM-ŠU*].
2. 1.61 1 SAL-*TUM* ᶠ*Ú-ta-ti* ᵐ*Te-me-it-ti-e-ni ŠUM-ŠU*.
*3. 1.61 1 DUMU.SAL ᶠ*Ú-da-ti ŠUM-ŠU*.
4. 1.63 1 SAL-*TUM* ᶠ*Ú-ta-ti Ta-ti-li-e-ni ŠUM-ŠU*.
5. 1.65 1 SAL-*TUM* ᶠ*Ú-ta-ti Za-ga-ša-lu-wa-aš-ši-e-ni ŠUM-ŠU*.
6. 2.1 1 SAL-*TUM* ᶠ*Ú-da-ti Za-kap-pa-u-te-ni ŠUM-ŠU*.
*7. 2.2a [1 SAL-*TUM*] ᶠ*Ú-ta-ti Za-ga-* . . . *-nu-e-ni ŠUM-ŠU*.
8. 2.3 1 SAL-*TUM* ᶠ*Ú-da-ti Pí-ip-ta-ru-wa-aš-ši-e-ni ŠUM-ŠU*.
9. 2.11 ᶠ*Ú-da-ti-iš Pi-iz-zu-ur-*.
*10. 2.31 1 DUMU.SAL ᶠ*Ú-da*[*-ti ŠUM-Š*]*U*.
*11. 4.11 ᶠ*Ú-da-ti-iš* ᶠ*Ma-ra-aš-ša-wi-y* [*a-aš*].

It should be noted that in every passage except 9 and 11, the presence of *ŠUM-ŠU* is to be expected, in accordance with the rule set forth above, for *Udati* is preceded by 1 SAL-*TUM* '1 woman' (in 1, 2, 4, 5, 6, 8, and probably 7) or 1 DUMU.SAL '1 girl' (in 3 and 10); and we do meet it in all these passages except 1 and 10, in both of which it is plausibly supplied. And wherever *ŠUM-ŠU* is present or plausibly supplied, we find the stem-form *Udati* except for one mutilated passage, 10, where OS certainly seem right in supplying *-ti ŠUM-Š* after *Ú-da* and before the end of [*ŠUM-Š*]*U*. On the other hand, in 9 and 11, where there is no *ŠUM-ŠU*, we find the nominative *Udatis*. In other words, *Udati*(*s*) behaves like a proper noun.[34] And a proper noun it certainly is in 3, 10, and 11.[35]

But what is it in the other eight passages? In all of them

except 9, where there is a lacuna,[36] it precedes a form ending in *-eni*.[37] This form has the masculine determinative in 2, and presumably the other forms, which all lack determinatives, denote males also. OS suggest very plausibly (49) that this *-eni* is a Zugehörigkeitssuffix.[38] Apparently the owner of the preceding feminine name was in such a distinctive relationship to the designated male that his masculinity could be taken for granted.[39] What relationship could this be except that of a wife or a widow?

Laroche had suggested (70) the meaning of 'widow' for *udati*. He does not recognize the *-eni* forms as exhibiting a 'Zugehörigkeitssuffix', but takes them as denoting the names of the women involved; thus he translates 6 'une femme veuve, Zakappauteni son nom', (64). Of course he recognizes that in 2, where the *-eni* form (*Temetteni*) has a masculine determinative, the name must denote a male, and he suggests that it is a genitive depending on *udati* (70).[40] In their treatment of the *-eni* suffix, OS seem to me to have improved on Laroche; but I must confess I cannot understand their failure to adopt his interpretation of *udatis* as 'widow'.[41]

Goetze in his review of OS declares (*JCS* 20.52): 'The authors are right (p. 42 fn. 1) that ^{sal}*ú-d/ta-ti* (against Laroche) cannot mean 'widow' '; and he adds in a footnote (52 fn. 10), 'In the meantime it has been demonstrated, confirming the suggestion of H. G. Güterbock, *IF* 60 (1950) 205 fn. 1, that the Hitt. word for 'widow' is *wannumi(ya)*- (A. Goetze, *Jaos* 74, 1954, 189)'.[42] This brings us to the question of *wannumiyas*.

Laroche discussed this word in *RHA* 9 fascicle 49. 14-15 (1948-9). He showed that it could be used of a child (he reports four occurences in *KUB* 17.4; the precise references are 2, 3, 6, and 12) or of a woman (*KUB* 8.12.2.5-6 with 34.16.15-16, 12.63.2.7, and 34.24.6),[43] and concludes that the Hittite word combines two notions for which French (and he might have added English too) lacks a single word, but which are both seen in Greek *orphanos* and Latin *orbus*.

Laroche does not suggest that one of these notions is 'widow';[44] the Greek and Latin words that he cites refer to the reciprocal relations of a parent bereft of children ('childless') and of a child bereft of parents ('orphan').[45]

The clearest of the passages cited by Laroche was also discussed at almost the same time by Güterbock in *IF* 60.205 (1949-50), where he refers to it as *KUB* 34.30.4.17-20. Considerably later, he incorporated it in his masterly edition of *Supp.*, in *JCS* 10; this particular passage appears on p. 98. It runs as follows: *an-zi-el BE-LÍ ú-e-ki-iš-ki-u-en an-za-a-aš-wa* EN-*NI ku-iš* ᵐ*Ni-ip-ḫu-ru-ri-ya-aš e-eš-ta nu-wa-ra-aš* BA-BAD DUMU-*aš-ma-wa-aš-ši* NU GÁL DAM *BE-LÍ-NI-ma-wa-an-na-aš wa-an-nu-um-mi-ya-aš*. He translates this passage in *IF* as follows: 'Unser eigener Herr, der Niphururiya war, ist gestorben, einen Sohn aber hat er nicht;[46] die Gattin unseres Herrn aber ist eine Witwe (?).' In *JCS*, however, he renders it thus: 'Nibhururiya, who was our lord, died; a son he has not. Our lord's wife is solitary.' His shift from 'a widow (?)' to 'solitary' is highly interesting.[47]

In *IF* 60 for his tentative translation 'eine Witwe (?)' he offers a possible parallel (205 fn. 1) from Kantuzzilis' Prayer to the Sun-God.[48] This Prayer he subsequently published in *JAOS* 78.237-45. His main copy, *KUB* 31.127.1.35-36, omits the crucial word *wannummiyas*;[49] this occurs, however, in the variant versions (see *JAOS* 78.240 fn. 19), in which form I quote the passage:[50] *Ištanuš dammišḫandaš kurimmaša wannummiyašša attaš annaš zik* 'Istanus, to the oppressed, *kurimmaš* and *wannummiyaš*, thou art father and mother'.[51] Goetze (*JAOS* 74.189[52]) states that this passage 'points with certainty' to the meaning 'orphans and widows'[53] for *kurimmašša*[54] *wannummiyašša*. But Güterbock even in *IF* 60 (205 fn. 1) had suggested just as Laroche had in *RHA* 9 (15) that Hittite *wannummiya-* and the modern term (his *Witwe* and Laroche's *veuve*) may not correspond precisely in denotation, *wannummiya-* perhaps being simply 'alleinstehend'. And ultimately for Kantuzzilis' Prayer just as for *Supp.* he selected a much more general term than 'widow', offering (*JAOS* 78.240 and fn. 19) for *kurimmas* and *wannummiyas* the non-committal 'lonely' and 'bereaved', and adding that both words 'may include the notions' of 'widow', 'childless', and 'orphan'.

And there the matter rests.

It seems to me that *wannummiyas* does indeed include all three meanings as posited by Güterbock, with the content determining which is particularly appropriate.[55] On the other hand, *udatis* in *Pud.* seems to me to demand the unequivocal meaning 'widow' and nothing else.

Finally, there is the additional circumstance that an excellent etymology is available for *udatis* if it really means 'widow'. Laroche deals with this admirably in a footnote to his discussion of the meaning of *udati* (70 fn. 2), connecting Hittite *udati* with Sanskrit *vidhava*, Latin *vidua*, Gothic *widuwo*, and Irish *fedb*.[56] I am well aware[57] of the fact that etymology is a difficult and dangerous foundation to build upon in the process of interpreting unknown words.[58] On the other hand if a suggested meaning based on the careful study of text and context, such as is demanded of the philologist, is supported by a sound etymology approved by the linguist, that seems to me a respectable means of reinforcing the plausibility of any given hypothesis. And this test the explanation of *udatis* as 'widow' seems to me to meet.

[1] This document is referred to here as *Pud.* Other bibliographical abbreviations in this article are to be interpreted as follows. *AAA* = *Annals of Archaeology and Anthropology*. *ANET* = *Ancient Near Eastern Texts Relating to the Old Testament*, ed. by James B. Pritchard (Princeton, 1950). Buck = Carl Darling Buck, *A Dictionary of Selected Synonyms in the Principal Indo-European Languages* (Chicago, 1949). Friedrich, *Wört.* = Johannes Friedrich, *Hethitisches Wörterbuch* (Heidelberg, 1952); *Erg.* 1 = *1. Ergänzungsheft* (Heidelberg, 1957). Güterbock, *Kum.* = *Kumarbi*, ed. by Hans Gustav Güterbock (Zurich and New York, 1946). Güterbock, *Supp.* = *The Deeds of Suppiluliuma as Told by His Son, Mursili II*, ed. by Hans Gustav Güterbock (reprinted from *JCS* 10.41-68, 75-98, 107-130). Güterbock, *Ull.* = *The Song of Ullikummi*, ed. by Hans Gustav Güterbock (reprinted from *JCS* 5.135-161, 6.8-40). *JAOS* = *Journal of the American Oriental Society*. *JCS* = *Journal of Cuneiform Studies*. Laroche, *Onom.* = Emmanuel Laroche, *Recueil d'onomastique hittite* (Paris, 1952). *Lg.* = *Language*. *PAPS* = *Proceedings of the American Philosophical Society*. *RA* = *Revue d'assyriologie et d'archéologie orientale*. *RHA* = *Revue hittite et asianique*. Sommer, *HAB* = *Die hethitisch-akkadische Bilingue des Ḫattušili I.* (*Labarna* II.), ed. by Ferdinand Sommer and Adam Falkenstein (Munich, 1938). Sturtevant, *Chr.* = *A Hittite Chrestomathy*, ed. by Edgar H. Sturtevant and George Bechtel (Philadelphia, 1935). Thieme, *Untersuchungen* = P. Thieme, *Untersuchungen zur Wortkunde und Auslegung des Rigveda* (Halle, 1949). *Wd.* = *Word*. *WP* = Alois Walde, *Vergleichendes Wörterbuch der indogermanischen Sprachen*, ed. and rev. by Julius Pokorny, 2 vols. (Berlin and Leipzig, 1927-30). *ZA* = *Zeitschrift für Assyriologie*.

[2] In references to *Pud.*, I quote the text as given by Otten and Souček, and employ the convenient numbering of the lines used in their translation. All references to Laroche (unless otherwise designated) and to OS (i.e. Otten and Souček) are to these two publications.

[3] The feminist notes with pleasure that three of the nine heads are women.

[4] Or her ghost-writer! But I have the feeling – purely subjective, I admit – that Puduhepas did compose the document herself.

[5] He is described (1.63) as 1 DUMU.NITA *E-TE-NU*, translated by OS 'einen alleinstehenden Knaben'. On this see below, fn. 55.

[6] An infant is designated as DUMU.NITA.GAB 'a boy nursing' (4.10) or DUMU.SAL.GAB 'a girl nursing' (1.54, 1.65, 3.2). Since these babies were not with their mothers, special provision must have been made for their needs; did the Hittites have bottles?

7 This woman, like the boy Palluwas (on whom see fn. 5), is called *E-TE-NU*. See below, fn. 55.

8 Cf. OS 48-51.

9 Cf. Laroche 76.

10 The only exception is *Su-na*-DINGIR-*LIM* in 2.7, 2.8, and 2.10. But a variant reading *Su-na*-DINGIR-*LIM-is*, as we would expect, also exists; see OS 23 fn. 10.

11 There are four exceptions. In three of these we find involved not one person but two, so that we would have needed 'their names' rather than the usual 'his name'; these are 1.13-14, 1.17-18, and 2.19-20. The fourth exception is 1.52, which is odd in other ways also; see fn. 16.

12 On *ŠU* see below, fn. 18.

13 There is considerable debate among scholars as to whether in English we should cite names in the nominative case (as we do Greek and Latin ones) or in the bare stem-form (as we do Sanskrit ones). The two leading American Hittitologists are divided on this point, Goetze favoring the former method, and Güterbock the latter. This moot point (which I discussed in *Wd.* 11.455-58, in the course of a review of Laroche's valuable *Onom.*, there giving my reasons for preferring to employ the inflected form, as I do in the current article) need not concern us here.

14 With peculiar ineptness syntactically, the two constructions can be combined in a single sentence, as in the very first set of names in the document, 1.10-11 ^{f}*A-ab-ba-a-aš* 1 DUMU.SAL-*ZU* ^{f}*Ni-wa ŠUM-ŠU* 1 DUMU.SAL-*ma* BA.UG$_6$ DUMU.NITA ^{m}*Du-du ŠUM-ŠU* 'Abbas, 1 daughter of her, Niwas her name, 1 daughter however died, a boy, Dudus his name'. Here, as is regular, we have three parallel entries, with *Abbas* in the nominative case, and *Niwa* and *Dudu*, being followed by *ŠUM-ŠU*, in the stem-form; but the march of the thought is interrupted by the interpolated clause '1 daughter died', where, however, no name is given.

15 There is just one example of the subject of a verb, 1.54-55 1 DUMU-NITA ^{m}*Te-me-it-ti ŠUM-ŠU A-NA* ^{m}SUM-*ya šal-la-nu-ma-an-zi pi-an-za* '1 boy, Temettis his name, (was) given to SUM-yas to bring up'. As an example of the object of a verb, I cite 2.5 1 DUMU.SAL ^{f}*Kum-mi-ya ŠUM-ŠU A-NA* ^{m}*Mu-ul-la šal-la-nu-ma-an-zi AD-DIN* '1 girl, Kummiyas her name, I gave to Mullas to bring up'; other examples of objects are 1.51, 1.56, 1.60, and 1.63-64.

16 The one exception is an amazing one, 1.52-53 1 DUMU.NITA ^{m}*Ta-ti-li-iš* ŠEŠ ^{f}*Ti-ta-i A-NA* ^{m}*A-pal-lu-ú šal-la-nu-ma-an-zi AD-DIN* '1 boy, Tatilis, the brother of Titais, I gave to Apallus to

bring up'. Here the usual formula would run '1 boy, a brother *of her*, Tatilis his name', with 'of her' referring to Titais (already mentioned in the preceding line). But instead we have '1 boy, Tatilis, a brother *of Titais*', and the presence *after* the boy's name instead of *before* it of the kinship phrase seems to have crowded out the *ŠUM-ŠU* which would have usually followed the boy's name. Therefore the name is given not in the stem-form but in a case-form. But the case-form is the nominative, not the accusative as the syntax demands. (Strangely, the editors make no comment on this solecism.) Perhaps Puduhepas had got used to the nominative as the only possible substitute for the stem-form elsewhere in the document. After all, she was not a native speaker of Hittite! However, she *could* use the accusative as object of a verb, as she shows in the very next line, 1.53, EGIR-*an-ma-an-ši-kán Ú-UL tar-na-aḫ-ḫu-u-un* 'however, I did not deliver him to him', where she correctly employs the accusative *-an* not the nominative *-as*; but this sentence is not formulaic. Still another oddity here is the form *Titai*, which is certainly not a genitive but the stem-form; for its use in this passage, see below, fn. 21.

17 Sommer, *HAB* 114, points out in opposition to Sturtevant that the names so treated are not themselves necessarily Akkadian. But that need not have prevented the scribe from writing them in Akkadian; he might have felt free to borrow an Akkadian form for a non-Akkadian name just as he often gave a Hittite form to a non-Hittite name. (I discuss this rather complicated question in *Wd*. 11.456, in the review already cited in fn. 13).

18 In Akkadian, *ŠU* is 'his' only, but the Hittites used it erroneously for 'her' as well, because their own *set* had both meanings.

19 I am accordingly writing the names with prepositions in Akkadian, thus departing from the practice of Hittite scholars in general (e.g. for the Märchen Friedrich, *ZA* 15.214-42, and for the epics Güterbock, *Kum*. and *Ull*.).

20 Thus we find Akkadian possessives in combination with nouns written in Sumerian as well as with those written in Akkadian.

21 Here again I am writing the names in Akkadian; see fn. 19. I should perhaps in the same way write ŠEŠ *TI-TA-I* in 1.52 of our own *Pud*., where the use of the stem-form with the kinship term ŠEŠ is perhaps to be accounted for in the same way as those noted here with AMA etc. This would in the interest of consistency require any one convinced that the stem-forms in *Pud*. before *ŠUM-ŠU* are Akkadian to write them in capitals also – which might seem too startling an innovation. The same problem again arises in connection with the

list of nine 'houses' later in *Pud.*, where in each instance the stem-form of the head's name follows the Sumerian É 'house'. But here as with *ŠUM-ŠU* a different explanation is possible; see fn. 32.

22 I doubt whether the construction really existed in any other language as a native one. (For possible borrowings, see fnn. 23 and 24.)

23 Tocharian A *ñom* and Tocharian B (or, better, Kuchean) *ñem* behave like Sanskrit *nāma*, and indeed the usage may be a Sanskritism. (I owe this information to my valued friend George S. Lane, to whom I am most happy to dedicate this article.)

24 In the interest of clarity and simplicity, I paraphrase all my formulas in Latin, no matter how barbarous this Latin may be. Actually, the construction in question is wholly alien to Latin. Vergil's use of *nomen* as an accusative of specification (*Aen.* 3.614 and 12.515), if the reading is correct (there is in each case a variant reading *nomine*), is clearly a Grecism, as the comparable usage in Tocharian may be a Sanskritism (see fn. 23).

25 The earliest certain instance known to me of 'in name' as an accusative of specification is the occurrence of *epiklēsin* in the Homeric Hymn to Apollo (1.385-86). Herodotus uses in this way both *epiklēsin* and the non-Homeric *epōnymiēn*; also possibly, though not positively, *ounoma* (4.12.1, 7.176.5, 8.138.3), and Xenophon probably so uses *onoma* (e.g. *Anab.* 1.2.23). But I know of no sure instance of *onoma* as an accusative of specification until Plutarch (*Solon* 12.4 *paida nymphēs onoma Baltēs*).

26 A much odder type of attraction of gender is regular in Old Persian, where the word for *nomen* is represented by what is to all intents and purposes an adjective *nāmă nāmā nāmă* in agreement in gender as well as in case with the word denoting the possessor of the name. (The form *nāmă* as a neuter might give us pause, since we would expect *nāmam*; but I suggest that the form owes its being to the analogy of the pronominal adjectives such as *aniyă aniyā aniyă* 'other'.)

27 Thieme (*Untersuchungen* 32) explains *dhenu* on the ground that a noun used as an appositive (or as a predicate) may assume the gender of the noun that it qualifies; but for my point it makes little difference whether we call *dhenu* a noun in apposition with *nāma* or an adjective modifying it.

28 *Tarquinio* can hardly be viewed as a noun in apposition with *nomine* (cf. fn. 27) because the ablative *nomine* used without a qualifying adjective would in such a passage as this probably not be possible.

29 For the complete passage, see Friedrich, *ZA* 15.220. To deal with

their meaning and construction in detail here would take us too far afield; I discuss them at length in my monograph.

[30] In part because *laman* in 3.7 has another adjective modifying it, *sanezzi*. But I think that this is not a serious objection, since *sanezzi laman* seems to constitute a single unit, *sanezzi* being a sort of stock epithet.

[31] The situation is further complicated by the fact that elsewhere in the story 'apparently the two brothers . . . bear names in *-a*-stems different from those in the earlier part of the text'. Certainly there can be no doubt that the older brother is not treated as being called HUL-*lus*, i.e. *Idalus*, for he is referred to repeatedly as HUL-*as*; I suggest that HUL-*as* represents *Huwappas*, another Hittite adjective (this one borrowed from Luwian) meaning 'bad'.

[32] It has occurred to me that we may have the same state of affairs in the enumeration of the nine 'houses', where É 'house', representing the Hittite neuter noun *pir*, is always followed by the name of the head written not in the genitive but in the form ending in *-a* (e.g. *A-ab-ba-a*, 3.26), *-i* (e.g. *Ši-mi-ti-li*, 3.40), or *-u* (*Ku-uk-ku*, 3.49). Can these too be adjectives, 'the Abba-house', 'the Kukku-house', etc.? But here as in 1.52 ŠEŠ *Ti-ta-i*, the juxtaposition of the word written in Sumerian may account for the use of the stem-form; see fn. 21.

[33] And nowhere else, according to Laroche (70). But OS (42 fn. 1) cite an instance from an unpublished text, *Bo.* 1602.10 ^{f}*Ú-da-tiš* ^{f}*Ú-wa-šu-na-tiš*, where *Udatis* is the name of a girl (does this text perhaps belong to our *Pud.*?), and also an instance from *KBo* 10.10.3.4, where it is the name of a woman.

[34] For this reason I write it everywhere with a capital, although this is not done by either Laroche or OS. And I transcribe its determinative everywhere as F (i.e. 'female'), departing from the custom of OS, which is evidently to use f for a proper noun denoting a female and to keep the Sumerian SAL for a common noun denoting a female.

[35] Laroche, who declares that the word cannot be a proper noun (70), did not know these three passages.

[36] We have *Pí-iz-zu-ur-*. Is it not likely that this mutilated form also ended in *-eni*?

[37] We also find a form in *-eni* in 1.59 1 SAL-*TUM* ^{f}*Kat-ti-it-ta-ḫi* ^{m}*Ta-ti-li-e-ni ŠUM-ŠU* and in 2.34 DUMU.SAL ^{m}*Pár-zu-u-e-ni* (the latter not commented on by OS). In the first of these the preceding female noun *Kattittahi* is clearly a proper name; it recurs in the following line as the name of a second individual, the niece of the

first one. In the second, the preceding noun is a kinship term ('daughter'), like ŠEŠ in 1.52 (on which cf. fn. 21) and – in my opinion – our own *udati*.

38 In that case all the *-eni* names with *Udati* are presumably to be viewed as bare stems, and are to be explained just like the other stem-forms as either Akkadian spellings influenced by the following *ŠUM-ŠU* (and thus influencing the preceding *Udati*), or neuter adjectives agreeing with the preceding proper name *Udati* (which is then also a neuter adjective, agreeing with *ŠUM*, i.e. *laman*).

39 Note that in 1.59 and 2.34 (both quoted in fn. 37), in which there is no such clear indication of the sex of the male person involved, the *-eni* form does have a masculine determinative.

40 In his *Onom.* (135) he lists *Temetteni* and *Zakappauteni* as examples of formations with the suffix *-ni*, along with names in *-ani*, *-ini*, and *-unni* (note that he cites all names in their 'forme non fléchie'; see his Préface, p. 5). As will be noted directly, he considers the stem-form *Temetteni* in *Pud.* as representing a genitive (*RA* 70), but obviously he would take the stem-form *Zakappauteni* (likewise presumably the other *-eni* forms) as representing a nominative.

41 They take cognizance of it 42 fn. 1, but do not seem to me to offer any conclusive argument against it; and they propose no substitute for it.

42 To the discussion by Goetze and Güterbock here referred to, I shall return presently.

43 We may compare *KUB* 13.2.3.21-32, cited by Güterbock, *IF* 60.205 fn. 1.

44 On the contrary, he says specifically that 'widow' is *udati*, and adds 'voir les détails ailleurs', by which he doubtless refers to his edition of *Pud.* However, Goetze (*JAOS* 74.189) definitely interprets *wannummiyas* as 'widow' in two of the passages cited by Laroche, *KUB* 8.12.2.5-6 (with duplicate 34.16.15-16) and 31.127.1.35-38; to Goetze's view of the latter I shall return below, as already noted in fn. 42.

45 Friedrich follows this in his *Wört.* (244), rendering *wannummiya-* by the general meaning 'alleinstehend', and following this with the more specific alternatives 'elternlos' and 'kinderlos'.

46 Laroche's rendering 'elle n'avait pas, dit-elle, d'enfants' is certainly incorrect; *-ši* must refer to the king, as Güterbock takes it, not to the queen.

47 There is no need to assume that the queen is called a widow here, for the point can certainly be not that she lacks a husband but that she lacks a son. The lack of a son of the royal couple is frequently

referred to in relation to both the king and the queen: see A.3.11, 23-24, 47-48, 53-54, 4.6, E_3.4.15 (probably), 19.

48 In the same note he adds that the situation is complicated by Laroche's recent explanation (in *RA* 43.70, i.e. his edition of *Pud.*) of *udati* as 'widow'.

49 I suppose there is no way of knowing which recension represents the original version. But it seems to me that a departure from the original version involving either the omission or the insertion of *wannummiyas* would be more likely to occur if the word is more or less a synonym of *kurimmas* than if the two constitute a specific and contrasting pair like 'widows and orphans'.

50 Since the precise Hittite spelling is irrelevant to our problem, I follow Güterbock's 'normalized' transcription.

51 The use of the words 'thou art father and mother' to generally oppressed persons is readily understandable. We find the same phrase similarly used in a general sense in line 21 of the same hymn (*JAOS* 78.239) and also in Mursilis' hymn to the Sun-Goddess of Arinna C.1.46 (as edited by Gurney, *AAA* 27.24) KUR-*e-aš ḫu-u-ma-an-da-aš at-ta-aš an-na-aš zi-ik* 'to all the countries thou art father and mother'. But as soon as we get down to specific relationships, it seems to me that the situation changes. Am I being too literal-minded if I point out that the aid of the Sun-God as 'father and mother' is appropriate for orphans but distinctly less so for widows?

52 This is Goetze's discussion (cited by him in *JCS* 20.52 fn. 10 as confirming Güterbock's suggestion of 'widow' as the meaning of *wannumiya-*) to which I indicated (fnn. 42 and 44) that I would return.

53 An interpretation already referred to above in fnn. 49 and 51.

54 Laroche in his citation of this passage in *RHA* 9.14 had rendered *kurimmas* by 'de l'estropié', but he showed his doubt by his use of an interrogation-point after this rendering, and he acknowledged in fn. 8 that this translation was 'entièrement conjecturale', being based on a supposed etymological connection with *kuer-* 'couper (un membre)'. This explanation seems to me highly dubious, but Friedrich tentatively accepted it in his *Wört.*, defining *kurimma-* (117) as 'Krüppel (?)'. However, in *Erg.* 1 (11) he offers 'Waise', following Goetze.

55 The same seems to be true of Akkadian *E-TE-NU*, used in 1.63 of a boy given to Utatis Tatilienis to bring up, and in 3.38 of a woman added to Sunailis' house, which consisted of four males and only one female. In both instances OS use 'alleinstehend' as a translation. Did this Akkadian word perhaps stand for Hittite *wannummiyas*?

(Friedrich, *Wört.* 307, defines *E-TE-NU* in 1.63 as 'Baumeister, Maurer'; this seems to me very strange.)

[56] We may compare WP 1.239-40 and Buck 131.

[57] As I have already shown by the skepticism expressed in fn. 54.

[58] Cf. the frequent strictures of the great Hittitologist Ferdinand Sommer, expressed by him *passim*. Also see Edgerton, *Lg.* 4.172-73 and *PAPS* 79.705-14, on the Mimansa theory of *yoga* vs. *rudhi* (in this connection I may perhaps refer to my mention of his views on the subject in my obituary of him, *JAOS* 85.4).

Ablaut, Accent, and Umlaut in the Tocharian Subjunctive

Warren Cowgill
Yale University

In this volume honoring George Lane, the dean of American Tocharianists and the man who first introduced me to these fascinating languages, it is a pleasure to contribute a study of a small corner of Tocharian verb morphology. May he find his pupil worthy of his teaching!

The various formations of the Tocharian subjunctive are listed and described by Sieg, Siegling, and Schulze 1931: 363-84, 421-84 and Krause 1952: 110-47, 218-309. This material is recapitulated in briefer form with additions and corrections by Krause and Thomas 1960: 221-33 and 1964: 77-263. The principal work so far on elucidating the prehistory of these formations is Lane 1959.

Most varieties of Tocharian subjunctive do not show root ablaut within the subjunctive stem. This is particularly true of those whose stems end in P(roto-)T(ocharian) **ä* alternating with **æ* (> A *a*, B *e*) according to the pattern of the Indo-European thematic vowels *e* and *o*. Just as Greek pl. *phérousi* 'they carry' has the same root vowel as sg. *phérei* 'he carries', so Toch. B *śanmeṃ* 'they will come' has the same root vowel as *śanmäṃ* 'he will come'.

But two varieties of subjunctive have vowel variation that can fairly be called ablaut. These are the subjunctives with endings added directly to a root ending in a consonant (the athematic subjunctive, class I of Krause and Thomas) or to a stem ending in PT **a*[1] (which becomes A *ā*, *a*, *ä*, or zero, depending on the neighboring sounds, and B *ā* when accented, *a* when unaccented; this is the *ā*-subjunctive, class V of Krause and Thomas).

The vocalism of the *ā*-subjunctive of language A is described by Sieg, Siegling, and Schulze 1931: 363-70. A basic vowel *ä*, *i*, or *u* remains unchanged in most forms built on the subjunctive stem-viz. the plural active and entire middle of the subjunctive itself, the optative, the verbal adjective in *-l*, and the verbal noun derived from this adjective - but is changed to *a*, *e*, or *o* respectively in the singular active subjunctive. Since A *e* and *o* generally result from monophthongization of Proto-Tocharian diphthongs, including **æy* and **æw*, and Tocharian *i* and *u* are morphophonemically *äy* and *äw*, the rule can be simply stated: replace PT **ä* by **æ*. Thus to the base *kälka-* 'go' the plural subjunctive is *kälkāmäs* 'we will go', the optative is *kälkim* 'I would go', and the verbal noun is *kälkālune* 'going', but the singular active subjunctive is *kalkam*, *kalkat*, *kalkaṣ*. To the base A *klisa-* 'sleep' the subjunctive active singular is *klesaṣ* 'he will sleep' but the optative is *klisiṣ* 'he would sleep'.

But a basic vowel *ā*, *e*, or *o* (continuing **a*, *ay*, *aw*) remains unchanged in all forms built on the subjunctive stem, e.g. sg. *āraṣ* 'will cease', pl. *āreñc* 'they will cease'.

While the prehistory of these non-ablauting bases is not yet clear, Lane 1959: 160, 173 has observed that the vocalism of the ablauting subjunctives corresponds exactly to that of the Proto-Indo-European perfect indicative (PT **æ* is the regular outcome of PIE **o*, as observed above). Whether this is indeed their source is not clear to me; in all respects except vowel timbre of the strong grade, the athematic root present (and aorist) would fit much better. At any rate, the formation indubitably continues a Proto-Indo-European ablaut pattern of the most archaic type.

A similar ablaut has not been observed in the athematic (class I) subjunctives of A; roots in *ä*, *i*, and *u*, that might be expected to show it, do not happen to be attested in the active singular subjunctive. Thus *tränk-* 'adhere' has a middle subjunctive *tränktär*, but no active **trankäṣ* has yet appeared.

But the more ample B materials show plentiful ablaut in the athematic subjunctive. Here PT **æ* appears regularly as *e*, and **ä* becomes *a* when accented (in the standard dialect)[2], *ä* or zero when unaccented. Thus to the root *pärk-* 'ask' the plural is *parkäṃ* 'they will ask', but the singular is *prekäṃ* 'he will ask' (with a 'metathesis' faithfully reflecting the PIE root shape *TReT* against the zero grade *TR̥T*, PT **TäRT*). Three other roots with this ablaut are listed by Krause 1952: 114-5 (note that for consistency the root 'touch' should be posited as *täk-*, not *tek-*, and that the zero grade *plätk-* 'emerge' is presumably analogic for **pältk-*).

Krause did not see that the ablaut pattern here is exactly like that of the A *ā*-subjunctive, because his only example of an active plural subjunctive was the *parkäṃ* cited above, and this seemed contradicted by *kweleṃ* 'they will drag along(?)'; but this word has a thematic ending and also can belong to a nonablauting *e*-root (*ekwalatte* 'irresistible', cited as possibly related by Krause 1952: 243, diverges in meaning and looks like a form from a base *kwäla-*). Lane 1959: 160 is clearly right in limiting full grade to the active singular of the subjunctive.

In the root *ku-* 'pour', morphophonemic *äw* appears as *u*: act. sg. *kewu*. 'I will pour', mid. *kutär* 'will be poured'. *Ru-* 'open' lacks strong forms; but note the active plural *ruwäm*. In *yäp-*'enter', *yänm-* 'attain', and *wätk-* 'separate, decide' the adjacent labial has umlauted **æ* to *o*: *yopäṃ*, *yonmäṃ*, *wotkäṃ* (the latter two are the only athematic forms of their roots, which otherwise act like *a*-bases); *kewu* may have restored *e* analogically on account of *kowu** 'I will kill'.

Otherwise, athematic B subjunctives to roots in *ä*, *i*, and *u* are mostly not attested in the active singular. Note *nakäṃ*, Sieg and Siegling 1949: 27a5, which is third plural 'they will destroy' of the athematic transitive subjunctive regularly paired with the medio-passive *e*-subjunctive *nke-* 'will perish', not singular as supposed by Sieg and Siegling in their translation. It is a third example, along with *parkäṃ* and *ruwäm*, for zero grade in the active plural of the subjunctive. Significant lack of ablaut coupled with palatalization of root-initial consonants permits assignment of several subjunctives securely to the thematic class. Thus *śilmaṃ-ne* 'will give him permission' (*śalmäṃ** without the enclitic) would be **kelmäṃ* if it were athematic; similarly *klyin-ne, klin-ne* 'will have to [do] it' must be from thematic **kl(y)iñäṃ*, not athematic **kleynäṃ*. *Campäṃ* 'will be able', pl. *campeṃ*, is also clearly thematic, and there is no reason not to assume the same of it in language A and when used in indicative value.

A different case is *yä-* (< PIE **i-*) 'go'. This subjunctive is unquestionably athematic, but there is no trace of a full grade **eyu*, **eyt*, **eyṃ*. Instead the present indicative *yam, yat, yaṃ* etc. functions as subjunctive also. Athematic presents have no ablaut in Tocharian, and it seems likely that *yam* etc. are primarily indicative, used secondarily as subjunctive (in A a distinction in mood was made – or kept – by using different roots).

At least one ablauting root seems to have gotten fixed in the strong grade. Corresponding to A *träṅk-* 'adhere', B has non-ablauting *treṅk-*, which plausibly arose in the strong grade of the subjunctive; generalization of *e* would have been favored by the existence of a second root *träṅk-* 'lament'.

In B, as in A, athematic subjunctives to roots in vowels other than *ä, i, u* normally show no ablaut. Only two roots with **a* show *o* rather than the expected *ā* in the active singular subjunctive. These are *kaw-* 'kill', subj. *kowän*, verbal noun *kāwälñe*, and *ara-* 'cease', whose causative *ārṣäṃ* 'leaves' is formed – like all causatives – without the final *-a-* and has in its subjunctive besides optative *āri* and infinitive *ārtsi*[3] a 3d. sg. subj. *oräñ-c* 'will leave thee' (there seems no need to set up a separate root *or-* to accommodate this and some preterit forms, as Krause does, 1952: 226). With these contrast *āyu* 'I will give' and *yāmu* 'I will make'; I cannot explain the difference.

A single ablaut pattern thus underlies both the A *ā*-subjunctive and the B athematic subjunctive, and is latent in the A athematic subjunctive. That the same pattern applies to the *ā*-subjunctives of B has not yet been clearly stated in print to my knowledge, owing principally to complications introduced by umlaut and accent.[4]

As in A, so in B, *ā*-subjunctives to roots in PT **a, ay, aw* (B *ā, ai, au*) do not ablaut. E.g. the base **taka-* 'be' has subj. sg. *tākaṃ* 'will be', pl. *tākam* 'we will be', *tākaṃ* 'they will be', opt. *tākoym* 'I would be'; **tsayka-* 'shape' has subj. *tsaikaṃ* 'will shape', opt. *tsaikoṃ* 'they would shape'; **kawta-* 'split' has subj. act. *kautaṃ* 'will split', mid. *kautatr* 'will get split'.

As far as the evidence goes, all these subjunctives – they number at least 64 – have root accent; this is indicated by the regular writing of PT **a* as *ā* in the first syllable and as *a* in the second. Apparent exceptions are so few that they can confidently be labeled nonstandard spellings, even in the base **nana-* 'show oneself' where the three attested forms have only *a* in the first syllable and *ā* beside *a* in the second.

This root accent does not fit the rule for accent in Tocharian B given by Krause 1952: 10 and repeated by Krause and Thomas 1960: 43, according to which disyllables were accented on the first syllable and longer words on the second. To be sure, the *ā*-subjunctive is mentioned (Krause 12, Krause and Thomas 44) as an exception, but the explanation offered does not account very well for an exception to an accent as regular and automatic as Krause and Thomas suppose it. Instead, as Winter has several times observed to me, the accent of Tocharian B does not depend merely on the number of syllables in a word, but must be determined empirically for each word or category. Krause's rule works for the preterits associated with the *ā*-subjunctive, where the accent is basically on the second syllable, as in *takāwa* 'I was', *takās* 'ye were', *takā-ñ* 'was to me', but is automatically retracted to the initial of disyllables ending in vowel or *-ṃ*, as in *tāka* 'was'; but it does not work for the subjunctive, and there is no reason a priori to label the one formation regular and the other irregular.

Again as in A, the B *ā*-subjunctives to roots in *ä*, *i*, and *u* do exhibit vowel variation. But the strong grade to *ä* is not *e*, as we should expect from the *a* of A *kalkam* and the *e* of B *prekäṃ*, but *ā*; thus to the base *kärsa-* 'know' the 1st singular active subjunctive is *kārsau* and the 3d sg. *kārsaṃ*; to *pälska-* 'think' the 1st singular is *plaskau* (with *a* a dialectal spelling for *ā*) and the 3d *plāskaṃ*. *i-* and *u*-roots are less clearly aberrant, since no sure example of an *i*-root in full grade occurs in the material known to me,[5] and the spelling *au* in *u*-roots like *sraukaṃ* 'will die' to the base *sruka-* is a frequent outcome of PT **æw* as well as of **aw*, especially in the 'standard' dialect of Šorčuq. But it is remarkable that beside the seven occurrences of *au* given in Krause 1952 there is no instance of e_u, which in other morphemes occurs beside *au* as a spelling for the reflex of PT **æw* (Krause 1952: 6).

Lane 1959: 169 saw that the distribution of strong and weak grades in the B *ā*-subjunctive is the same as in A, but did not try to explain the unexpected timbre of the strong grade. Krause and Thomas 1960: 60 say that ablaut of *ä* and *ā* is 'offenbar analogisch neu aufgebaut,' but not what it is analogic to. The true explanation is an umlaut first called to my attention by Werner Winter in 1960, and since briefly mentioned by him in print, Winter 1962: 32-3.

PT **æ* followed in the next syllable by **a* developed in the daughter languages like PT **a*. This change of **æ* to **a* was later than the hypothetical undifferentiated parent language of A and B, since the rules for the two languages are slightly different (a point not mentioned by Winter). While in B every **æ* before **a* was affected, in A it appears that **æ* was umlauted only when, to judge by the B evidence, it was unaccented. Thus in the subjunctive, where B forms like *kāskat* 'you will scatter' and *tsāṅka-ne* 'there will arise to him' indicate root accent in strong forms regardless of the accent elsewhere, A *kalkam,* not **kālkam,* exhibits no umlaut. (Similarly B *śtwer,* A *śtwar* 'four (m.)' and B *śtwāra,* A *śtwar* 'four (f.)' are regular from PT masc. **śtwǽr,* fem. **śtwǽra,* although here B *śtwāra,* being a disyllable ending in a vowel, furnishes no direct evidence for the position of the prehistoric accent). But the reduplicating syllable of the past participle, which is normally **Cæ-*, as in B *kekamu,* A *kakmu* 'come', appears as **Ca-* in both languages before a root syllable containing **a,* e.g. B *papaikau,* A *pāpeku* to the base **payka-* 'paint, write', B *kakārpau,* A *kākärpu* to **karpa-,* Similarly the negative prefix, which is regularly **æ(n)-*, as in B *ekamätte* 'not (yet) come', A *asinät* 'insatiable', appears as **a-* in B *aknātsa,* A *āknats* 'ignorant' from PT **æknátsa.* Both reduplicated past participles and combinations with the negative prefix clearly have root accent in B; if we suppose the same accent once existed in A, we can neatly explain the contrast between *pāpeku* etc. with umlaut and *kalkam* etc. without it. This would mean in turn that the accent of B is essentially that of Proto-Tocharian, and that the vocalism of A forms like *kākku* 'called' vs. B *kakākau* reflects a secondary accent shift in A.[6]

Outside the active singular of the subjunctive proper, the vocalism of these *ā*-subjunctives to roots in *ä, i, u* has been puzzling in that the first syllable often has *a* instead of *ä* or zero, e.g. *karsatsi* 'to know', while the second often has *a* instead of *ā,* as in *karsatsi, srūkalñe* 'dying', *rītatsi* 'to seek'. Krause (1952: 116; cf. Krause and Thomas 1960: 221, 227) was led by his a priori accent rule to suppose that some of the *karsa-* forms contained the same basic vocalism as *kārsaṃ,* but with a different accent, while others might reflect a root vocalism *ä.* But this ignores the ablaut pattern observable in all the other ablauting subjunctives of Tocharian, and does not account for the *a* of the second syllable in *karsatsi, srūkalñe, rītatsi* etc.

Lane 1959: 169 correctly stated that the radical *a* of *karsatsi* etc. comes from PT **ä*, but did not expressly disavow Krause's accent rule. But in fact these *ā*-subjunctives with *a* in the second syllable have root accent, just like *tākam*. The only difference is that while all B *ā*-subjunctives to roots in *ā, ai, au* accent the root syllable, some roots in *ä, i, u* accent the first syllable and some accent the second. Determination of which group a particular root belongs to is not always easy; decisive forms may be lacking, or the dialectal and scribal fluctuation in use of *ä, a,* and *ā* may make the evidence conflicting. Thus the form *maskālläññe* 'being' is impossible as it stands, but can be equally well emended to *maska-* from **máska-* or to *mäskā-* from **mäská-*. Of 71 or so relevant roots, I find 31 where initial accent seems probable, 24 candidates for postinitial accent, and 16 where I wouldn't care to hazard a guess. Some good examples of noninitial accent are *tsäma-* 'grow', 3d pl. mid. subj. *tsmāntär* (opt. *tsamoy*, if rightly segmented and translated, has regular retraction); *lipa-* 'remain behind', 3d sg. mid. subj. *lipāträ*; *muska-* 'get lost', inf. *muskātsi*[7].

Understanding of the basic patterns helps to sort out aberrant spellings. Thus inf. *tārkatsi* 'to abandon', mentioned by Lane loc. cit., is probably not an Ablautentgleisung but rather only a misspelling for *tarkatsi*, which occurs. The 3d sg. *krāstäṃ* 'will cut off' is, as Lane implies, a spelling for *krāstaṃ**, not an intruder from class I as supposed by Krause 1952: 126. *kätka-* 'cross over' does not really lack ablaut, since the only active singular forms, *katkat* and *katkaṃ*, are from an area where confusion of *a* and *ā* is particularly frequent.

Ablaut seems really lacking in *iya-* 'fahren', *śuwá-* 'eat', *läká-* 'see', and *tättá-* 'place'. Here in *śuwat, śwāt* 'thou wilt eat', *śūwaṃ, śwān-* 'he will eat', and *iyaṃ* 'he will go' the lack of ablaut is transparent; and in *lakau* 'I will see', *lakaṃ* 'he will see', *tattaṃ* 'he will place', *a* is only **ä* secondarily accented in disyllables ending in vowel or *ṃ*, as is shown not only by its frequency and lack of variant spellings, but also by unretracted *lkāt* 'thou wilt see', *lkā*(*n*)- 'he will see'.

But *iya-*, *läká-*, and *śuwá-*, like the *yä-* discussed previously, function also as indicatives (in A, *lkā-* is only indicative)[8] and so admit the same explanation as it. And *tättá-*, competing with a thematic subjunctive *tāṣäṃ*, *tāseṃ* to a base with *s*-extension, appears to be closely related to the past participle *tättā*$_u$, indeed may be a back formation on it. Since this past participle is clearly reduplicated, it is strictly the *a*, not the *ä*, of *tättá-* that is the root vowel, and so it belongs to the same nonablauting group as *táka-* 'be', *ay-* 'give'. The same explanation applies to *iya-* if it is a straightforward development of PIE **yā-*, and may apply to *läká-* and *śuwá-*, whose etymologies I do not know; but it cannot apply to *yä-* from PIE **ey-*, *i-*.

An inverse case would be *pärska-* 'fear', in which it seems that subj. sg. *prāskaṃ*, pl. *parskaṃ* is used as indicative also. But the A present *praskmār*, *praskatär* (B **proskotär*) implies a present base PT **praska-*, and the B present may result from contamination of this base with the **pärska-/præska-* (> **praska-*) of the subjunctive.

It appears then that when the results of accent and umlaut in B are taken into account, the ablaut of *ā*-subjunctives and athematic subjunctives in both Tocharian languages follows a single pattern: roots with PT **a*, **ay*, **aw* (B *ā*, *ai*, *au*, A *ā*, *e*, *o*) keep these vowels unchanged (except for the *o* in B *kowän*, *oräñ-*) while roots with PT **ä*, **i*, **u* replace these vowels with PT **æ*, **æy*, **æw* in the active singular subjunctive. Although the Proto-Indo-European source of these formations has not been discovered with certainty, it is clear that the athematic and the *ā*-subjunctives of Tocharian are in origin one, the difference depending only on the shape of the verb base, and that they continue the well known pattern of Proto-Indo-European athematic verb formations, in which only the predesinential morpheme ablauted.[9]

[1] The source of this **a* is a matter of controversy. I follow Werner Winter in thinking it not a mood sign but a component of the verb base, partly for reasons expressed at the conclusion of this paper and partly because it regularly recurs outside the subjunctive in the imperative, the preterit, the past participle, and often in the present as well.

[2] On graphic alternation of *ä*, *a*, and *ā* in B see Krause 1952: 1-4, Krause and Thomas 1960: 48.

[3] In B the infinitive is usually made on the subjunctive stem.

[4] The ideas set forth below owe very much to the stimulus and helpful hints of Werner Winter, in whose teaching and publications they are largely implicit. But to the best of my recollection, the points on which I do not give specific credit to Winter were worked out independently by me between September 1965 and August 1966.

[5] In a version of this paper read to the Linguistic Society of America in July 1966, I suggested that *saikaṃ* 'will step' beside present *siknaṃ* might be full grade to a base *sika-*. But Winter pointed out that we probably have here rather a contrast between present base *sika-* and nonpresent base *sayka-*, of the same type as e.g. pres. *päla-*, nonpres. *pala-* 'praise' in B pres. *pällātär* (< **päl-n-á-*), subj. *pālamar* (< **pála-*), pret. *palāmai* (< **palá-*), past part. *papālau* (< **pæ-pála-*).

[6] I do not know why negative prefix and reduplication have PT **æ(n)-* and **Cæ-* instead of the **ä(n)-* and **C'ä-* that seem regular from PIE **n̥-* and **Ce-*. Perhaps there is some connection with the **æ* instead of **'ä* in the subjunctive.

[7] There is some indication of a similar accent dichotomy in athematic subjunctives, e.g. *taśim* 'I would touch' from **tắk-* but *yamim* 'I would make' from **yam-́*. Winter tells me there is a simple rule by which the accent of Tocharian verbs can be predicted, but the rule as communicated to me encounters several exceptions.

[8] Indeed, none of the examples which Krause 1952: 223 gives for *iya-* are subjunctive in value.

[9] Since writing this article I have seen that already in 1944 A. J. van Windekens, *Morphologie comparée du tokharien* 267, compared the vocalism of the ablauting Class I subjunctives of A to the Indo-European perfect indicative.

REFERENCES

Wolfgang Krause, 1952: *Westtocharische Grammatik*, Band I (Heidelberg, Winter).

Wolfgang Krause and Werner Thomas, 1960: *Tocharisches Elementarbuch*, Band I (Heidelberg, Winter).

Idem, 1964: *Tocharisches Elementarbuch*, Band II (Heidelberg, Winter).

George Lane, 1959: 'The formation of the Tocharian subjunctive', *Language* 35.157-79.

E. Sieg and W. Siegling, 1949: *Tocharische Sprachreste*, Sprache B, Heft 1 (Göttingen, Vandenhoeck & Ruprecht).

Emil Sieg, Wilhelm Siegling, and Wilhelm Schulze, 1931: *Tocharische Grammatik* (Göttingen, Vandenhoeck & Ruprecht).

Werner Winter, 1962: 'Die Vertretung indogermanischer Dentale im Tocharischen', *Indogermanische Forschungen* 67.16-35.

The Correspondences Among the Mid Vowels of Tocharian

Thomas G. Reitz
Columbia University

George Lane wrote in 1938, 'It is . . . the problem of the relationship of Tocharian to the other Indo-European dialects which has most interested scholars from the very beginning, while very little time has been devoted to the comparative study of the two dialects themselves'.[1] This statement still holds true. Although the first step in tracing the prehistory of the phonology of related languages is ordinarily to compare the languages and to reconstruct from the evidence they provide, this procedure has not been followed in the case of the Tocharian dialects. Without such a reconstruction by means of the comparative method, further etymological work is very difficult.[2]

The apparent irregularity of the correspondences among the mid vowels has posed some of the most complex problems of Tocharian phonology, and students of Tocharian have had to be content with rules of correspondence which have many exceptions. Lane discusses these problems at length in his 1938 article.[3] It is from the groundwork laid by Lane in that article that this paper proceeds.

The correspondence of A *a* to B *e* is extremely common. A few examples are A *ak*, B *ek* 'eye'; A *pats*, B *petso* 'husband'; A *mañ*, B *meñe* 'moon'; A *kam*, B *keme* 'tooth'; A *wak*, B *wek* 'voice'; A *saku*, B *sekwe* 'pus'; A *pracar*, B *procer* 'brother'. Also, A *a* corresponds to B *o* in such words as A *pracar*, B *procer* 'brother'; A *praski*, B *proskiye* 'fear'; A *aratär*, B *orotär* 'listens'; A *oṅkaläm*, B *oṅkolmo* 'elephant'; A *orpaṅk*, B *orpoṅk* 'platform'; A *potatär*, B *pautotär* 'flatters'.

There are, however, a number of words in which the correspondence of A *e* to B *e* occurs: A *eṃts*, B *entse* 'envy'; A *erkät*, B *erkatte* 'unfriendly'; AB *eṅkäl* 'passion'; AB *tseṃ* 'blue'; AB *lek* 'appearance'; A *ke*, B *kete* 'whose'. Many examples of the correspondence of A *o* to B *o* are also found: A *oṅkaläm*, B *oṅkolmo* 'elephant'; A *orpaṅk*, B *orpoṅk* 'platform'; A *okät*, B *okt* 'eight'; A *klyom*, B *klyomo* 'noble'; A *orkäm*, B *orkamo* 'dark'; A *yoñi*, B *yoñiya* 'domain'.

The situation is further complicated by the occurrence of the correspondence of A *o* to B *e*. Some examples are A *ñom*, B *ñem* 'name'; A *cmol*, B *camel* 'birth'; A *omlyi*, B *emalya* 'heat'; A *porat*, B *peret* 'axe'; A *opyāc*, B *epiyac* 'zur Erinnerung'; A *oṅk*, B *eṅkwe* 'man'.

These various correspondences among the mid vowels may be represented in the table

A	*a*	*a*	*e*	*o*	*o*
B	*e*	*o*	*e*	*o*	*e*

From these correspondences it is possible to reconstruct Common Tocharian[4] phonemes by means of the comparative method, employing the principle of reconstructing a unit for each correspondence for which no phonological conditioning can be found. For the correspondences of A *e* to B *e* and of A *o* to B *o* the obvious reconstructions are **e* and **o* respectively. A *a*, B *e* cannot be derived from **e*, nor can A *a*, B *o* be derived from **o*, as no phonological conditions can be determined. It is necessary, therefore, to consider these correspondences to be the reflexes of other CT phonemes: A *a*, B *e* may be viewed as the reflex of CT **ε*, and A *a*, B *o* as the reflex of CT **ɔ*. The correspondence of A *o* to B *e* occurs only in the proximity of certain labial consonants and appears to be due to a sort of assimilation of vowel quality to be labiality of neighboring consonants, or labial attraction,[5] in A. It is not possible to derive A _o_, B _e_ from *_ε_, since *_ε_ becomes A _a_ in all environments, including labial, as in A _mañ_, B _meñe_, A _pats_, B _petso_, and A _saku_, B _sekwe_. But CT *_e_, reflected by A _e_, B _e_, apparently does not occur in labial environment, and so the correspondence of A _o_ to B _e_ may be considered to be the reflex of CT *_e_ before and after *_p_ and *_m_ and before *_kw_. *_e_ apparently remains in A in the proximity of *_w_, as shown by A _twe_, B _tweye_ 'dust'. CT *_e_, then, would remain in both dialects, except when it would become A _o_ because of labial attraction; *_o_ would remain in both dialects; *_ε_ and *_ɔ_ would merge with *_e_ and *_o_ respectively in B and both would become _a_ in A. The correspondences of these CT vowels with the mid vowels of A and B would be

CT	*_e_	*_e_[6]	*_o_	*_ε_	*_ɔ_
A	_e_	_o_	_o_	_a_	_a_
B	_e_	_e_	_o_	_e_	_o_

Following are a few examples of the development of the CT mid vowels in the two dialects.

CT *_e_ > AB _e_: CT *_entse_ > A _eṃts_, B _entse_; CT *_tsen_ > AB _tseṃ_; CT *_lek_ > AB _lek_.

CT *_e_ > A _o_, B _e_: CT *_ñem_ > A _ñom_, B _ñem_; CT *_perεt_ > A _porat_, B _peret_; CT *_enkwe_ > A _oṅk_, B _eṅkwe_.

CT *_o_ > AB _o_: CT *_onkɔlmo_ > A _oṅkaläm_, B _oṅkolmo_; CT *_klyomo_ > A _klyom_, B _klyomo_; CT *_yoñiya_ > A _yoñi_, B _yoñiya_.

CT *_ε_ > A _a_, B _e_: CT *_εk_ > A _ak_, B _ek_; CT *_mεñe_ > A _mañ_, B _meñe_; CT *_pεtso_ > A _pats_, B _petso_.

CT *_ɔ_ > A _a_, B _o_: CT *_prɔcεr_ > A _pracar_, B _procer_; CT *_onkɔlmo_ > A _oṅkaläm_, B _oṅkolmo_; CT *_ɔrɔtär_ > A _aratär_, B _orotär_.

The reconstructions proposed in this paper offer a solution to some of the problems relating to the Tocharian mid vowels, namely, the seemingly irregular correspondences between the two dialects. Many problems of course remain, since no account has been taken of the correspondences with Proto-Indo-European. But reconstruction by means of the comparative method is a vital step in the study of the prehistory of these vowels; it is only by way of this initial step that the remaining problems can be solved.

1 'Problems of Tocharian Phonology', *Language* XIV, p. 20.

2 Krause and Thomas remark, 'Wie schwer würde es vergleichsweise sein, etwa das Mittelhochdeutsche ohne jegliche Kenntnis anderer germanischer Sprachen mit anderen indogermanischen Sprachen systematisch zu vergleichen!' (*Tocharisches Elementarbuch* I, Heidelberg, 1960, p. 6) And, 'Es ist noch nicht möglich, den toch. Vokalismus, von gewissen Grundzügen abgesehen, mit dem des Indogermanischen zu vergleichen, weil uns jegliche Vorform des Toch. fehlt'. (P. 52) Usually, if no earlier form of related languages is attested, one is reconstructed before work proceeds.

3 *Language* XIV: the mid vowels are discussed on pages 28 to 36. Cf. Krause and Thomas, *Tocharisches Elementarbuch* I, pp. 53-57. The words cited here were taken from these two sources and from the glossary in *Tocharisches Elementarbuch* II, Heidelberg, 1964.

4 Hereafter abbreviated CT.

5 Krause and Thomas use the term Labialumlaut (*Tocharisches Elementarbuch* I, pp. 55 and 57). They try to derive A *o* from an earlier **a*.

6 Before and after **p* and **m* and before **kw*.

Latin *sōns*

Calvert Watkins
Harvard University

It has been recognized for almost a century that the Latin words *sōns* 'guilty' and *īnsōns* 'innocent' are by origin simply the present participle of the verb 'to be', and thus supply – from the purely formal standpoint – the element missing from the paradigm of *esse*.

This discovery goes back to W. Clemm in a study of 1870, *Curtius' Studien z. griech. u. lat. Gramm.* 3.328-44, who compared the group of derivatives exemplified by Skt. *satyá-* Goth. *sunja* (f.), ON *sannr* (*sađr*) 'true'; it received a 'glänzende Bestätigung' from Sophus Bugge in the following year (*ibid.* 4.204-6), who made the specific comparison of ON *sannr* in the expression *sannr at* 'guilty of'.

The cognates may be grouped into three semantic areas: those meaning 'true, real', 'sin', and 'guilty'. The facts are well known, and readily available in the dictionaries of Pokorny, Feist, Fritzner, de Vries, Jóhannesson, and Grein-Köhler. The first is found in the forms Ved. *satyá-*, Av. *haiθya-*, OP. *hašiya-*, Goth. *sunja* (**sunjis*), all of which presuppose **sn̥t-i̯ó-*, Gmc. **sun(đ)jáz*, and ON *sannr*, OE *sōđ*, OHG *sand* presupposing **sónto-*, Gmc. **sánþaz*. From these forms we have likewise denominative verbs, which have a characteristic legal meaning: ON *sanna* 'affirm, declare solemnly', OHG *ist sandonti* 'testificatur' (Gmc. **sanþōn*); OE *ge-sēđian* 'testificari' (Gmc. **sanþjan*); Goth. *sunjon sik* 'ἀπολογεῖσθαι', gasunjon 'δικαιοῦν' (Gmc. **sun[đ]jōn*). Both Gothic and Vedic Sanskrit show also a derivative in *-īno-*: RV *satīná-* (in composition) and Goth. *sunjeins*; but in view of the productivity of this suffix in both languages, particularly Gothic (Kluge, *Nom. Stammbildungslehre* § 199), the two may well be parallel but independent creations.

Finally we have in Latin the adjective *sonticus*, attested from the XII Tables (2.2) in the expression *morbus sonticus* and from Naevius (128 Ribb.) in *sontica causa* (both in Festus p. 372 Lindsay, cf. ibid. 99.464). Festus quotes the definition: *sonticum morbum in XII significare ait Aelius Stilo certum cum iusta causa*, which is quite correct: 'true, real, genuine, legally valid'. The legal connotation of *sontica causa*, and its clear derivation from *morbus sonticus*, is likewise apparent in Tibullus I 8.51 *parce, precor, tenero: non illi sontica causa est/sed nimius luto corpora tingit amor*. We have an exact parallel in the form *sunnis* in the Lex Salica (1,2) meaning 'legally valid hindrance (from appearing)', which is a Germanic loan word in the Latin text: cognates are OS *sunnea* 'Behinderung, Krankheit', OHG *sunna* 'rechtsgültiges Hindernis, vor Gericht zu erscheinen', and ON *syn* 'Leugnung', with the denominative verb *synja* 'leugnen, verweigern, freisprechen', which is formally identical with Goth. *sunjon sik*, *gasunjon* above. Lat. *sonticus* is important in that it shows the productive Italic suffix *-iko-*, and was in all likelihood formed only in Italic or Latin times. Since it preserves the meaning 'true, genuine' which is found in non-derived cognate forms, it follows that the Italic or Latin participial base *sont-* must have still had the basic meaning 'true' in Italic or Latin times, and thus that the development of the meaning 'guilty' is a Latin innovation which must be independent of the semantic development of ON *sannr*.

In all these forms we may observe the strong legal association; and it should be pointed out that the same legal context of the oath, testimony, or other solemn declaration is evident in Gothic from John 8.13-14: *so weitwodiþa þeina nist sunjeina* 'ἡ μαρτυρία σου οὐκ ἔστιν ἀληθής' . . . *sunja ist so weitwodiþa meina* 'ἀληθής ἐστιν ἡ μαρτυρία μου'.'. In his orginal study W. Clemm alluded to the meaning 'true' of the

Sanskrit participle *sánt-* as well as to the derivative *satyá-*. It is worthwhile noting that in the Rig Veda *sánt-* and its negative *ásant-* occur in a context which is specifically both legal and religious: In RV 7.104 = AV 8.4 is figured the oath of innocence professed by Vasiṣṭha accused of being a sorcerer. Lines 12b-d preface this with

> *sác cā́sac ca vácasī paspṛdhāte*
> *táyor yád satyám̥ yatarád ṛ́jīyas*
> *tád it sómo avati hánti ā́sat*

> 'The true and the false word are
> contending with one another. Which
> (ever) of the two is the true, which
> the right, that one does Soma favor;
> he smites the false one'.

The same clear association with solemn legal declarations is evident from the numerous compounds of the derivatives meaning 'true' with words meaning 'speech', 'word', or the like in many of the Indo-European languages. Thus we have RV *satyá-mantra-*, *satya-vā́c-*, AV *satya-vādín-*; ON *sann-ráđenn, sann-ordr, sann-yrdi, sann-sagđr*; OE *sōđ-cwide, sōđ-word, sōđ-gid*. The importance and antiquity of this legal and religious context, and in particular the fact of a ritual public profession of guilt or innocence, will be apparent below.

Since Jakob Grimm the group of Germanic cognates of English *sin* have been related to these forms: OHG *suntea*, OS *suntea*, OE *synn*, ON *synd* (?), on the assumption of Gmc. **sun(đ)jō* (= Goth. *sunja*), perhaps **sundī/sun(đ)jāz*, or finally also **sunjiþō*, a collective from **sun(đ)ja-*, if ON *synd* is not simply a Middle Low German loan word.

This etymology has periodically been questioned, but I can see no valid formal or semantic objection to it, so long as the semantic connection is properly appreciated (v. infra); for the sequence 'truth, reality' → 'sin' is scarcely a direct one.

What is important is to separate the forms meaning 'sin' in Germanic from the other cognates. In view of the formal identity with such forms as Goth. *sunja*, it is clear that there was a Germanic semantic development from 'truth, reality' to 'sin' which still requires an explanation. Despite the universal Christian acceptation of these derivatives in North and West Germanic, the formal identity with the East Germanic form requires the assumption of a pre-Christian Common Germanic term somehow connected with ritual religious usage.

The final meaning attested in derivatives is that of 'guilty', which is attested for Lat. *sōns* with its negation *īnsōns*, and for ON *sannr* (*saðr*). Both *sōns* and *īnsōns* are quite rare and poetic words in Latin, particularly the former (only once in Plautus); the monosyllabic nom. sg. *sōns* indeed appears to be attested only in Festus and the epitome of Paulus. In earlier authors they are used often predicatively, virtually as substantives (*TLL* s.v. *insons*), and usually absolutely, 'guilty' or 'innocent' both legally and morally, whether as attribute or predicate; the construction 'innocent of s.th.' is attested only from Ovid, Met. 13.149 *fraterni sanguinis insons*, and is quite infrequent thereafter.

It is clear from Plautus, as well as from *sonticus* of the XII Tables, that *sōns* is basically a legal form: Capt. 476 *ut in tribu sontes aperto capite condemnant reos*, where there is an intended contrast of a solemn ritual action with the preceding *de foro tam aperto capite ad lenones eunt*. But it is equally clear that both *sōns* and *īnsōns* are archaisms preserved only in poetic language in later Latin, since both are unknown as legal technical terms; *īnsōns* is wholly absent, and *sōns* only once appears (just to be glossed by *nocens*), in the *Vocab. Iurisprud. Rom.* We have to deal with very old Latin forms indeed. Yet as we have seen above from *sonticus*, the basic meaning of the stem *sont-* must have been 'true, real' still in Italic or prehistoric Latin times. Hence we are left with the same semantic problem as with the words for 'sin'; for the bridge between 'true, real' and 'guilty' is as unclear as that between 'truth, reality', and 'sin'.

The case of ON *sannr* is different. Here the basic meaning is clearly 'true', from the earliest times to the present-day Scandinavian languages, and the problem is to account for the secondary meaning of 'guilty' which is attested to my knowledge only in ON. The answer is not hard to find. For the meaning 'guilty' is found in earlier usage in only one syntactic context: the legal expression *sannr at* 'guilty of (s. th., always specified)': the one case which is specifically late and rare in Latin. Not only have we a particular syntactic acceptation of *sannr* 'true', but also one reinforced by a particular stylistic figure associated with a definite legal meaning, and most clearly exemplified in legal texts. The full expression is *kunnr oc sannr at*. Compare the following examples: *Gulaþingslov* § 24 *sannr at udáþom* 'guilty of the evil deed', *sannr at sokenne* 'adjudged guilty of the charge', *ibid.* § 26 *en ef madr verdr at þvi kunnr oc sannr at hann a gudsiviu sina* 'and if a man is accused and convicted of having possessed a spiritual kinswoman, (tr. Larson); Grágas 2.189 (1829 edition)*kuđr oc sađr orþinn at þiofscaþ* 'become known and proven to be a thief'.

The whole group of Scandinavian derivatives has now been subjected to a thoroughgoing philological and juridical examination by Klaus von See, *Altnordische Rechtswörter* (*Hermaea* NF 16) 222-35 (Tübingen, 1964). Since the views of this distinguished scholar of early Scandinavian legal texts are virtually identical with my own independent preliminary findings, I may simply here repeat his conclusion, founded on an impressive body of evidence, that 'die Verwendung von *sannr* i. S. von 'schuldig' sich Wahrscheinlich allein aus dem anord. Sprachgebrauch entwickelt hat'. The basic meaning of 'true', from 'das Seiende', is alone that which may be attributed to Gmc. **sanþaz,* and the Scandinavian forms do not constitute a valid parallel to Latin *sōns*.

The meaning of *sannr* is not 'guilty' in the abstract, but

rather 'found guilty of, convicted of' whether by a regular juridical process or not. The full expression *kunnr ok sannr at* (*þiófskaþ* etc.) may well be by origin a quasi-hendiadys; not so much 'recognized and convicted of (theft, etc.), erkannt und überführt (v. See)' – which has too 'modern' a ring – as simply 'known to be really (a thief, etc.)', with the full etymological sense of *sannr*.

It has been noted quite rightly by Benveniste, '*Être* et *avoir* dans leur fonction linguistique', *BSL* 55.114 (1960), and followed by V. V. Ivanov. *Obščindoevr., praslav., i anatol. jaz. sistemy* 266 (Moskva, 1965), that the semantic value of these nominal derivatives from the root **es-* preserve the original full lexical meaning of this verb as 'really, actually be, exist'. One may note the archaic use of the verb in the Hittite ritual phrase *apāt ešdu*, virtually 'so be it', quoted with a Luvian parallel by Ivanov (*op. cit.*, p. 56) from Götze, Tunnawi 33 n. 50, and Gurney, Hitt. Prayers 35 n. 11, 37 n. 4, 116.

The semantic development of a participle from 'really being, existing' to 'true' makes no difficulties. Lat. *est* on the plane of *parole* is precisely the equivalent of 'yes, right, true' on the plane of *parole* in modern European languages, witness the very interesting little metalinguistic poem *De est et non* in the Appendix Vergiliana. Norwegian *ikke sant*? with a form going back to the participle of the verb 'to be', is essentially similar in usage to German *nicht wahr*?, Spanish ¿*no es verdad*?, or for that matter colloquial American English *right*?

Yet while we can explain the meanings 'true, truth' for **sont-/sn̥t-* and derivatives, we are still equally distant semantically from the meanings 'guilty' and 'sin' which are in fact attested from Latin and Germanic respectively. From 'true' to 'guilty', or 'truth' to 'sin' (even abstracting the Christian association), is not an immediately self-evident semantic leap. Indeed E. Schroeder, in a formally unconvincing yet still rich article on 'Sünde and Schande', *KZ* 56.106-16 (1929), aptly qualified it as 'eine Luftbrücke'. If it is possible to understand 'der, welcher es war' (Jóhannesson), 'celui qui est réellement (l'auteur du délit)' (Benveniste), as the guilty party in a specific social context, on the plane of *parole*, it is far less easy to see how such an expression would come to be the general word for 'guilty' in the absence of such a context, and on the plane of *langue*. Still less easy is it to understand why 'that which really is' should mean 'sin', as in West Germanic.

It is doubtless for such reasons as these that Meillet in the *Dict. étym. de la langue latine*[4] s.v. *sōns* was led to say: 'Pour expliquer tout à fait le sens de *sōns*, il faudrait connaître les anciennes formules où figurait le mot'.

It is a tribute to Meillet's acuity of judgment that the ancient formula in fact exists; it is found in Hittite. In the second Plague Prayer of Muršiliš (ed. Götze, *Kl. Forsch.* 1. 161-251 [1929], cf. *ANET* 394-6) we read the following:

> § 6.3 *nu-za-kan kāš[a ANA PANI* ^{d}*IM waš]tul tarnaḫḫun ešziy-at iyawen-at* 'and lo!' I confessed my sin before the Storm-god (and said): 'It is (so). We did it'.
>
> § 9.5. *n-at-za-kan kāša ANA* ^{d}*IM* ^{uru}*Hatti* EN-*YA U ANA* DINGIR.MEŠ *BELU* MEŠ-*YA piran tarnan ḫarmi ešziy-at iyawen-at* 'and lo! I have confessed it to the Storm-god of Hatti and to the gods, my lords, (saying): 'It is (so). We did it'.
>
> § 10.6. *ammuk-ma-za-kan ŠA ABI-YA waštul tarn-[aḫḫun] ašān-at iyanun-at* 'but I confessed my father's sin, (saying): 'It is (so). I did it'.

In the first two passages we have the 3 sg. pres. finite verb *ešzi* in the archaic, pregnant sense 'is truly'. But in the third passage we have a syntactic nominalization, to the neuter singular participle 'truly being'. The verbal sentence is transformed to a nominal sentence, and the resultant form is identical with Latin *sōns*.

In both cases we have an overt suffixed subject pronoun; the neuter gender and the agreement in *ašan* make it clear that the pronominal subject stands for the sin itself, *waštul* (nt.) of the preceding sentence. It is the 'sin' or 'guilt' which exists, and the purpose of the confessional formula is to assert that existence.

We may note that in the first two passages it is a question of the general guilt of both father and son: *iyawen-at* 'we did it'; while in the third passage, syntactically transformed, it is his own personal guilt which the son Muršiliš formally avows, and undertakes to make restitution if this is necessary. For this reason one cannot accept Goetze's translation of *ašān-at* in *ANET* as 'it is only too true', an expression already used in § 9.3 to render the rather different *kikkištari QATAMMA*, and his omission of quotation marks wholly obscures the fact that *ašān-at* is an equally solemn verbal formula as *ešzi-at*, and quite possibly more so.

If we transpose the Hittite formulas into Latin, using *sōns*, the result is 'id est; id fecimus', 'id sons; id feci.' I suggest that Latin *sōns* is by origin specifically 'he who says *sōns*; and Gmc. **sunjō* 'sin' from **sn̥t-i̯ā* is the abstract-collective formed from just such an utterance in the Germanic confessional formula.

That is to say that we have in *sōns* and **sunjō* to deal with 'delocutory' forms, in the sense described by Benveniste in 'Les verbes délocutifs', *Studia Philologica et Litteraria in honorem L. Spitzer* 57-63 (1958). The same is clearly suggested by the *sác cā́sac ca vácasī* of the Vedic ritual discussed above, and by the many compounds meaning 'true word' and the like. An interesting onomastic parallel from the same general semantic sphere, though outside the legal and religious context, is furnished by the Polish family name *Ozajst*, derived from the exclamation *o za iste* 'oh, really', as Kuryłowicz informs me. The putative semantic bridge from 'existent, true' to 'guilty', from 'existence, truth' to 'sin' is thus a pseudo-problem; the semantic development of the Latin and Germanic forms must be explained through the channel of a ritual formula in a particular cultural sphere.

In view of the textual attestation of the participle in the Hittite formula, and the direct or indirect reflexes in Vedic, Germanic, and Latin, we are justified in terming our reconstruction not only an Indo-European form, but an Indo-European utterance: a fragment of the confessional formula, both for religious and for secular transgressions. This fact deserves to be put together with the remarkable equation of Hittite *tarna-* in the expression (in the passages above) *waštul tarna-* 'confess one's sin' with Tocharian A *tärnā-* in the phrase *puk maṅkant tarneñcäm* 'they absolve him of his sins' (*Toch. Sprachr.* 230 b 6) as shown by Ivanov, *op. cit.* 180; *Toch. Jazyki* 35).

The Truth, the Whole Truth, and.... Problems in Old Norse Linguistics

Ole Widding
The Arnamagnean Dictionary of Old Norse, Copenhagen

The widely held opinion that there are very few secrets left in the field of Old Norse linguistics, and that essentially the whole truth about the Old Norse language is accessible to anyone who cares to consult the works of such giants as Adolf Noreen and Finnur Jónsson, is unfortunately not true. The problems are numerous, and details badly needing further investigation can be found in every extant text from medieval Norway and Iceland. Whether it is desirable or not to find the whole truth about Old Norse, I do not know, but it would be regrettable if an overly optimistic view of the state of scholarship in this field were to hamper further research in Old Norse language and literature.

The initial work towards a new dictionary of the Old Norse language (Icelandic until 1540, Norwegian until c. 1370), to be published in Copenhagen under the auspices of the Arnamagnean Commission, has taught the staff that there are problems enough in the Old Norse material to keep many generations of Old Norse scholars busy and happy, and I think it proper and fit on this occasion to draw attention to the intricacies of Old Norse linguistics by a discussion of a related group of prepositions and adverbs. Investigations of details, like the one presented here, often enable us to give a more accurate description of, or reveal a little more of the truth about, the history of literature or Old Norse stylistics. It can now be positively stated, for example, that the language of the so-called legendary saga of King Olav the Saint is of a different kind than that of the miracles told at the end of the saga; a result that makes Sigurður Nordal's theory about the origin of the saga unlikely, as already on quite other premisses has been demonstrated by Anne Holtsmark in the introduction to the photographic reproduction of the MS (Corp. cod. Norvegicorum Medii Aevi, Quarto Serie vol. II). To take another example: It is now possible to demonstrate that the final chapters of *Heimskringla* (referring to chapters after 1130) make use of a language that is more modern in several ways than that employed in the rest of the book, and it is unsound to neglect this fact in speculations about the origin or composition of *Heimskringla*.

The problem I want to discuss here is the use of prepositions or adverbs as *mót, á mót, á móti, í mót, í móti, at móti* or simply *móti*.

A look in the older dictionaries yields very little information as to the use of these prepositions. In the dictionary by Johan Fritzner (s. *mót*) we find the different meanings: 'against', 'in return', 'towards' and so on, and further (s. *móti*) the information that *móti* can be used for *í móti*. From the dictionary of Cleasby and Vigfusson (*Icelandic-English Dictionary*, 1874, s. *mót* B II) we learn that all these forms (*móti, í móti*, and more rarely *at móti*) are used indiscriminately, as also an apocopated *mót*, qs. *móti* (*á mót, í mót*).

These are the main attempts so far to classify the forms and to describe their meaning.

The problems arise as soon as the total findings of the various prepositions in the oldest preserved Icelandic and Norwegian texts, registered in the two concordances mentioned below, are included in the investigation.

From ten manuscripts from the oldest literary period Ludvig Larsson (*Ordförrådet i de äldste isländska handskrifter*, 1891) has collected the combinations *á mót* and *á móti* as the most common. Besides, *at móti* is found; and the expression *í mót* is unusual.

In thirteen manuscripts or records representing the oldest extant Norwegian Anne Holtsmark (in *Ordforrådet i de eldste norske håndskrifter til ca. 1250*, 1955) has registered *á mót, í mót*, and *á móti*, the prepositions *í móti* (7 exs.), and the dative *móti* (10 exs.).

From this survey it is clear that in the oldest literary period (c. 1150-1250) there was a distinct difference in the use of these prepositions in Icelandic and Norwegian literature. The difference is stressed when the distribution of the forms characteristic of the Norwegian literature is included in the investigation. The forms are not used indiscriminately by the fifteen scribes whose vocabulary is listed. While *móti* is found with six of the scribes and thus can be said to be widespread, the combination *í móti* is only found with one of the fifteen scribes, and furthermore only in two of the chapters written by him, viz.: one group p. 126-127 in the homily 'In ascensione domini nostri Jesu Cristi. Sermo ualde necessaria' (Indrebø's edition (1931) p. 89-92), and a second group including examples from pp. 147-151 in the chapters dealing with Saint Olav 'In die sancti Olaui regis' and in 'Fra jartæinum hins helga Olafs konungs (Indrebø's edition pp. 108-111 and 112ff.).

About the year 1200 the preposition *móti* was in fairly common use in Norway, but apparently not in Iceland, and the preposition *í móti* was not used in Iceland, and, it seems, only in local use in Norway. To the explanation in Cleasby-Vigfusson's dictionary it should be added that *í mót* is not simply an apocopated form for *í móti*, used in Icelandic, where no *í móti* is registered, but must be dependent on the context (common in the connections *hér* or *þar í móti*).

To verify this result I consulted the vocabulary to the collection of old Norwegian laws compiled by Ebbe Hertzberg (1895). His references can be summarized like this:
í mót (2), *móti* (9), *á mót* (2), *mót* (1), *á móti* (1), and from the youngest set of laws *í móti* (2).

Of course, a survey like this cannot give an idea that is correct in every detail of the use of these prepositions in Norwegian laws; still, the material gives a hint that supports the theory of *móti* as an innovation of predominant character in the Norwegian language.

In that connection another observation becomes significant. It is a well-known fact that *mót-* and *móti-* alternate in compositions. One finds *móti-* and *mótburðr*, *móti-* and *mótganga*, *móti-* and *mótmæli*, *móti-* and *mótstaða*, and so on. In deverbatives and compositions of this kind, we can learn from the references in the dictionaries that the words with *móti-* as a first component most frequently – if not exclusively – represent Norwegian sources.

I have not followed up these facts by investigations in the vocabulary of scaldic poetry and the Edda poems because of metrical restrictions and heterogeneous manuscript tradition. Information is found in *Lexicon Poeticum*² 412b and in Gering, *Vollständiges Wörterbuch*, 1903 col. 698.

When this is compared with the use in modern Icelandic and in Faroese, we learn that a great simplification has taken place. In Icelandic the preposition *á móti* is dominant, while *móti* can be used in certain connections, in Faroese on the other hand *ímót* and *ímóti*, *mót* and *móti* are used side by side, as it seems with a semantic restriction as to the use of the two last-mentioned, which are used for 'towards' in chronological but not in spatial meanings.

The use of *mót* and combinations of *mót* as a preposition seems to be an innovation in the Scandinavian languages. For centuries there was competition between the old preposition *gegn* and *í gegn* and these newer prepositions. It is possible to follow this competition in several manuscripts. It is often seen that *gegn* in old MSS is being replaced by a construction with *mót* in copies, whereas the opposite is a very rare phenomenon. The legal language is of a very conservative nature;

in it *gegn* and *í gegn* is in common use. One can read nearly one hundred pages in the lawbook *Grágás* in search of *mót* (and the like), and when it appears at last, it is in a heading, where the text itself reads *gegn*.

We have seen that the use of *mót* alone, or preceded by *í* or *á* followed by either an accusative or a dative, or by *at* followed by a dative, is a fact from the oldest literary period; it is more surprising, perhaps, that the dative alone can be used with the same function, at least in Norwegian from the oldest literary period.

The use of a case of a noun as a separate preposition is not quite exceptional. From the Old Norse language can be mentioned e.g. *handa honum* used instead of *honum til handa*, and likewise *sakar* or *sakir e-s* (generally with the genitive, not with the accusative as suggested by Johan Fritzner and Leiv Heggstad in their dictionaries) which can be traced back to the construction *fyrir sakar* (*sakir*) *e-s*. In quite the same way one sometimes finds *móz* instead of the fuller expression *til móz við*.

As a comment to the following investigation it must be mentioned that it does not build on a mere counting of occurrences of the different words. In any single case it has been considered whether the different combinations occur as prepositions or as adverbs. Moreover, when they occur as prepositions, the *Aktionsart* of the preceding verb has been noticed, whether it indicates a movement or is an iterative or an imperfective. These observations are generally not mentioned here, except in cases where they seem to be of some interest.

As we have seen, there is a pronounced discrepancy between the use of prepositions built on the noun *mót* in Norway itself, in Norwegian compared with Icelandic, and in the oldest period of the preserved language compared with modern spoken language. Two questions arise now: is the information about the oldest period due to a statistic defect, and insufficient for any assurance; and is it possible to build a bridge across the centuries to connect the modern stage with the old one? It surely would be a formidable task to answer these two questions, and it is not possible to do it here. Still, I think it is possible to throw some light on a few minor questions that arise from the material already mentioned: to investigate whether it can be confirmed that the dative *móti* used as a preposition was a novelty in Norwegian that spread to Icelandic, and to find out what was the fate of *í móti* found in a few old Norwegian sources and in modern Faroese, but not in old Icelandic, and only in restricted use in modern Icelandic.

First a few words about the preposition *móti*. One cannot be deceived by the statistics gathered from the concordances mentioned above (Larsson, Holtsmark) for the use in Norwegian sources, and as a whole it can be asserted that this preposition is of much greater frequency in Norwegian sources than in Icelandic sources, where it is rather unusual especially in pure Icelandic texts. A survey of the use in some texts will prove that.

Thomas saga erkibyskups is a Norwegian product, preserved in MSS from before the year 1300, telling the sad story of Thomas Becket, the archbishop who was killed in Canterbury cathedral in 1170. The Norwegian main manuscript is dated back to c. 1280. In this manuscript *móti* dominates to such a degree that other possible constructions have been noticed only in a few places (e.g. *Her i mote* 56^4 and *i mote* 209 in Unger's edition 1869). This manuscript shows very clearly that *móti* in Norwegian could be used in all situations, and in all the different meanings of the word.

An investigation of other Norwegian texts confirms this result; an example is *Speculum regale*, or in Norwegian *Konungs Skuggsjá*. It is a work dealing with (1) geography, seamanship, commerce, (2) the king's duties, and (3) ethics. It has been suggested that the book was composed of three parts (as indicated). If so – and linguistic evidence really points in that direction – it can be said that *móti* is a common feature of all three parts of the text. Besides *móti á mót* and *á móti* are used as adverbs in a few cases.

We have seen that the authors (and/or scribes) of two of the most important Norwegian texts from the Middle Ages have accepted the dative *móti* as a preposition. It can be added that several MSS of Norwegian laws from the time 1275-1325 also make use of *móti* as a preposition and adverb; thus the older ecclesiastical law of the Frostathing, the ecclesiastical law of the Gulathing and that of archbishop *Jón* (1268-1282). From the last *móti* in some cases has been transferred to Iceland, as seen in the ecclesiastical legislation of bishop *Árni* of Skálholt (1269-1298). Closely connected with the law texts is the *Hirðskrá* (MS from c. 1325) where *móti* is the common form in the chief manuscripts from Norway, while the most important copies have converted into *í móti*, but since *í mót* and *í móti* are found in one of the chief Norwegian manuscripts, it cannot be stated with full certainty which form was the original one in the *Hirðskrá*.

The translation of Gauthier de Chatillon's poem *Alexandreis* to ON prose, known under the title *Alexanders saga*, is of primary interest on this point. In Icelandic MSS we are told that the translation was made by the Icelandic cleric Brandr Jónsson the winter he stayed in Norway before his consecration as a bishop. But a wealth of details in the language of the saga indicates that this statement, made more than a hundred years after the translation, cannot be true; and further, there is no indication of Brandr as the translator in the oldest MS; there is just an anonymous translator mentioning himself in this role.

Even if it is possible to distinguish between Norwegian parts, and Icelandic (or Icelandicized) parts of the translation, one cannot accept the theory of E. O. Sveinsson that the bishop during his stay in Norway had a Norwegian assistant;

for quite the same distinctions can be made in another old fragment of the saga; only the change is not found in the same places in these two MSS. All details lead to the conclusion that the translation was made by a Norwegian, and that a copy later was brought to Iceland, perhaps by Brandr Jónsson. To the many Norwegian features in the chief MS may now be added the fact that the translation generally uses the preposition *móti*, only now and then *ímót*, corresponding to what was found in old Norwegian MSS. It is almost unnecessary to mention that the fourteenth century Icelandic copies use *í móti*.

Also in the booklet *'En Tale imod Biskopperne'* (a speech against the bishops from c. 1200, but preserved in a much later MS) *móti* is dominating, while *á móti* is being used once, and *í móti* four times.

Another series of texts gives an idea of the way in which Norwegian translations lived on in Icelandic copies. In his edition of *Mariusaga* C. R. Unger edited a great many MSS, the correlation of which never has been fully investigated. In the course of preparation of The Arnamagnean Dictionary, we have been compelled to look into the problems connected with this collection of legends told about the Holy Virgin. It is in order to mention one of the results here. Three of the MSS used in the edition are closely related (namely L, S, and E). In S a part of the legends found in L are left out, whereas E has been shortened in another way. In E the characteristic stylistic features of the ornate style ('florissant stil') have been left out, to make the style more plain and simple. All three MSS make use of the preposition *móti*, but L more often than the others, L being closer to the Norwegian type of language in all the points where Norwegian and Icelandic differed, and in many cases the two Icelandic copies make use of *í móti* instead of *móti* in good accordance with current usage in Icelandic texts from the same time.

The use of *í móti* is surprising in more than one respect. In the oldest literary period it is found, as previously mentioned, only in certain parts of the Old Norwegian book of homilies and not in the group of Oldest Icelandic MSS. On that background it is surprising that *í móti* in the period 1250 until c. 1400 occurs in almost all sources and in most of them as the most current of the different combinations, and it is just as surprising that *í móti* in Icelandic has been subdued in favor of *á móti*, which is now dominating. The different features and various stages of this development cannot be described here in detail; but some about certain MSS must be given.

In the legendary saga of Saint Olav preserved in a manuscript of the 13th century (the text redacted c. 1240) *í móti* dominates, *móti* being found only now and then.

Strengleikar is the name of a translation into ON prose of some of Marie de France's poetic romances preserved in a MS of the 13th cent. There *í móti* is dominating as also in *Gyðingasaga*, a renarration of parts of the first book of the Maccabees and of Josephus's work on the history of the Jews. It is preserved in a MS of c. 1350, and *í móti* is also found in an old fragment of the *Gyðingasaga* of c. 1300.

The saga of king Sverre is preserved in five MSS and some fragments on vellum. A look into three of these MSS yields interesting information. The principal MS (AM 327,4^{0} of c. 1300) as a rule makes use of *ímót* or *ímóti*, both of them being used as preposition and adverb. Even if there are pages where *ímót* is dominating and sections where *ímóti* dominates, it is not possible to divide the text on the basis of this distribution or to describe the use as dependent on the context. More seldom *móti* is used; and only seldom *ámót, ámóti* and *at móti* are found. The question arises: does this mixed usage reflect the language of the author (or authors) or perhaps of the scribe?

To answer that question it is necessary to examine this point in other MSS of the saga. The saga is also found in the *Eirspennill* (AM 47 fol. of c. 1325), written by two scribes. The first one has preferred *móti* and *í móti*; the second one almost invariably writes *ámót* and *ámóti*. It can be added here that the same usage as found with the second scribe also is the standard in the *Fagrskinna* version of the saga of the Norwegian kings, but only in the A-version of *Fagrskinna*.

Also in the famous *Flateyjarbók* the saga of king Sverre is found. In that version we find to some extent the same usage as in AM 327, 4⁰: *ímót* and *ímóti*. It is obvious from other criteria that the scribe has copied from two different MSS belonging to two different versions of the saga; but the use of *mót* (etc.) gives no clear indication of where the change took place: we find alternately *á mót* and sometimes *á moti* and even *mót* both before and after the change.

On the whole it therefore must be said that the MSS of the saga of king Sverre with regard to the preposition discussed here reveal the writing habits of the different scribes more than anything else, but this of course does not exclude the possibility that some of the variations are due to influences from the original.

Closely related to the group of oldest Icelandic MSS is AM 623,4⁰ ed. by Finnur Jónsson under the title *Helgensagaer*. The most common preposition in that MS is *á mót(t)* (13 exs.) used both as a preposition and as an adverb; *á móti* occurs twice after verbs indicating a movement; *at móti* and *í mótt* each occurs once.

According to this survey, AM 623,4⁰ could be a MS from the oldest period. But it is wrong, though generally believed, that the MS is of c. 1250/1275. It must with all certainty be dated to some year after 1300. However, it is written by a novice who tried to copy his original, which must have been quite old, most likely of c. 1200.

It would certainly be of enormous interest to have a full survey of the usage in all the sagas of the Norwegian kings. However, an investigation on that scale would demand a renewed exact reading of all the texts in question. Only a little contribution to this noble project can be made here. One of the oldest MSS in this connection is the Ágrip (AM 325,4^{0} II of c. 1225 ed. Dahlerup 1880 and Finnur Jónsson 1929). The findings are as follows:

á mót 7^{5}, $9^{1,8}$, 16^{4}, 31^{9}, 48^{1}, 49^{7}

á móti 34^{9}, 36^{5}, 45^{17}

at móti 11^{1}, 36^{18}, 40^{17} used after verbs indicating a movement

í mót 9^{20}, $10^{4,8}$, 28^{6}, 44^{15}, (evt. 9^{12} mot>moti)

í móti (9^{12}), 45^{17}, 46^{5}, $56^{2,17,19}$

The result is of great interest. As for the first three mentioned combinations, there is nothing exceptional in this survey of a MS of c. 1225. Only the last five examples deserve a special commentary; *í móti* is found only on the last pages, two examples towards the end of the part written by hand I (ends col. 88, in Jonsson's ed. 52^{7}). The other three are found in the part supposed to be written by hand III – if there are more than two hands? – (begins col. 93, in Jónsson's ed. p. 54^{12}), and this last hand in the MS is generally held to represent an Icelander.

The phrase used by Cleasby and Vigfusson comes to mind when the possibilities are reviewed: 'used indiscriminately'. Still it is possible to make some distinctions and form a notion of the usage. Perhaps the most astonishing thing in this connection is the use of *í móti*. It begins, so to speak, in a corner of the literature about 1200; but already 1300 it is found all over the area of Old Norse. Some examples will show it.

In the old fragments of the *Orkneyingasaga* (the story of the Norwegian earls of the Orkneys) of c. 1300 *í móti* is dominating.

The great saga of King Olav the Saint is printed from a MS that dates back to shortly before 1300. This MS belongs to those in which *í móti* is favored; and the same is true of the parallel saga adopted in *Heimskringla*. In some cases *móti* is used in the saga, but generally the *Heimskringla* text in such cases writes *í móti*, as also some of the fragments (e.g. AM 75 a fol.); but this investigation has not been followed up, for regrettably, on this point, the editors have conquered the temptation to give complete variants from the different MSS used in the edition. The preposition *í gegn* is used very sparingly, and in younger MSS it has been replaced by *í móti*.

About the middle of the 14th century one finds Icelandic texts where *í móti* is quite dominating. As an example can be mentioned the *Laxdælasaga* as it is in *Möðruvallabók* (AM 132 fol). In that MS of the saga *ímót* and *ímóti* are used more than fifty times (*í móti* more than forty times), while other combinations (*á, at mót, at móti*) are found only ten times – most of them in the beginning of the saga – and *í gegn* is used only once. It may be added that other MSS of the saga do not yield quite the same result; still there is an obvious favoring of *ímót* and *ímóti* also in the old fragment of c. 1300.

As a last attempt towards a description of this innovation in usage, I shall list my counting of examples from the manuscript *Frísbók* (*Codex Frisianus*), written in the beginning of the 14th century, or shortly after 1300. This manuscript is of special interest since it contains the sagas of the Kings of Norway in a recension that agrees with the *Heimskringla* version in parts, in parts with the *Morkinskinna* version.

In four sagas of the *Heimskringla* type (pp. 33-96 in C. R. Unger's ed. of 1871) the scribe uses:

	Codex Frisianus	*Heimskringla*
móti	15	8
í móti	1	5
þar í mót	2	2
Verb + *í mót*	1	3
Verb + *á mót*	1	1
á móti	—	1

These figures should be compared with the figures from a section of the manuscript where the text is of the *Morkinskinna* type (although a few chapters are still directly dependent on *Heimskringla*). I have excerpted all the sagas from *Magnús saga berfœtts* through *Inga saga ok brœðra hans* (pp. 261-347), and the figures are as follows:

	Codex Frisianus	*Morkinskinna*
móti	8	2
í móti	13	17
á mót	3	—
á móti	5	—
í mót	—	6

For the sake of completeness I add my figures from a saga younger than any of the others in *Codex Frisianus*: *Hákonar saga Hákonarsonar,* probably compiled by the Icelander Sturla Þórðarson (d. 1284) on the basis of Norwegian material. The figures are compared with those of the corresponding parts of *Eirspennill,* and it is to be understood from the figures that only part of the saga has been excerpted:

	Codex Frisianus	*Eirspennill*
móti	4	2
í móti	5	—
í mót(t)	6	—
á mót	—	9
á móti	—	2

A word of caution is in order here: The figures clearly show that the division of *mót* (etc.) represents the usage of the scribes of the manuscripts in question, and not that of the compiler/author of the common source. The extract from *Eirspennill* analyzed here is from the part of the manuscript written by the scribe who favours the use of *á mót(i)*.

It is never possible to bring an investigation like this to a proper conclusion; but perhaps those who have followed my analysis this far will subscribe to my view that it can be useful to track down the peculiar usages of every and all manuscripts to arrive at an understanding of the difference between the stylistic intention of the scribe, and the textual tradition carried over from older sources. If, however, one prefers to judge about the distribution of a group of adverbs/prepositions like *mót* (etc.) from a comparison of the occurrences within similar quotations from different manuscripts, one is compelled to confess that Cleasby and Vigfusson were right to state that the forms were 'used indiscriminately'. The following example will emphasize how difficult it is to arrive at a simple truth.

My starting point is an example from *Ágrip* (45^{17}, col. 76), 'menn scvldo ganga imoti liki hans. oc gec aller lvþr amoti oc flestr allr grataNdi'. In *Fagrskinna* (311^{1}) the same quotation reads, 'at menn skylldu ganga i mote liki Haconar konongs oc sva giecc allr lyðr oc flester aller gratande'. *Morkinskinna* (298^{28}) has a shorter version, 'gengo menn þa ímoti lici hans. oc allir gratandi', and an almost similar reading is found in *Codex Frisianus* (262^{11}), 'gengo menn þa i moti liki hans ok nær allir gratanndi'. *Heimskringla* (236^{14}) refers to the same event in the following words, 'gekk þá allr bœjarlýðr, ok flestr grátandi, móti líki konungs', a variant reading has 'en moti liki hans gekk allr lýðr ok flestr allr grátandi'.

It will be noticed that only *Ágrip* has the variation *í móti/á móti*, and it is tempting to interpret the difference as a genuine semantic distinction, since 'standa upp í móti' is a common phrase (also in manuscripts that predominantly use other constructions) in the meaning 'rise to greet' or 'stand up in honor of somebody', whereas *á móti* in this example can be taken to mean 'towards'. An interesting parallel to 'standa upp í móti' is found in Danish ballads: e.g. – ind ad døren tren/ – stod ham op igen; the last word must be read with the second (stressed) vowel long, a pronunciation still found in Danish dialects. In 'igen' we have a true correspondence to ON *í gegn*.

To describe the truth behind the distribution of forms on the basis of the above quotations would lead to confusion, unless the analysis is checked and supplemented by an independent investigation of the general and typical usage of each manuscript. My survey of the use of *mót* (etc.) should rightly be understood as a partial contribution to such investigations; and I have chosen to shed some light into a corner of Icelandic linguistics in honor of George S. Lane, with whom I have shared an interest in *Islandica* since we first met in Iceland almost forty years ago.

The Origin of Irregular *-t* in Weak Preterits like *sent* and *felt*

Norman E. Eliason

University of North Carolina

In Old English weak verbs, the suffix of the preterit and of the past participle was regularly *t* after a voiceless consonant (e.g. *cēpan – cēpte – cēpt, cȳ̆ssan – cȳ̆ste – cȳ̆st, mētan – mētte – mett*[1]) and *d* after a voiced consonant (e.g. *lǣfan – lǣfde – lǣfd,*[2] *fēdan – fēdde – fēd, fēlan – fēlde – fēld, dwĕllan – dwĕalde – dwĕald, sēndan – sĕnde – sĕnd*). This well-established and phonetically governed distributional pattern of *t/d* was disrupted, however, in late OE or early ME, when *t* began to supplant *d* in the preterit and past participle of a number of verbs like *send,*[3] *feel,*[4] *dwell,*[5] and *leave.*[6] For this odd development various explanations have been proposed, none of which seems to me really satisfactory.

The problem cannot be properly explored without first taking note of the vowel quantity in weak verbs. In early ME, the preterit and past participle were distinguished from the present either by the dental suffix alone or also by a difference in vowel quantity.[7] There were five fairly distinct vowel-quantity patterns, of which the first and second were decidedly the most common:

1. V̄ – V̆ – V̆: kēpen – kĕpte – kĕpt, fēden – fĕdde – fĕd
2. V̄ – V̄ – V̄: dēmen – dēmde – dēmd, fēlen – fēlde – fēld
3. V̆ – V̆ – V̆: kĭssen – kĭste – kĭst, dwĕllen – dwĕlde – dwĕld
4. V̆ – V̄ – V̄: sĕllen – sǭlde – sǭld
5. V̆̿ – V̆ – V̆: sē̆nden – sĕnde – sĕnd

These patterns were of course not rigid, nor do the illustrative examples cited above invariably conform to the patterns assigned them there. *Dēmen*, for example, also had a preterit and past participle with a short vowel, thus conforming to pattern 1. instead of 2. Especially variable in this respect were verbs like *fēlen*, *dwellen*, *sellen*, and *senden*. But despite such variation, vowel quantity in weak verbs was not a willy-nilly matter, as we shall see in the next paragraph. Worth noting here is the marked tendency for the vowel quantity (and quality) to be the same in the preterit and past participle whether or not it was also the same in the present.

The variation in vowel quantity, which accounts both for the different patterns and for the shifting of verbs from one pattern to another, was due to analogy or to either of two phonological changes. In *dēmen*, for example and many other verbs like it, the vowel of the preterit, which should have become short, remained long by analogy with the vowel of the present. In *dwellen*, and a few other verbs like it, the vowel of the preterit, which should have become long, remained short by analogy again with the present. The important role of analogy in thus regulating the vowel quantity of weak verbs is of course generally recognized. In *kēpen*, on the other hand, the vowel of the preterit and past participle, which was originally long as in the present, was shortened before consonant groups. This phonological change, which occurred in the 9–10th century, had – as is also generally recognized – a profound effect on the vowel-quantity pattern of weak verbs, for verbs like *kēpen – kē̆pte – kē̆pt* and *fēden – fē̆dde – fē̆d* were very common. Less profound in its effect, but only because of the small number of verbs to which it could apply, was another phonological change of about the same date (i.e. 9-10th c.), whereby vowels were lengthened before *nd*, *ld*, and *rd*, thus accounting for the long vowel in the preterit and past participle of verbs like *sē̆llen – sǭlde – sǭld* and in some other forms to be noticed later.

Irregular *t*, we should note, apparently occurs only when

the preceding vowel is short, e.g. preterits or past participles like *fĕlt(e)*, *dwĕlt(e)*, and *sĕnt(e)*. But the reverse is not true, for when the vowel is short, the preterit suffix may be *d*, e.g. preterits like *fĕdde* and *frĕmde*.

Irregular *t*, as is suggested by the examples cited in the first paragraph, occurs after three types of stems:

1. Stem ending in *n*, *l*, *r* + *d* (e.g. *send*, etc. – see fn. 3)
2. Stem ending in *n*, *l*, *r* (e.g. *feel*, *dwell*, etc. – see fns. 4 and 5)
3. Stem ending in some other voiced consonant, such as *v*, *z*, *m* (e.g. *leave*, *dream* – see fn. 6).

Again, however, the reverse is not true, for after such stems *d* may also occur, e.g. *minded*, *kneeled*, *seemed*.

Thus, though the occurrence of irregular *t* correlates neither with the short vowel of the stem nor with the stem ending of the types just cited, it seems likely that the origin of irregular *t* is to be sought in a combination of these two factors. This likelihood is strengthened by the fact this *t* is first found in verbs like *senden – sente – sent*. '*It is here* [in verbs like *senden*] *that the irregular weak pattern receives its first impetus*', says Marckwardt,[8] who later (p. 307) adds, 'Beginning in the southeast of England in the late eleventh or the early twelfth century, these voiceless inflections [i.e. with irregular *t*] were found in both the preterit and the past participle of Old English first-class weak verbs with originally long stems ending in a liquid or a nasal followed by *d*'.

Marckwardt's analysis of the evidence is so careful and thorough that it must be accepted, but not, I think, his explanation of why or how irregular *t* originated. Before considering his explanation, however, two others[9] merit brief notice.

1. Analogy with preterits and past participles like *kĕpte – kĕpt*, *mĕtte – mĕt* and *kĭste – kĭst*.[10] The explanation is unsatisfactory, for it fails to explain why the analogy operated when it did (i.e. in the 10-11th centuries, when irregular *t* first appears) or even why it operated at all. Because such preterits

and past participles as *kepte – kept,* etc. existed long before *t* supplanted *d* in the preterit and past participle of verbs like *send* and *feel,* the delay in the operation of the analogy is inexplicable. Between forms like *kĕpte, mĕtte,* or *kĭste,* on the one hand, and *sĕnte* or *fĕlte,* on the other, there is a basic dissimilarity, for in the former the *t* after the voiceless consonant was entirely regular, whereas in the latter the *t* after the voiced consonant was not. There is no reason why analogy should have operated to produce this irregularity, resulting in *sĕnte* and *fĕlte* rather than *sĕnded* or *fēlde.* Thus this analogical explanation simply dodges the real crux of the problem.

2. Phonological change whereby final *-d* after *n, l,* and *r* became *t,* thus producing past participles like *sent,* the *t* of which was then extended to preterits like *sente.*[11] Although this phonological change may have helped to establish irregular *t,* as Marckwardt also believes, it cannot have been the primary cause, since the change occurred in West Midland in the 13th century, too far removed in place and time from the development in *sente* (see Marckwardt's statement above).[12] Luick, it should be noted, thought the extension of *t* from the past participle to the preterit was aided by the fact that the resulting pattern *sēnden – sĕnte – sĕnt* conformed to that of *kēpen – kĕpte – kĕpt,* both sharing the vowel-quantity pattern $\bar{V} - \breve{V} - \breve{V}$, a very common one, as we have seen. Thus Luick, though sensing that vowel quantity was somehow related to the development of irregular *t,* failed to realize the actual relationship of the two phenomena.

Marckwardt attributes the irregular *t* to analogy, but, unlike the unsatisfactory analogical explanation in 1. above, does not dodge the crucial issue, why irregular *t* first developed in verbs like *senden.* He shows that verbs like *senden* are precisely like verbs like *mynten* 'to intend' at one particular point, the third person, singular indicative, where each might end in *-nt* (i.e. *sent* < *sendeþ* and *mynt* < *mynteþ*). This, he argues, served as the transfer point between the two types of verbs, whereby the regular preterit *t* of *mynten* was analogically extended to the preterit of *senden*, i.e. *mynt* (3 pers sing) : *sent* (3 pers sing) : : *mynte* (preterit with regular *t*) : *sente* (preterit with irregular *t*).

Pat as this seems, it is not really convincing, I think,[13] for it gives rise to several questions which remain unanswered. The proportion *mynt*: *sent*:: *mynte*: *sente* might just as well have worked otherwise, i.e. *mynt*: *sent*:: *mynde*: *sende*. Why did analogy produce *sente* and not *mynde*? Other verbs also were alike at this same point, e.g. OE *fēdan* – *fĕdde* and *mētan* – *mĕtte*, where syncope and assimilation resulted in similar third person singular forms, *fēt*(*t*) and *mēt*(*t*), but this did not act as a transfer point here, altering the preterit to either *fĕtte* or *mĕdde*. Why did the analogy work in one type (*senden*) but not in the other (*fēdan*)? In verbs like *senden*, syncope and assimilation produced *t* in the third and also the second person singular, *sent* and *sentst*, but this *t* was not regularly extended to other forms of the present. Why not? Why was it extended only to the preterit and past participle?

A satisfactory explanation of the origin of irregular *t* must take into account the following facts: It dates from as early as the 11th century. It is not confined to the West Midland or any other region where final *-d* became unvoiced. It developed and persisted in the preterit and past participle. It first appeared in verbs like *senden*.

Besides the irregular *t* of their preterit and past participle, weak verbs like *senden* are exceptional in that they were subject to one of the phonological changes mentioned earlier, vowel lengthening before consonant combinations like *ld*, *nd*, and *rd*. Marckwardt pretty well ignores this vowel lengthening,[14] but surely this is a mistake, for the two developments are remarkably close in date,[15] and, as I have mentioned above, the occurrence of *t* seems to be related somehow to the quantity of the preceding vowel.[16] It is to the vowel quantity in verbs like *senden* that our attention must now turn.

Before consonant combinations such as *nd*, *ld*, and *rd*,[17] vowel lengthening occurred under conditions that remain somewhat obscure. As I understand it,[18] the lengthening originally occurred in dissyllables,[19] where it was dependent on syllable division, occurring when the division was *send-en* but not otherwise. If a third consonant followed, as in the preterit *sendde,* and such division was impossible, vowel lengthening failed. As a result, the vowel-quantity pattern regularly developed was *sēnden – sĕndde – sĕnd,*[20] the same pattern as that of *kēpen – kĕpte – kĕpt.*[21] Although this pattern $\bar{V} - \breve{V} - \breve{V}$ was a very common one and may therefore have been influential in establishing and extending irregular *t* in verbs like *senden,* it was not the primary cause.

It is, I believe, in preterits like *sendde* that irregular *t* first developed, as the result of a phonological change whereby, after *n*, *l*, or *r*, *-dd-* first was simplified to *-d-* and then became *-t-*.[22]

Whether the simplification of *-dd-* to *-d-* was at first merely orthographic is impossible to say, nor is it of any real consequence. The fact that the vowel remained unlengthened in preterits like *sĕnde*[23] suggests either that they continued to be pronounced for a while as *sĕndde* (where the syllable division can only have been *send-de*) or that the syllable division was *sen-de.*[24] In *sen-de,* where *d* was thus initial in the syllable, it is reasonable to suppose that *d* was fortis,[25] whereas in *send-en* it was lenis. This phonetic difference, I think, caused the fortis *d* to be apprehended as an allophone of the /t/ phoneme and then to be written as *t* in preterits like *sĕnte.*

From such preterits, *t* was quite naturally extended to past participles like *sĕnt,* for the past participles of weak verbs regularly share not only the same vowel as the preterit but also the same dental suffix.[26]

Irregular *t,* which – according to my view – thus originated as the result of a phonological change in the preterit of verbs like *send,* was probably first extended to verbs resembling *send* in the preterit[27] and then to others unlike *send.* The process, I suggest, was as follows:

In verbs like *feel* (*fēlen – fēlde/fĕlte – fēld/fĕlt*), irregular *t* may have developed phonologically as in *sēnden – sĕnte – sĕnt*, but it seems more likely that here the vowel pattern $\bar{V} - \breve{V} - \breve{V}$ of *sēnden* and *kēpen* was first adopted and then, because of the irregular sequence in the preterit *fĕlde* (short vowel followed by *ld*),[28] this was resolved by substituting *t* for *d* as in *sĕnte*.

In verbs like *dwell* (*dwĕllen – dwĕlde/dwĕlte – dwĕld/dwĕlt*), the same irregular sequence in the preterit *dwĕlde* was resolved in the same way. On the other hand, in verbs like *sell* (*sĕllen – sǭlde – sǭld*), the vowel of the preterit was lengthened,[29] and, because the sequence was accordingly regular, the *d* was retained.

In verbs like *dream, earn,* and *learn,* where the sequence in the preterit *drĕmde, ĕrnde, lĕrnde* was regular[30] and accordingly *d* might have been retained,[31] the substitution of *t* was due to analogy with preterits like *dwĕlte, fĕlte,* and *sĕnte,* which likewise had *t* preceded by a short vowel.

In verbs like *leave* and *lose,* the *t* of the preterit was also due to analogy and then the *t* caused the preceding consonant to become voiceless.

Briefly recapitulated, the view I have tried to expound here is that irregular *t* originated as the result of the phonological change *-dd-* > *-d-* > *-t-* occurring in the preterit of verbs like *send,* from which the *t* was then analogically extended to the past participle. In other verbs, like *feel, dwell, sell,* where the preterit suffix *d* was also preceded by *n, l,* or *r,* the development of irregular *t* was influenced by its development in *send* but not in so simple a way that the process can be described merely as analogy. Only in verbs like *dream, earn,* and *leave* was irregular *t* due simply to analogy, and here it was the analogy of verbs like *dwell, feel,* and *send* that prevailed.

This explanation not only accounts for the fact that irregular *t* first developed in verbs like *send* but also takes into account the phonological change that such verbs were subject to, i.e.

vowel lengthening before consonant combinations like *nd, ld,* and *rd,* and shows how the two developments are related. As a result, the vowel quantity variation in such verbs (e.g. *sēnden* vs. *sĕnde/sĕnte*) becomes explicable, thus shedding further light on this vowel lengthening and helping to confirm my view that the lengthening originated in dissyllables and that it was dependent on syllable division, occurring in *sēnd-en* but not in *sĕn-de.*

[1] Since my primary concern is the t/d variation, I ignore differences that have no bearing on it, such as variant forms of the preterit and of the past participle. Some past participles had *d* whereas the preterit had *t*, but this difference was regularly leveled out, e.g. *cy̌ste – cy̌ssed* and *mētte – mēted* becoming *cy̌ste – cy̌st* and *mētte – mēt(t)*.

[2] Where *f* = *v*, for *f* as well as *s* and *þ* became voiced between voiced sounds in early OE.

[3] And also *bend, build, gild, gird, lend, rend, spend,* and *wend.* For a more complete list of each type, see pp. 153-55 in Albert H. Marckwardt, *Origin and Extension of the Voiceless Preterit and the Past Participle Inflections of English Irregular Weak Verb Conjugation* in *Essays and Studies in English and Comparative Literature,* U. of Michigan Publications, Language and Literature, XIII (1935), 151-328.

[4] And also *deal, kneel, lean,* and *mean.*

[5] Also *smell, spell, spill.*

[6] Also *bereave, cleave, lose; dream; earn, learn.*

[7] Difference in vowel quality (e.g. *sēken – sǒhte – sǒht* and *sellen – sǭlde – sǭld*) is irrelevant here and will be noticed below only when necessary.

[8] Op. cit., p. 222 – italics his.

[9] The only ones, besides Marckwardt's, still given any credence. For a survey of other explanations, see Marckwardt, pp. 156-168.

[10] Thus Joseph and E. M. Wright, *An Elementary Middle English Grammar* (London, 1934), § 270.

[11] Thus Karl Luick, *Historische Grammatik der englischen Sprache* (Leipzig, 1940), § 713, anm. 3.

[12] On the change of *-d* to *-t*, see also Jordan-Matthes, *Handbuch der mittelenglischen Grammatik* (Heidelberg, 1934), § 200, where, oddly enough, the development of irregular *t* is ignored. That irregular *t* was not due to this phonological change is also the judgment of Karl Brunner, *Abriss der mittelenglischen Grammatik* (Tübingen, 1953), § 70, anm. 3, and *Die englische Sprache,* II (Tübingen, 1962), p. 266.

[13] My doubts are shared by others. Brunner, who adopts Marckwardt's explanation, nevertheless says, 'Die Entstehung und Ausdehnung dieser Stammbildungsart [i.e. with irregular *t*] ist nicht leicht zu erklären' (*Englische Sprache,* p. 266). Jespersen, though admitting that Marckwardt's explanation is more convincing than the analogical explanation in 1. above, does not regard it as a final solution (*A Modern English Grammar,* VI [Copenhagen, 1942], § 4. 32).
Worth noting, since it bears on a point of crucial concern later, is

this comment of Jespersen's: 'I have often thought that the ME innovation *sent(e)* may have originally stood for *sendd* with a long, emphatic *d* to distinguish it from the present form' (ibid).

[14] And so also does Luick, as I have noted above. In fact no one seems to have realized that this vowel lengthening is inextricably related to the development of irregular *t*.

[15] Although irregular *t* is apparently of later date (11-12th c.) than the vowel lengthening (9-10th c.), the discrepancy is not surprising. If the two developments are related as I believe they were, vowel lengthening ought to have occurred first. The lag in the appearance of *t* may be due either to scribal conservatism or to the time required for the phonological change involved, whereby preterit *sendde* > *sende* > *sente* (see below).

[16] And also to the kinds of preceding consonants, i.e. *nd*, etc., or precisely the consonant combinations before which vowel lengthening occurred.

[17] And other combinations of liquids or nasals followed by voiced homorganic consonants that are irrelevant here.

[18] See my discussion of the vowel lengthening in *Studies in Philology*, XLV (1948), 1-20. I did not concern myself there with vowel lengthening in verbs like *sēnden* and its failure in *sĕnde*. If my explanation of this is sound here, then my view as expounded in *SP* is significantly augmented and strengthened.

My view, I might add, differs from that of others only in the two essential respects mentioned above, i.e. that the lengthening originated in dissyllables and that it was dependent there on syllable division.

[19] And then by analogy was often extended to monosyllables, e.g. *āld*, *cīld*, *gōld*, *hūnd*, *wīnd*, etc., where the lengthened vowel, I believe, was due to dissyllabic inflected forms *āld-*, etc. To attribute the long vowel of monosyllables to the analogy of their dissyllabic forms is not only a tenable hypothesis but a necessary conclusion if I am right in thinking that vowel lengthening originated in dissyllables. That such lengthening did occur in dissyllables cannot be doubted, for, as Luick points out (§ 267, anm. 1) it took place in some words that existed only in dissyllabic form.

[20] Where, according to my view, the vowel regularly remained short in the monosyllabic past participle and regularly was lengthened in the dissyllabic infinitive. In *sēnden*, and other verbs like it, it is generally recognized that the vowel was either long or short in ME (cf. the MED entry-forms *gĭ̄lden*, *gĭ̄rden*, etc.). The short vowel, I believe, was due to analogy with the preterit, past participle, or present forms like *sent*, *sentst*.

[21] Where the short vowel of the preterit (and thence, by analogy, the past participle) was due to vowel shortening before consonant combinations where the syllable division was necessarily *kep-te*. Worth noting is that this vowel shortening is of the same date as vowel lengthening before *nd*, etc. See my *SP* paper, pp. 7-9.

[22] The only exceptions I have noted (in K. Bülbring, *Altenglisches Elementarbuch* [Heidelberg, 1902], § 519) are *ðirda* (< *ðirdda*) and *birdas* (< *birddas*), where *-dd-* simplified to *-d-* in accordance with the change but failed to go on to *-t-*. The failure, I presume, was due to the influence of their metathetic variants *ðridda* and *briddas*. The change did not occur when *-dd-* was followed by *n*, *l*, or *r* (e.g. *nǣddre*) or when *-dd-* was intervocalic (e.g. preterits like *fědde*), where *-dd-* remained until c. 1400, when all double consonants were simplified.

[23] In OE such preterits were usually written as *sende* rather than *sendde*, for, as Campbell, who cites a couple of examples of the latter, states, 'Etymological writing of *dd* is rare' (*Old English Grammar* [Oxford, 1959], § 476 n. 4).

[24] There is, of course, no direct evidence, orthographic or otherwise, that the syllable division differed in *sende* (*sen-de*) and *senden* (*send-en*). It is an inference warranted on the one hand by the difference in vowel quantity, which remained short in *sĕnde/sĕnte* but became long in *sēnden*, and on the other by the difference in the development of *d*, which became *t* in *sente* but remained *d* in *senden*.

[25] Cf. Jespersen's comment, cited in fn. 13, about this *d*. Although I agree in a sense with him, I disagree about how and why this *d* was exceptional.

[26] In the earliest instances of irregular *t* cited by Marckwardt (p. 196), it occurs more often in the preterit (51 times) than in the past participle (14 times). But the evidence is conflicting (see especially Luick, § 713, anm. 3), and probably Marckwardt is right in thinking that there is no significant difference in the incidence of *t* in the two forms (pp. 200-201).

[27] For like *sende*, they too had preterits where *d* was preceded by *n*, *l*, or *r*.

[28] Which should have caused the preceding vowel to lengthen. Note that in *felde*, the *d* was not originally *dd* as it was in *sende*.

[29] And then extended to the past participle.

[30] For *md* is not a lengthening combination, and, though *rn* is, vowel lengthening did not occur if a third consonant followed.

[31] As it frequently was, of course, accounting for the Mod. E. preterits and past participles *dreamed*, *earned*, *learned* as against their variants *dreamt*, *earnt*, *learnt*.

Atertanum Fah

W. P. Lehmann
University of Texas

In a highly developed area like Germanic philology, one of our obligations and pleasures is to continue to examine problems of detail which escaped the authors of our comprehensive handbooks. These problems often involve the inadequately described sections of the language, such as the weakly stressed syllables; they may then require minute concern with rare phonological sequences in the older languages. Moreover, for their clarification we may need to draw on various branches of Germanic philology – besides linguistics also metrics and the discussions of Germanic pursuits, mostly warfare, which made up much of the stuff of its literature. In paying my respects to Professor Lane, I should like to reflect his command over the broad spectrum of philological disciplines and his concern with the data transmitted in documents. My own essay will deal with the background of Old English verse, with reference to phonological problems of pre-Old English, starting from a discussion of the difficulties found in a half-line of the *Beowulf*

1459b ātẹrtānum fāh

This half-line is not among the most disputed in the *Beowulf*, but its meaning is by no means clear. There are also phonological problems, and a morphological difficulty that I discuss below.

Syntactically there is no problem: *fāh* is interpreted to mean 'variegated, decorated, shining',[1] and in this meaning or its second meaning 'blood-stained' it may be used as a predicate adjective accompanied by a dative, as in

1038a sadol searwum fāh

'a saddle decorated skilfully [with skills)'. In

2671a fȳr-wylmum fāh

'brilliant with surges of fire' we find the same construction. Accordingly we can analyze 1459b as consisting of a dative plural, used adverbially with the descriptive adjective *fāh*.

Morphologically, however, the half-line presents a problem; *āter-tān*, as it is interpreted, 'poison-stripe' < 'poison-twig' is the only *-tān* compound in the poem. The first component is conventionally equated with the word found in *Beowulf* 2715 as *attor*, in 2523 as *(h)attres* 'poison, venom' – a cognate of ON *eitr*, OS *ettar*, OHG *eit(t)ar*. The second component has been related to Goth. *tains*, ON *teinn*, OHG *zein* 'branch'. Though we have no evidence for assuming that the Germanic author and his audience related designs on a sword with 'poison-twigs', the noun is assumed to refer to a damascened pattern in the sword.

To be sure, the Sutton Hoo ship-burial find gives us evidence for damascened or pattern-welded swords, with inscribed patterns.[2] Yet this patterning agrees better with the description of Beowulf's own *wrǣtlīc wǣgsweord* 'ornamented sword with waves', 1489a, which he leaves behind than with Hrunting.

Although the construction of Hrunting may be obscure, the unique occurrence of the compound *atertanum* is possibly the chief reason for the reluctance of commentators to accept the cited interpretation and the half-line without emendation. P. J. Cosijn in two comments suggested the substitution of *ātertēarum* 'poisoned tears': in PBB 8 (1882) 571 he supports this interpretation by a reference to Bugge's proposed Old Norse parallel, *eitrdropum fáðr*; in his *Aanteekeningen op den Beowulf* (Leiden, 1892) p. 24 he compares *Andreas* 1333 *earh āttre gemǣl* 'spear poison-stained' – a half-line in a Christian context. The proposed emendation would remove the troublesome *-tān-*, but it would still leave a phonological difficulty, as would Trautmann's *-tācnum* 'marks of poison, ' introduced in his *Das Beowulflied* (Bonn, 1904). Both of these proposals also suggest rather prosaic compounds. Apparently the *Beowulf* editors continue to cite them because of an antiquarian piety that assists bibliographers more than readers of the text. We may therefore pass over the suggested emendations.

Yet we cannot dismiss a metrical problem which the normal interpretation of the line as well as the proposed changes leave. Because a half-line of the pattern $\acute{-} \smile \grave{-} \smile \acute{-}$ is unique, editors propose deleting the second vowel of *āter-*, as does Klaeber. Such a deletion, however, is contrary to the phonological observances of the *Beowulf*. If a long syllable precedes a pre-Old English resonant, the resonant has syllabic value in the earliest Old English verse. This value is regularly observed in the *Beowulf*, as in the numerous uses of *(e)aldor*, e.g.

1644b ealdor ðegna

and in 2839a þæt hē wið attorsceaðan.

I have examined all such syllables in 'Post-consonantal *l m n r* and metrical practice in *Beowulf*', which is to appear in the *Einarsson Festschrift*, pp. 138-157, and have found remarkable consistency of usage. After short syllables, as in

2013b setl getǣhte

resonants have no metrical value; and vowels written in the manuscripts should be deleted, as does Klaeber in

1082b on þǣm meðęlstede.

To remedy the problem in 1459b, we could suggest that the initial element has been wrongly identified with *āter* 'poison' and that the compound has not been properly interpreted. For the long quantity supplied by editors may not be justifiable.

In the three occurrences of 'poison' in the *Beowulf*, the word is spelled each time with double *t*. Line 2839a *þæt hē wið attorsceaðan* refers to the dragon itself; line 2715a *attor on innan* refers to the dragon's poison affecting Beowulf. Line 2523a reads in the manuscript *reðes* 7 *hattres* and is amended to *oreðes ond attres*, an emendation not without problems – cf.

Klaeber 215; but I will not deal further with it here. In these occurrences the word refers to the poison of the dragon as it would affect a man; there is no evidence for the assumed etching of a sword-blade by means of such poison.

If we wish to examine 1459a without preconceptions, we have no grounds for departing from the transmitted text. There are no problems with the manuscript at this point which might lead us to propose an emendation. And the passage is carefully composed. In the epic description of Beowulf arming himself for the battle with Grendel's mother, the first piece of his armor is the corselet; the second is the helmet; and the last is the sword here described, the magnificent Hrunting which Unferth lent Beowulf. Although Hrunting was to fail and we might then look tentatively for the author's forecast of its inadequacy in 1459b, we are told at the end of the poem that Beowulf's strength was too great for any sword. 2682b

	Him þæt gifeðe ne wæs,
þæt him īrenna	ecge mihton
helpan æt hilde;	wæs sīo hond tō strong . . .

'That was not fated for him, that the edges of iron swords might help him in battle; his hand was too strong'.

We may therefore assume that the description of Hrunting in lines 1457-1463 is straightforward, not ironical:

wæs þǣm hæftmēce	Hrunting nama;
þæt wæs ān foran	ealdgestrēona;
ecg wæs īren,	ātẹrtānum fāh,
āhyrded heaþoswāte;	næfre hit æt hilde ne swāc
manna ǣngum	þāra þe hit mid mundum bewand,
se ðe gryresīðas	gegān dorste,
folcstede fāra;	

'The name of that haft-sword was Hrunting. It was unique among all ancient treasures. The edge was iron; it was decorated with . . . , hardened in the sweat of battle; it never failed in combat for any man who grasped it with his hands, who dared to go about perilous ventures, the battle-places of the hostile . . .'.

In interpreting this passage, we find everything clear and obvious, except for 1459b. The designation of the sword, *hæft-mēce*, like the earlier *beado-mēcas* of 1454a, is to be sure a hapax in Old English poetry; but it has long been connected with the *heptisax* of the parallel passage in the *Grettissaga* 66. While unique, the 'hafted sword' may belong to the story of the monster slain under water – cf. Klaeber xviii; the equally unique *atertanum* may be a characteristic feature of a hafted sword.

In examining the other passages in which there are references to 'hafted swords' and swords termed *mēce*,[3] we may find some evidence on their construction which may help in the interpretation of *atertanum*. We may be assisted in such interpretation by examining their role in the accounts which have reference to them.

The *heptisax* is described in its sole occurrence in Old Norse as having a wooden shaft. Its role in the account of Grettir's fight with the underwater giant is one of failure. Though the author of the *Grettissaga* puts it in the hands of the giant, not the hero, it fails as did the *hæft-mēce* in the *Beowulf*, and Grettir's opponent, like Beowulf, must turn to a different sword. While details of the use of the hæft-sword vary, both the Icelandic and the Old English story recall it as an inadequate weapon associated with a monster who lives under water.

If we pursue the story of the underwater fight, we find that it was apparently taken over from Irish tradition. The hæft-sword may then be an importation into the Germanic accounts.

Presumably Beowulf accepted the *hæft-mēce* Hrunting from Unferth and left him his own 'ancestral sword with its wave-patterned blade' in the belief that Hrunting would be more successful against Grendel's mother. The motivation recalls the motif of the giant who can only be killed with a unique deadly weapon, often one he carries.[1] One of the giants killed in this way is the Searbhan Lochlannach of *The Pursuit after Diarmuid O'Duibhne and Grainne*. Another is the giant Uath, Terror, of the *Feast of Bricriu*.

The Searbhan Lochlannach affords a remarkable resemblance to Grendel and his mother in being a 'giant of the children of wicked Cam, the son of Naoi'; see O'Grady 121. Elsewhere I have commented on the *Beowulf* passages referring to Cam, which editors unfortunately modify to Cain; see *JEGP* 59. 140-141 (1958). Both descendants of Cam, Grendel's mother and the Searbhan Lochlannach, may apparently only be killed in particular ways, the Searbhan Lochlannach with his own iron club. As did Beowulf, Diarmid killed the Searbhan Lochlannach in the *Pursuit* story after casting his own weapon to the ground; see O'Grady 139.

In the *Feast of Bricriu* Cuchulainn uses the giant Uath's axe to cut off his head, in accordance with a sequence followed later in *Gawain and the Green Knight*. The giant, beheaded, vanished beneath the sea, to return the next day restored, so that one monster may do the work of Grendel and his mother. Accordingly, as has been pointed out before, there are remarkable resemblances between the *Beowulf* account of the monster slayings and Irish story. Presumably the Germanic accounts were taken from the Celtic; we may then find further survivals of the Celtic traditions hidden in the *Beowulf* text, possibly even in 1459b.

The entire line 1459, and 1460a, apparently describe the construction of Hrunting. Before we return to it, however, we may note that the notion of the opponent who must be killed by a special weapon is not only found in Irish literature; in section 30 of *Njálssaga* Hallgrim carries such a weapon, a halbard. Like the *heptisax* in the *Grettissaga* and the Irish weapons this has a handle of wood. And as in the *Grettissaga*, the weapon also fails its owner; Gunnar cuts it with his sword.

It is characteristic of all of these venerable weapons that they were constructed of wood. Remnants of swords with wooden bases have been found in Denmark, one remarkably with a runic inscription containing the word *makia*[5]. The hilts of these swords are distinctive; circular ferrules protect the head of the sheath of the sword from Torsbjærg. The ferrule from Vi on which the runic *makia* was inscribed was also circular. Hrunting may have been similarly constructed. For in 1521 it is described as *hring-mǣl,* in 1531 as *wundel-mǣl.* And 1459a tells us explicitly that the edge was iron, presumably to indicate that Hrunting had an 'iron edge' covering a wooden shaft, rather than to refer to the weapon itself as *ecg* is often used in metonomy.

If the edge is so described, we may ask the purpose of the further description. It may not be accidental that the two *mæki* in the *Edda* described as *mál-fán* 'decorated with inlaid ornaments' were also used against giants and dragons. In the Skirnismál the *mál-fán* sword belongs to Freyr, who gives it to Skirnir when Skirnir goes to woo the giant maiden Gerþr for him. And in the Sigurðarkviða in skamma the sword that Sigurð laid between Brynhildr and himself is *mál-fán.* Besides the monsters involved in each of these stories, both share the motif of halls protected by a ring of fire. Moreover Freyr's sword is peculiar in two further ways: it fights by itself; it does not come back to its owner. As H. Gering and B. Sijmons point out in their *Kommentar zu den Liedern der Edda I* (Halle, 1927) p. 221, the loss of the sword is poorly motivated in the Skirnismál. They also suggest that the subsequent battle of Freyr without his sword is surely based on an age-old tradition. Whatever the motivation, we find some of the same motifs as in the *Beowulf*: the sword distinctively marked – with excellent characteristics, yet it fails and its bearer must fight without his original weapon. Hrunting with its *atertanum* may resemble the Eddic swords with their distinctive marking.

A more obvious parallel to the Eddic swords was noted by Bugge in his comments on the Eddic lays, *PBB* 22.131, a description of a sword in the *Andreas*. This sword is in the hands of heathen soldiers who are seeking to kill Andreas.

1132b	Sceolde sweordes ecg,
scerp ond scurheard,	of sceaðan folme,
fyrmælum fag,	feorh acsigan.

'The edge of the sword, sharp and battle-hardened, in the enemy's grip, adorned with fire-marks, was about to take his life'.

However different the passage from the *Beowulf*, the swords here too 'melted, much like wax', Andreas 1145-46[6]. Apparently the author of the *Andreas* also knew of the *mál-fán* swords, with decorations (shining) like fire, that failed their owners.

I suggest that Hrunting too was a sword of magical powers, of construction similar to the wood-based weapons found in monster-slaying stories, and that like these it had special adornments to which the author refers by *atertanum*.

The *Andreas* passage associates the adornments with fire, possibly because of their gleaming brilliance. The Eddic passages suggest that this brilliance results from inlays, and for these the English were famed. An illustration of a comparable sword found at Sutton Hoo is given by Green, *Sutton Hoo*, Plate xxiv and Fig. 24. On the sword found there the 'cross-bar of the hilt is of gold with filigree-work on its upper surface; the grip is fitted with two shaped gold mounts which are filigree-decorated and the pommel, also of gold, is embellished with garnets set in stepped and quatrefoil cloisons'. (Green, 81). The decorations of Hrunting may have been similar, and the phrase *atertanum fāh* may refer to them.

Krause also gives illustrations of the pommels of the wood-based sword of Torsbjærg, Fig. 97, p. [179] and that of Vi,

Fig. 99, p. [180]. These may date from as early as the third century and are far less elegant than the Sutton Hoo sword. But we may assume that they are part of the line of *mēce* which with their magical powers occupied a special place in the stories of combat with giants and monsters. Like the *mál-fán* swords in the *Edda*, they were specially decorated. Other examples are given in the *Beowulf*. The huge sword with which Beowulf killed Grendel's mother and cut off Grendel's head had a hilt decorated with treasure:[7]

1615b ond þā hilt somod
since fāge.

And the sword with which Wiglaf killed the dragon was *fáh ond fæted*, 2701a, decorated and ornamented (with gold). 1459b may then refer to the ornamented hilt of Hrunting.

Yet we have few means of identifying the components of *atertanum* with certainty. We do not know the terms used for the inlays on the hilts and purses which are patterned after the fanciful decorations which we see in the Old Irish manuscripts. Yet if the patterns were borrowed, the terms may too have been taken over. If however we attempt to determine possible interrelationships between Old English and Celtic lexical items, we are unfortunately less well-informed than for the older period, which Professor Lane clarified in a number of articles.[8] We can therefore do little but conjecture. For the terms we are concerned with are virtually unknown in both languages, let alone relationships between them.

One of the remarkable Irish swords is found in 'The Irish Ordeals'.[9] The sword is described as having a 'hilt of gold and a belt of silver: gilded was its guard, diverse-edged its point' (Stokes' translation, 218). Like Hrunting, it was an ancestral bequest. In the suit for it the owner asserts his rights to it *7 a atharchtu 7 a imdhenom* (200; ms. B has *atharachtu*). Stokes translates the passage: 'its trappings (?) and ornaments' (219). The dictionaries do little more than repeat Stokes. Hessen, *Irisches Lexikon* 66, glosses *atharchtu* 'Pferdeschmuck?; trappings?'. Kuno Meyer, Contributions 143, simply cites the passage with Stokes' queried translation.

In the paucity of our information it may be rash to speculate about a more certain definition for *athar(chtu)*, or on its source. I would like to suggest that it may be related to Goth. *fodr* 'sheath', Skt *pā-tra-m* 'container', which are derived from PIE *pō-* 'protect'; cf. S. Feist, *Vgl. Wb. der Gotischen Sprache* p. 157-8, and H. Pedersen, *Vergleichende Grammatik der keltischen Sprachen* 2.45, who relates Ir. *e-thar* 'boat', connecting the Indo-European root 'drink'; see Walde-Pokorny 2.71-73. If we derive *athar-* from the root *pō-*, it might refer to the protecting part of the sword, the hilt or pommel, as readily as to the sheath as it does in Gothic. In Germanic the term came to be used even more generally for 'clothing-ornament', as illustrated in NE *fur*. Like MIr *arathar* 'plough', < PIE *arə-tro-, arā-*, it would have had weak grade of the root.

The *-tan-* component may be related to Welsh *tan* 'fire, gleaming', which Förster takes to be the basis of the river-name *Tanad*, NE *Thanet*; see *Der Flußname Themse und seine Sippe* 581-2. If we may posit a compound from which the Old English *atertan-* may be derived, it would be comparable in formation to Ir. *etharglan* 'of bright vessels'. It would mean 'of gleaming/fiery hilt/pommel'.

Yet, although such an interpretation may be plausible, we lack the evidence to support this suggestion, and it is difficult to see where we can find it. Unless we can, the meaning and the etymology of *atartan-*, even a possible source in Celtic names for weapon-ornaments, will be subordinate in importance to the search for data on comparable swords in Germanic story and on their characteristics. Metrical analysis of 1459b suggests that the tentative interpretations given in our *Beowulf* editions is not correct. In attempting to provide better interpretations however we find ourselves hampered by fragmentary information on the Germanic lexicon, on that of neighboring languages, and on the relationship and analysis of both. But even attempts to increase our control over these areas, and over early Germanic linguistic data, may lead to little more than a display of our inadequate information and to disclosure of the unsolved problems.

[1] Lines are cited in accordance with the edition of Fr. Klaeber, *Beowulf and the Fight at Finnsburg*, Boston: D C Heath and Company, 1950. Klaeber has a lengthy note on the uncertain interpretations of 1459b, p. 185. C. L. Wrenn is equally guarded in his comments; see his *Beowulf*, pp. 211 and 233, as is the Heyne-Schücking Commentary – the 16th edition of Else von Schauberg, Paderborn, 1949, says of the half-line: 'Nicht sicher erklärt'.

[2] See Charles Green, *Sutton Hoo*. The Excavation of a Royal Ship-Burial. London: Merlin Press, 1963, especially pp. 81-83, 135, and the excellent illustrations, such as Plates xxiv and xxv.

[3] In discussing problems in the *Beowulf* it is difficult to know which references to include. Any study involving metrics, would rely on J. C. Pope's *The Rhythm of Beowulf*; the metrical pattern in 1459b is discussed pp. 367-71. – For comments on *mēce*, besides the dictionaries, pp. 126-8 of K. Sisam's *Studies in the History of Old English Literature*. Oxford: Clarendon, 1953 is useful.

[4] See Tom Peete Cross, *Motif-Index of Early Irish Literature*. Bloomington: Indiana University Press, 1952, especially p. 536. – For the texts, see: *The Pursuit after Diarmuid O'Duibhne, and Grainne*, ed. by S. H. O'Grady. Dublin, 1857; *The Feast of Bricriu*, ed. by G. Henderson. London: David Nutt, 1899.

[5] See Wolfgang Krause, *Runeninschriften im älteren Futhark*. Halle: Max Niemeyer, 1937, pp. [178-183]. In the edition included in the Schriften der Königsberger Gelehrten Gesellschaft, Geisteswissenschaftliche Klasse, 13, Heft 4, the pages are numbered 600-605.

[6] For the text see George Philip Krapp, *The Vercelli Book*. New York: Columbia University Press, 1932. p. 34. Jacob Grimm in his edition of *Andreas und Elene*. Cassel: Fischer, 1840. glossed the line: ensis igneis signis rutilans, p. 127.

[7] In attempting to visualize the swords mentioned in the *Beowulf*, we might recall that the Sutton Hoo find included the 'ring' of a ring-sword. Green says of it, p. 82: 'Of gilded bronze, it appears to have been removed from its parentsword . . . and deposited in the grave as a separate piece'. The *fetel-hilt* of the sword with which Beowulf killed Grendel's mother and cut off Grendel's head, and brought back with him, may have been an idealized version of such a 'ring-sword'.

[8] See especially 'The Germano-Celtic Vocabulary'. Language 9. 244-64 (1933). Other discussions are modestly entitled notes: Language 7. 278-83, 8. 295-8, 13. 21-8; and they are less directly concerned with Germanic. – For the later period, two works by Max Förster are of fundamental importance: *Keltisches Wortgut im Englischen*. Halle: Max Niemeyer, 1921; and *Der Flußname Themse und seine Sippe*. Sitzungsberichte der Bayrischen Akademie der Wissenschaften. Phil.-hist. Abt. 1941.1 München. – For an essay on the language with which the English came into contact see Kenneth Jackson, 'The British Language during the Period of the English Settlements', pp. 61-82 of *Studies in Early British History*. Cambridge, 1959.

[9] See *Irische Texte*. Hrgb. von Wh. Stokes und E. Windisch. Dritte Serie. 1. Heft. Leipzig: Hirzel, 1891. pp. 183-229.

European Clothing Names and the Etymology of *Girl*

Fred C. Robinson
Cornell University

George S. Lane's exemplary monograph on clothing names[1] brings into prominence many interesting patterns in the development of the various European vocabularies. In examining his lists, one is impressed, for example, by the frequency with which words denoting an article of clothing subsequently come to denote the *wearer* of the article of clothing. Thus the words he records for 'skirt' in Spanish (*falda*), Danish (*skørt*), and English (*skirt*) all come to denote 'woman' at one level of usage or other. Spanish *gorra* 'cap' has had since the seventeenth century the figurative meaning 'persona que tiene por hábito comer, vivir, regalarse, o divertirse a costa ajena'.[2] Danish *sok* 'sock' in colloquial usage means 'spineless person'. The word *cassock*, which, as a name for a military coat, may have derived ultimately from the proper noun *Cossack*,[3] comes almost full circle later and, in ecclesiastical context, refers in English to 'a wearer of a cassock; *esp.* a clergyman'.[4] Numerous clothing terms like OIcel. *hǫttr* 'hood', *mǫttull* 'mantle' and *vǫttr* 'glove'[5] come to be used as personal names; the Germanic word which serves for 'glove' in Danish, Swedish, OIcel., German, etc. occurs in OE solely as a proper name: *Hondscioh*.

This semantic tendency has not passed wholly unnoticed, of course. In *'Enfant', 'Garçon', 'Fille' dans les langues romanes* (Lund, 1919), Ivan Pauli remarks,

> C'est un phénomène extrêmement fréquent qu'une personne soit désignée par un détail du vêtement. C'est ainsi que le franç. *cotillon*, l'ital. *gonnella*, l'esp. *falda* se disent pour

'femme', surtout en parlant des femmes en général. Dans Cotgrave on relève *courtes chausses* au sens de 'femmes', mot que nous retrouvons avec la même signification dans le patois rouchi: *courtes cauches*. Dans les patois picards, wallons, et dans le parler messin, on dit *blancbonnet* pour 'femme' ou 'fille'; et, dans les mêmes contrées, les hommes sont appelés *les chapeaux*. Rappelons que, dans *Werther*, Goethe fait dire à Lotte: 'Mein Chapeau walzt schlecht'.[6]

It is not difficult to add to these examples. Pauli himself cites as terms for infants or children in various Romance dialects *culottier, hannard, maronier, braiet, robichon,* etc.,[7] and there are further instances to be found in other European languages. Spanish *capa negra, capa parda, capa rota,* all occur as designations for persons,[8] while *chancleta* 'little shoe' appears as a playfully pejorative term for a female infant in the Carribean.[9] According to Du Cange, Latin *albati* was used to refer to a newly-baptized child,[10] and nursery terms like *Rotkäppchen* and *Baby Bunting* remind us of the pervasiveness of this type of semantic transference. Further, OIcel. *piltr* 'boy', Danish, Swedish *pilt* 'small boy' and the Breton loanword *paotr* all seem likely to be related to Danish *pjalt,* Swedish *palt* 'rag', while Swedish, Norwegian *plagg* 'piece of clothing' appears in Swedish dialects with the meaning 'rascal, impudent boy'.[11] Swedish *flicka* 'girl' has been convincingly connected with OIcel. *flík* 'a piece of cloth, loose end of a garment',[12] and German *Schlafmütze* 'nightcap' has for centuries been used to denote 'a sleepyhead, dullard'. Clothing terms designating special groups are extremely common, as witness *bluestocking, blousons noirs, Braunhemd, redcap, Schwarzrock, starched shirt,* and the like. Even the primary Germanic word for 'woman', represented in German *Weib,* English *wife* and *wo*(*man*), OIcel. *víf,* etc., is thought to be derived ultimately from the name of an article of clothing worn by women.[13]

English is well provided with examples of this semantic

pattern. Aside from those already cited, we have *brat* coming from OE *brætt*, a Celtic loanword meaning 'pinafore, cloak'. *Clout*, a late ME pejorative term for 'young man', derives from OE *clūt* 'cloth, patch, piece of clothing'. Björkman (p. 272) thought that the puzzling English word *lad* might come from a Scandinavian word meaning 'stockings, slipper'. A particularly good area for observing this semantic trend in English is American slang. Berry and van den Bark list as either current or passé terms for 'girl' or 'young woman' many such slang forms as *bobby sox(er)*, *drape*, *dress goods*, *fluff*, *frill*, *hairpin*, *muff*, *piece of calico*, *petticoat*, *rag*, and, of course, *skirt*.[14]

Bearing these points in mind, we might profitably turn to that common English word of baffling etymology, *girl*. *The Oxford Dictionary of English Etymology*, our most up-to-date authority on the subject, has the following entry for *girl*:

> *girl* . . . youth or maiden XIII [i.e. thirteenth century]; female child XVI. The ME. vars. *gurle*, *girle*, *gerle* suggest an orig. *ü*, and an OE. **gyrela*, **gyrele* has been proposed, based on **gur-*, repr. prob. in LG. *göre* boy, girl; but, as with *boy*, *lad*, and *lass*, certainty is not obtainable on the evidence.

In short, the word first appears in thirteenth-century ME, and before that it has no discernible history. The attempts to connect it with Low German *göre* are, as the *Oxford* concedes, problematic; and although the hypothetical OE etymon **gyrela* (which was authoritatively proposed by Luick[16]) has been generally accepted, no convincing connection between this hypothesized form and any known OE word has been established. *Webster's New World Dictionary*[17] proposes a connection with southern English dialect *girls* 'primrose blossoms', but the presumed semantic relationship is not entirely clear. Holthausen[18] relates the word with OE *gor* 'dung, filth', but again, the semantic (and even phonological) development is not clarified. I believe the *OED* makes a shrewd guess, however, when, after declaring *girl* 'of uncertain etymology', it remarks that *girl, boy,* and similar etymological enigmas 'probably . . . arose as jocular transferred uses of words that had originally a different meaning'.[19] As has been shown, one type of transference of particularly high probability is the shift from clothing name to personal name. Therefore, in seeking an OE word similar in form to the conjectured etymon **gyrela,* it would be well to look especially closely among the OE clothing names.

Doing so, we are led to the documented OE word *gyrela* (also spelled, although less frequently, *gerela* and *gi(e)rela*), a noun of common occurrence which has the meaning 'dress, apparel (worn by either sex)'. Apparently this word is presumed by the dictionaries (Bosworth-Toller, *Dictionary* and *Supplement*; Holthausen, *Etymologisches Wörterbuch*; and Clark Hall-Meritt, *Concise Anglo-Saxon Dictionary*) to have died out at the end of the OE period, leaving no trace in later English. But considering that words for clothing tend to shift their reference to the wearers of the clothing, and remembering that the earliest meaning of *girl* recorded in ME is 'youth or maiden', one is tempted to conclude that the ME word is the direct descendant of the OE word, though in a previously unrecorded sense. For it is quite conceivable that OE *gyrela* had already developed the transferred meaning 'young person of either sex' in pre-Conquest times, but that the usage was limited to the domestic sphere and never got into literary record, where an ample series of non-colloquial terms such as *bearn, byre, cnafa, cnapa, cnæpling, eafora, fæmne, geonga, geongling, hyse, lytling, mægeþ, meowle, umbor,* etc. adequately served this expressive need.[20] But after the Conquest, all these native literary words began to fall out of common use, thus depleting the wordstock for this semantic category. Meanwhile, *gyrela* in its primary sense of 'dress, apparel' was being displaced by a rush of French loanwords such as *array, attire, cloak, habit, mantle, robe, roket, vestment* (all first recorded in thirteenth-century writings), *apparel, coat, frock, garment, gown, livery, ray, vesture* (all first recorded in early fourteenth-century writings). Having been rendered superfluous as a clothing term and being in high demand as a term for 'a young person', *gyrela* would seem, then, to have passed, during the centuries when it is absent from written record, into exclusive use in this latter, originally secondary sense.[21] In this respect, *gyrela* may be said to have followed the same pattern of development as *brat*, mentioned above. OE *brætt* meant 'pinafore, cloak' exclusively. Subsequently, however, the word appears to develop the meaning 'young person' as well, and now this is the only meaning of the word in standard usage.

Rather than being an etymological puzzle, English *girl* would seem then to have a fairly clear history – once we recognize the semantic trend evidenced in *brat, clout, flicka, falda,* etc. and reunite ME *girle*, which had been thought to have no ancestry, with OE *gyrela*, which had been thought to have no descendant. For if my explanation is correct, they belong together in a single etymological continuum, and the hypothesized OE etymon **gyrela* can be disburdened of its asterisk.

[1] *Words for Clothing in the Principal Indo-European Languages.* Language Dissertations, IX (Baltimore, 1931). Subsequently this study was incorporated into Carl Darling Buck's *A Dictionary of Selected Synonyms in the Principal Indo-European Languages* (Chicago, 1949), a monumental compilation to which Professor Lane was a major contributor, especially on questions of Celtic and Germanic etymology.

[2] Martín Alonso, *Enciclopedia del Idioma* (Madrid, 1958), s.v. *gorra.* (Cf. OIcel. *motra* 'a woman wearing a *motr*', and Danish *hat,* which is used metonymically of persons.) My primary source for OIcel. has been the Cleasby-Vigfusson *Icelandic-English Dictionary*; for Danish, Verner Dahlerup's *Ordbog over det Danske Sprog* (Copenhagen, 1919-1954); for Swedish, the *Ordbok öfver Svenska Språket* utgifven af Svenska Akademien (Lund, 1898 -).

[3] Lane, pp. 22-23.

[4] *OED,* s.v. *Cassock,* 4.b., records this metonymical usage for the Renaissance period.

[5] Cleasby-Vigfusson includes in each of these instances the common noun and the proper name under a single entry. I shall not here go into the possibility of one or another of these examples being homonyms of different etymological origin.

[6] Pauli, p. 269, n.

[7] Pauli, p. 269.

[8] Alonso, s.v. *capa.*

[9] Communicated to me by Professor Emerson Brown of the University of Puerto Rico. Alonso, s.v. *chancleta,* indicates a colloquial figurative use of the word with the meaning 'persona inepta'.

[10] *Glossarium Mediæ et Infimæ Latinitatis* (Paris, 1840-50), s.v. *alba,* p. 161, col. 2. Cf. Pauli, pp. 269-270.

[11] Erik Björkman, 'Neuschwed. *gosse* 'Knabe, Junge', eine semasiologisch-methodologische Studie', *Indogermanische Forschungen,* XXX (1912), 272.

[12] George T. Flom, 'Semological Notes on Old Scand. *Flík* and Derived Forms in the Modern Scandinavian Dialects', *JEGP,* XII (1913), 78-92. On p. 89 Flom cites several other examples of Swedish personal nouns deriving ultimately from clothing terms.

[13] Friedrich Kluge, *Etymologisches Wörterbuch der deutschen Sprache,* 19. Auflage bearbeitet von Walther Mitzka (Berlin, 1963), s.v. *Weib.* Cf. Ernest Weekley, *An Etymological Dictionary of Modern English* (London, 1921), s.v. *wife*[1].

[14] Lester V. Berry and Melvin van den Bark, *American Thesaurus of Slang,* 2nd ed. (New York, 1952).

[15] *The Oxford Dictionary of English Etymology*, ed. C. T. Onions, with the assistance of G. W. S. Friedrichsen and R. W. Burchfield (Oxford, 1966), s.v. *girl.*

[16] Karl Luick, 'Die herkunft des ne. *girl*', *Anglia Beiblatt*, VIII (1897), 235-36.

[17] College Edition (Cleveland and New York, 1964), s.v. *girl.*

[18] *Etymologisches Wörterbuch der englischen Sprache*, 3rd ed. (Göttingen, 1949), s.v. *gore*[1].

[19] *OED*, s.v. *girl* sb. Buck, *Dictionary*, p. 87, similarly remarks that 'a noticeable number of the modern words for 'boy', 'girl', and 'child' were originally colloquial nicknames, derogatory or whimsical, in part endearing, and finally commonplace'.

[20] The OE gloss *gyrlgyden* to Latin *Vesta* is cited in *The American College Dictionary* (New York and Syracuse, 1963), s.v. *girl*, as carrying the meaning 'virgin goddess', and if this is so, then we might have here a solitary instance of OE *gyrela* 'girl' preserved in writing. But since the earliest ME occurrence of *girl* carries the meaning 'young person of either sex' rather than 'girl, virgin', the *ACD*'s interpretation of *gyrlgyden* seems dubious. The more likely explanation of the gloss is that it means 'clothing goddess', the OE glossator having associated *Vesta* with *vestis* 'garment'. See H. D. Meritt, *The Old English Prudentius Glosses at Boulogne-sur-Mer* (Stanford, 1959), p. 69.

A possible, remote survival of OE *gyrela* with its original meaning is the otherwise inexplicable ME form *garlement* 'clothing, apparel', which is instanced once in the *OED* s.v. *garlement* and twice in the *MED* s.v. *garnement*, all three occurrences being from the fourteenth century. This may be a blend of *girl* 'apparel' with *garment.*

I should add here that although no previous commentator has hit on the interpretation of *girl* as a descendant of OE *gyrela*, two have struck close. Rolf Berndt, *Einführung in das Studium des Mittelenglischen* (Halle, 1960), pp. 339-40, suggested as the OE etymon of *girl* **gyr(w)ela*, which he connected with the verb *gierwan* 'dress, clothe, adorn', a word with which the documented *gyrela* 'apparel' has also been related. But instead of drawing this connection, Berndt conjectures that his starred form is a unique derivation retaining an original Germanic meaning of the root – 'der, die Reifende, Heranwachsende'. The *MED*, after offering the traditional etymology for *girl*, adds '? akin to OE *gierela* . . .' but does not go any further. Rolf's derivation of a noun with the form **gyrela* (rather than **gierela*) from the root underlying *gierwan* 'dress, clothe', it should be added, is the most satisfactory phonetic form to assume for the documented word *gyrela* 'apparel' if this word is to be understood as the antecedent of modern *girl*, for in that case we should expect the OE word to have precisely the form we find in modern *girl* (with the initial stop) and in the ME variant spellings *gerle*, *gurle*, and *girle*. If the original form were *gierela*, as some have suggested, then the initial stop in modern *girl* would have to be explained as the result of Northern dialect or foreign influence (as is the case with English *giefan*, *giest*, *gietan*, *gilde*, etc.). Although OE spelling is not to be trusted in this respect, it should be mentioned that of the fifty-nine quotations in Bosworth-Toller, *Dictionary* and *Supplement*, containing the element *gyrela*, thirty are spelled with *y*, fifteen with *i*(*e*), and fourteen with *e*. These spellings may well reflect *y* developed from 'unstable *i*' in late OE.

www.ingramcontent.com/pod-product-compliance
Lightning Source LLC
Chambersburg PA
CBHW020751160426
43192CB00006B/295
* 9 7 8 1 4 6 9 6 5 7 0 2 8 *